When Dad Hurts Mom

Also by Lundy Bancroft

Why Does He Do That?:
Inside the Minds of Angry and Controlling Men

The Batterer as Parent:
Addressing the Impact of Domestic Violence
on Family Dynamics
(with Dr. Jay G. Silverman)

When
Dad
Hurts
Mom

Helping
Your Children
Heal the Wounds
of Witnessing Abuse

Lundy Bancroft

G. P. PUTNAM'S SONS　　NEW YORK

The names, identifying characteristics, and other relevant details of the anecdotal cases in this book have been modified to protect the privacy of these individuals. This book is not intended as a substitute for advice from a trained counselor, therapist, or other mental health professional. If you are currently in counseling or therapy, check with your mental health provider before altering or discontinuing your therapeutic regimen.

While the author has made every effort to provide accurate telephone numbers and Internet addresses at the time of publication, neither the publisher nor the author assumes any responsibility for errors or for changes that occur after publication.

G. P. Putnam's Sons
Publishers Since 1838
a member of
Penguin Group (USA) Inc.
375 Hudson Street
New York, NY 10014
www.penguin.com

Copyright © 2004 by Lundy Bancroft

Library of Congress Cataloging-in-Publication Data

Bancroft, Lundy.
When dad hurts mom : helping your children heal the wounds of
witnessing abuse / Lundy Bancroft.
p.   cm.
ISBN 0-399-15110-9
1. Abused wives—Life skills guides.   2. Children of abused wives—
Psychology.   3. Abusive men—Family relationships.   4. Family
violence—Prevention.   5. Victims of family violence—Mental health.
I. Title.
HV6626.2.B254   2004   2003064680
362.82'923—dc22

Printed in the United States of America
1   3   5   7   9   10   8   6   4   2

This book is printed on acid-free paper. ♾

Book design by Lovedog Studio

Acknowledgments

As was true of my previous book, *Why Does He Do That?*, my largest debt of gratitude for this current work is owed to Carole Sousa, who was my first teacher and mentor on understanding and addressing the impact on children when a man abuses their mother. I first worked with Carole fifteen years ago, and she has been a tireless advocate for the children of abused women, and for their mothers, ever since. I cannot thank her enough for what I have learned from her, much of which is reflected in this book. Carole also reviewed the manuscript and, as always, made comments that have had a significant positive impact on the quality of the final product.

Next I would like to thank the abused mothers who made suggestions on the manuscript, including M-B.R., R.G., S.B., and M.P. The insights these women offered about what parenting strategies, and legal strategies, have worked for them and which have not have helped to ground this book in real-life experience. Their feedback also helped to guide the tone and content of the book toward information and support that would be most practically useful and contribute most to healing and recovery for abused mothers and their children.

Important comments and assistance were also offered by Joan Zorza, Susan Schechter, Ann Brickson, and Mo Hannah. For their general support of my work over the years I wish to thank again, without naming them all, the various people I mentioned in *Why Does He Do That?*, including my deep debt to the abuser program Emerge, where I was trained and educated about abuse.

I want to thank my agent, Wendy Sherman, for her ongoing encouragement and assistance in the development of my writing projects, and for once again finding a good home for the book. My publicist, Gail Leondar-Wright, did an incredible job of getting my writing into the public eye, where it could reach the women who needed the information. Several people at Putnam deserve gratitude, including Denise Silvestro, Martha Bushko, Beth Mellow, and Gilda Squire (who has moved on from Putnam).

I wish to acknowledge the Ford Foundation and the Wellesley Centers for Women, for their financial and logistical support of the research effort that I have been part of to examine the experiences of abused women in custody and visitation litigation, and the use of courts by abusive men as a way to continue their control over women and children.

For general inspiration on the subject of abuse and its impact on children I wish to thank Michelle Lambert, Jeff Edleson, Sandra Graham-Bermann, Betsy McAlister Groves, Kathleen Faller, Peter Jaffe, Anna Salter, Judith Herman, and Barbara Hart.

For their love, kindness, and friendship in a difficult time, I owe deep gratitude to the three people to whom this book is dedicated, and to several others: Amy Waldman, Dawn Faucher, Scott Laidlaw, Carrie Cuthbert, Karen Johnston, Flip Rosenberry, Anita Raj, Steven Holmes, Joyce Zimmock, Jason Patrissi, Felice Wolfzahn, Lucy Garbus, Blake Walton, and Caryn Markson.

I want to express my thanks to Gillian Andrews for first proposing a book for the general public on the impact that abusive men have on children. Her suggestion gradually grew into the book you have in your hands, which has become a guide for the mothers themselves.

As always, my utmost appreciation and admiration is for all the women, and men, who are pouring their dedication and energy into creating and staffing programs for abused women and activist organizations that are seeking to end the abuse of women and children.

For Carlene, Jay, and Karen B.,

who got me through

Contents

PART III   The Abusive Man and Your Children
Post-Separation

PART IV   Children Moving Forward

Preface

This is a book for women who have faced chronic mistreatment by their partners, and who are concerned about how their children have been affected by the events they have seen or heard. I describe how children are emotionally hurt by living in the atmosphere that abusive behavior creates, and how mothers can help their children heal. There is a place here for you even if your partner's selfish or bullying behavior does not rise to a level that you would call "abuse." What matters is not the precise labels we put on conduct, but how we help children come through intact when they have been stung by the disrespect, cruelty, or violence they have seen their mother subjected to.

Many readers will not be the abused mothers themselves, but friends, relatives, or professionals who are interested in finding ways to help a woman in their lives, because they are worried for her children. You will find in these pages insights into the challenges that she faces, and guidance on how you can best reach out to her and become part of her support system. You will also learn ways to make direct connections with her children so as to counter the unhealthy role modeling provided by the abusive man, and create an opening for them to share their feelings and experiences with you.

Although chapters 14 and 15 are the most directly focused on healing, practical suggestions for how mothers can assist their children are woven in throughout, and most chapters end with a collection of guidelines for action called "What Can I Do?" Although you will learn a great deal in this book about the nature of children's struggles, you will also come out with a tremendous range of strategies you can use to move your family toward emotional wellness, enjoyment of life, and hope.

Families in our times take many different forms. When I speak of "father" or "Dad" in this book, I am referring equally to stepfathers and live-in partners. I speak of the abusive person as "he" and the target of the abuse as "she," but I know that there are lesbian mothers who are abused by their female partners, and the dynamics that result can be quite similar to the ones I describe in this book. Adolescent girls and young women sometimes raise children while being abused by their own parents. Whatever the source of the abuse in a mother's life, she will find helpful insights here into managing and improving her family life. I recognize that there are also women who behave abusively to men, but the problem is substantially less common and involves a distinctly different set of dynamics, so I will not attempt to address it in this book.

The process of making recommendations to women about how best to assist their children is a delicate one, due partly to the strong influence that culture plays in determining what a person's beliefs are about how to raise children—and how children react to witnessing abuse. I have made an effort to suggest concepts and approaches that are adaptable to a range of cultural backgrounds and circumstances, and that can permit you to foster in your children those values which you hold most dear. At the same time, cultures are not united fronts; there is sometimes considerable tension between what women of a certain race or ethnicity believe about what is best for children and what the men of that culture believe. These differences can be sharpened in cases where the man is abusive to the woman. Part of the goal of this book is to assist women of all backgrounds to stay true to what they believe will promote their children's well-being in the long term.

At the risk of stating the obvious, I need to underline the fact that children's needs vary tremendously with their ages, as do the specific symptoms they tend to exhibit from witnessing abuse. To divide each of the points I discuss by age category would have made this book too long to be practical for mothers to use, and would require turning this into a child development text. If you are confused about whether certain approaches are appropriate for a child of a particular age, and some trial and error doesn't resolve the question for you, contact a child specialist at a program for abused women. There are also additional materials you can use listed in the Resources section in the back of this book, under "Children's Healing," page 343.

For the past sixteen years, I have been a counselor for men who abuse women, mostly leading groups. As part of my work, I have always interviewed the partner or ex-partner of my client, the woman who is the survivor of his abuse or violence. I make that contact in order to encourage each woman to use the services offered by her nearest program for abused women, and to get the straight story on my client's problem; abusive men themselves are, unfortunately, poor sources of information about their own history of abusiveness because they deny and distort so much. I have also worked extensively as a custody evaluator, a child abuse investigator, and a legal consultant, and a number of the accounts that I share come from times when I was wearing one of those hats.

As you read this book, you will notice that I stay carefully away from blaming abused mothers for their children's distress. I believe that the responsibility for an abusive man's actions, and therefore for the effects of those actions on children in the home, lies entirely with him. At the same time, I recognize that mothers are the people who are in the best position to help their children understand what they have seen, process and heal their emotional injuries, and move toward a life where they will no longer be exposed to cruelty or intimidation. Your children need your loving support, your compassion, and your leadership. Amid all the challenges you face, your children need you to find a way to shield them from witnessing abuse and assist them in recovering from what they have already been through. I have written this book because I believe you and other mothers in your position are anxious to find a way to do that for them, and because I also believe that you can succeed.

Chapter One

Partner Abuse Through Children's Eyes and Ears

Listen to the voices of these mothers:

"He's mean to me, not to the children, but later on they fall apart from seeing what he did. I feel like they're going downhill emotionally."

"My teenage daughter says to me, 'Why do you put up with the way Dad treats you? I'd never take that from a guy.' "

"My son keeps getting kicked out of daycare centers for being too aggressive."

"My husband says I just wasn't cut out to be a mother."

"The school says I need to give my children medication because they have been diagnosed with depression and attention deficits. No one has asked me anything about what's going on at home that is putting them under so much stress."

"My children are furious at me for leaving their father. He told them I made up lies about abuse because I wanted to be with another man, and they believe him."

"My son is starting to act more and more like his father, like he's becoming an abuser himself."

"My children don't listen to me at all. I can't leave their father because they would walk all over me if he weren't around to discipline them."

Nearly three-quarters of women who are chronically mistreated by their partners have children. For these mothers, the sting of the verbal abuse, emotional cruelty, or physical violence they are subjected to by their partners is sharpened by worry and concern for their children. If you have picked up this book, you are probably among the women who ask themselves, "Are my children being hurt by what my partner is doing to me? Can I find a way to bring them through this in one piece, emotionally and physically? Are they going to be okay?"

This is a book about emotional injury, but even more it is a book about healing, for your children and for you. Your well-being and that of your children are tightly interwoven. The better you can come to understand how your angry or controlling partner has affected both you and them, the more you will be able to shield your children from further harm and help them on the road to recovery, so that they can remain—or return to—the vibrant, hopeful, whole people they are capable of being. And that you are capable of being.

The pages ahead bring you inside the world of children who are exposed to a man who abuses their mother. When I write about "abuse," I am referring not only to physical assaults and threats, or even the most obvious forms of verbal degradation or humiliation. I am speaking also of an atmosphere where Mom is disrespected by Dad, where her voice is silenced, where she is bullied or made to feel worthless or treated like a servant. When a man repeatedly treats his partner in this manner, he sends shock waves through the whole family, in ways that not only bring distress to the children, but also can foster tense relationships between mothers and children and sow divisions among siblings. Life in the family changes when a man's abusiveness enters the picture.

At the same time, neither women nor children are passive victims. Mothers attempt in a great range of ways to stand up to the abusive man, and to try to protect the children from his scary or demeaning ways. Children fight back by becoming defiant, or by watching out for their siblings, or by pouring themselves into activities that they love and that help them forget the most painful aspects of life at home. Some mothers and children stay by each other's side with the most admirable loyalty and courage, even if the abusive man tries to drive them apart. Abused women keep trying to move toward the light of freedom and kindness, and to bring their children with them. Healing sometimes comes in powerful, deep ways that allow all family members to feel that they are embarking on a new life and leaving cruelty and abuse behind—with or without the abusive man, depending on whether or not he decides to face his problem.

You are your children's lifeline. They need you to be the very best you can be. Whether the abusive man is their father or stepfather, or is your live-in boyfriend, he cannot be their guide into healthy values and compassionate living; he cannot bring them deep nurturing for their souls; he cannot fully see and admire them for who they are. Abusiveness is incompatible with truly positive parenting, for a whole set of reasons that we will explore in the pages ahead. If the abusive man decides to change, then the children may be able to look to him more in the future. But overcoming abusiveness takes years, and even then can happen only if the man decides to take his problem very seriously and stop blaming other people, including you. So the most important adult love and influence for your children has to come from you, and from other loving, non-abusive adults in the children's lives.

If you are no longer involved with the man who mistreated you, your children may still be struggling with the aftershocks of his aggression. And if he is the children's father, you may be observing distressing reactions that your children are having to their ongoing contact with him, or you may be faced with a legal battle over custody, visitation, or child support. Many separated mothers find that their need to help their children process their father's intimidating or manipulative behavior is just as urgent as it was before, or more so. Whenever I use the term "partner" in this book, I am also including ex-partners in the points I am examining.

I want to thank you, on behalf of your children, for deciding to read this book. It would be so much easier, in some ways, to close it up and throw it on the shelf. When a woman lives day in and day out with a man who tears her down, intimidates her, or devalues her, she naturally becomes consumed with her own confusion and hurt, and the urgent search for solutions. Living with these challenges, you may feel overwhelmed when you consider shouldering your children's burden on top of everything else. But they need you to grasp their experience, and to reach in to put your arms around them, both literally and figuratively. They need to feel held by you, even during times when you are apart. You can make a tremendous difference to them. You probably already have in many ways, and you will gain insights and approaches in the chapters ahead that will make it possible for you to give your children even more.

Some parts of this book are difficult to read. You may start to notice distresses in your children that had not come to your attention before. You may become aware of serious problems in your partner's treatment of your children, when you thought up to now that he was a pretty good parent or stepparent. You may blame yourself for uncomfortable or traumatic experiences in your children's lives. But you will also learn about your children's sources of strength, and about your own. You will learn that the problems in your family are largely not caused by you—though you will probably have to be the one to repair the damage, because no one else will. And I will encourage you throughout to believe that you can get through these times, and bring your children through them and out the other side.

To introduce you to the themes that we will be exploring in this book, I want to now tell you a few brief stories of some families that are typical of the cases I become involved in. Aspects of the lives of these individuals are likely to feel familiar to you.

Grace and Matthew

Grace had grown up knowing Matthew as a local boy in her town. Late in high school they had become sweethearts and decided to get engaged, and when they graduated they began living together. Within a few months, though, Grace's hopefulness about the future had plummeted, as she increasingly found that Matthew was moody, possessive, and involved in almost daily pot smoking. She spoke with a couple of friends who had known Matthew for many years, as she had, and they told her, "He's acting really immature. This is typical for guys who are just getting out of school. He'll settle down and get responsible in a couple of years."

So Grace watched and waited as she pursued her associate's degree at the local junior college. Two years later, Matthew didn't show any serious signs of growing up, but he was at least willing now to take the leap and get married. They had a big wedding that drained their savings accounts and her parents' as well. Matthew promised he would stop taking (and losing) low-paying part-time jobs, and would get going on paying off their debts and building up some savings to buy a house. But he didn't. Meanwhile, his jealous tirades made it hard for Grace to have a social life. She felt increasingly lonely and depressed.

Grace's unhappiness and anxiety finally reached enough of a pitch that she decided to pour her heart out to her mother. Her mother reacted with horror at the prospect of a divorce. She advised Grace that the answer was to have a child. "Once you have his baby, he'll finally believe you aren't off with other men, plus he'll see it's time to stop partying like an adolescent and find a decent job." So Grace informed Matthew that she was going off birth control. He was less than enthusiastic about her decision but assented.

Matthew did stop his jealous accusations at the beginning of Grace's pregnancy. However, he soon switched to criticizing her about the changes in her appearance, telling her that she was gaining too much weight and even calling her "fatso." He was also upset that Grace wasn't making dinner every night as she had done before, and that the upkeep of the house was slipping. He told her, "You're using being pregnant as an excuse to be lazy." In the later months of her pregnancy she stopped being comfortable with having sex, and he responded to her refusals by going back to making accusations that she was sleeping with other men. Grace was shocked that Matthew could degrade her in this way while she carried their baby.

Matthew did seem genuinely excited when the baby was born, especially since it was a boy. They named him Gabriel. For the first three or four months of the baby's life, Grace felt that perhaps her mother had been right; Matthew was working steadily, had cut down a lot on smoking pot (though he didn't stop), and many days he helped her with the baby. On nights when he had gotten high he still slept like a rock, but other nights he would get up and attend to the baby during his frequent times of waking up.

But before so much as half a year had gone by, Matthew's patience had worn thin, and then disappeared altogether. He started to make comments such as, "I feel like this baby is ruining our lives," and, "You care more about Gabriel than you do about me." He stopped helping with the baby's care and went back to being out partying with his friends several nights a week. Home life became ugly as he would yell at Grace in front of Gabriel, calling her fat, ugly, and lazy. He would make disgusted faces when Grace nursed the baby and began to demand that she put him on a bottle, making degrading comments about the breast-feeding process.

Gabriel was startled and frightened by the yelling, and would sense his mother's tension or hear her crying. He also became aware that his mother was less receptive to him when his father was in the room. Gabriel responded to these disruptions by becoming colicky, clinging to his mother, and having trouble keeping food and milk down. Grace could see that as Matthew's behavior became increasingly hostile, the effects on the baby were becoming more pronounced, and she knew she had to get help. She began by calling a hotline for abused women several times a week, during hours when Matthew was at work and the baby was napping.

Breanna and Adam

Breanna lived a busy life, typical of a professional woman of our time. She was divorced and had primary custody of her three children, who spent alternate weekends with their father, Darren. He was a somewhat negative and depressed person, but the children had a good relationship with him. Three years had passed since the divorce, and the children were now twelve, nine, and seven.

Then Breanna met Adam through acquaintances at her company. She was drawn quickly to his liveliness and humor, so refreshing to her after years of living with Darren's bleak moods. The children were not happy about seeing their mother with another man, however, especially when Adam came to live with them. And they became increasingly upset as they began to witness events when Adam was mean to their mother. Adam, in turn, was angry that the children were aloof and at times rejecting toward him. He would yell at Breanna that his problems with the children were her fault, and that if she were a better mother she would be able to control them.

Within a few months, the children were becoming aware that Adam was a control freak. He would tell them which pots they could cook certain kinds of food in, how long they were allowed to be in the shower, and which friends they could have over to the house. He would say insulting things about their father in front of them, referring to him as a "loser" and saying that he was "in love with being miserable."

When Breanna's oldest child, Caleb, turned thirteen, he decided he wouldn't tolerate Adam's dictatorial control anymore. One day when the children were laughing loudly together and Adam snarled up the stairs at them to quiet down, Caleb came out of his room and yelled furiously, "Go fuck yourself! You're not our father, you can't tell us what to do!" Adam flew into a rage, ran up the stairs and grabbed Caleb's face hard, and said, "You're going to be sorry, smart-ass!" and pushed him against the wall. Caleb went back hard at Adam with his fists while the younger children screamed, and Breanna came running and pulled Caleb away. She yelled sternly at her son, "You show Adam some respect! I'm sick of you being so rude and hostile toward him! When are you going to accept that things change?"

In the following days, Breanna started to have qualms about the way she had responded to the fight. Her younger children insisted that Adam had attacked Caleb first (which Adam was hotly denying). She reflected on the fact that Adam's bullying and control were driving *her* crazy, so why wouldn't the children be getting exasperated as well? Maybe it wasn't just the children's loyalty to Darren that was causing them to be rejecting toward Adam; maybe Adam was part of the problem.

Alexandra and Greg

Like Breanna, Alexandra was divorced, but her problem wasn't her new partner; it was her old one. During her marriage, Alexandra had found Greg to be selfish, arrogant, and threatening. On a few occasions he had even been physically violent, poking her in the chest, hitting her with a set of car keys he threw at her, or grabbing her arm hard enough to hurt and bruise her. Since their breakup, his hostility and constant unreasonable demands had not let up at all—in fact, they had gotten worse. He was enraged about paying child support, saying, "I know you're spending my hard-earned dough on yourself, not on the children." He would also become furious anytime he found out she had left the children with a baby-sitter; one time he filed a motion at the family court asking the judge to forbid her to leave the children with anyone unless she checked with him first (a request the courts denied).

The most important problem, though, was that Greg was determined to turn the children against their mother and win them over to his side. He had visits with the children on alternate weekends and one evening per week, during which he would spend money extravagantly on gifts and clothing, take them to shows, go horseback riding, appearing to be SuperDad. He would also make dazzling promises about the future: that he was going to take them on a round-the-world cruise when they were older, that he was going to remodel his house so each of them would have a private bathroom, that he had a friend who knew Celine Dion and they would get to meet her personally. The children were enraptured by him.

Sometimes Alexandra would ask them, "What happened to all of the complaints you used to have about your dad? You used to say you couldn't wait for him to move out of the house because he was mean and scary. You tried to get me to call the police once, remember?" But the children would just respond, "Oh, he's not like that anymore, and anyhow, you're really exaggerating what it was like—it wasn't *that* bad."

Alexandra's oldest daughter, Marlene, became harder and harder to deal with as she approached adolescence. She began to call her mother a "bitch," and became openly defiant of anything her mother asked her to do. She would stay out late and refuse to explain where she had been, and Alexandra suspected strongly that she was drinking.

Greg made fun of Alexandra's worries about their daughter. "*I* don't have any trouble with her," he said cuttingly. "She's very well behaved when she's here with me. Maybe you should take a parent-training course to learn how to handle her. Or even better, get yourself some therapy."

Alexandra was not surprised that Greg had no trouble with managing Marlene's behavior, because he wasn't trying to. When Marlene was at her father's, he let her come and go as she pleased, didn't monitor whom she was with, and let her stay up until one or two in the morning. He also made ridiculing comments to her about her mother and encouraged her to disrespect her mother's authority. Life at Greg's house was a teenager's dream: no structure, no authority, no responsibility.

Alexandra became worried that Greg's goal was to take custody of Marlene away from her. She began collecting information about abusive men in custody disputes, and preparing legal strategies to stop Greg's divisive tactics from working, in addition to seeking professional help for her increasingly difficult relationship with Marlene.

Wanda and Leif

Wanda's four children, Kirk, Jenna, Hillary, and Jethro, were all adults and out living on their own. She had been a full-time mother for over twenty years, and now was struggling to reenter the work force. She craved a sense of independence after decades of being entirely dependent on Leif's income, but at times she wasn't sure she could succeed.

Wanda's third child, Hillary, was married and getting ready to start having children. One weekend Hillary came to visit without her husband, Sam, and confessed to her mother that she felt anxious about starting a family because Sam was prone to rages. Then, choking back tears, she told Wanda that Sam had slapped her on the side of the head a few days earlier and called her an "ignorant piece of shit" because he wanted to find a new house and she wouldn't agree to move.

Wanda responded by focusing on what seemed to be bothering her daughter's husband, and what Hillary could do to help Sam feel better. "Maybe he's right, maybe you really should get out of the neighborhood you're in. It would be better for your children to grow up in healthier surroundings."

Hillary began crying, and erupted with anger she had long suppressed around her mother. "I didn't come over here so you could take Sam's side against me. I can't believe you're doing this—he *hit* me, for God's sake, he *hurt* me. This is just the way you always were with Dad. It didn't matter how he hurt you, or how he hurt us, you always had an excuse for him. He treats you like dirt!"

Her daughter's harsh words cut Wanda to the quick. "Your father has *never* laid a hand on me," she shot back defensively, "or on any of you children."

"So what?" Hillary responded through her tears. "You think hitting someone is the only way to hurt them? Why do you think Jethro hasn't spoken to Dad for two years? Because he got sick of being put down by him!" Hillary stormed out of the house.

Wanda spent the next several days drawn up inside herself, struggling to digest Hillary's words. Leif responded to her withdrawal with irritability and blame.

One evening Wanda called her older daughter Jenna and described what had happened during Hillary's visit. Jenna's words were kinder than Hillary's but her message was the same: "It's uncomfortable to talk about, Mom, but Jethro and I have been commiserating for a long time about how badly Dad treats you, and trying to figure out what to do about it."

Wanda snapped hotly, "I don't think this is all your father's fault. You children have to look at your part in your difficulties with him. He and Kirk get along fine."

Jenna paused for a few moments. "Mom, the reason those two don't clash is that Kirk is just like Dad. Kirk's lost two girlfriends because of the way he walks on them. We've been putting off telling you, but his last girlfriend has a restraining order against him. She says Kirk threatened to kill her if she left him."

Wanda sputtered impatiently, "That's *ridiculous,* Jenna. Kirk would never do something like that. That's terrible that you would believe a lie like that about your own brother."

Wanda spent weeks reeling internally from these interactions with her daughters, but gradually began to take in the realities they were confronting her with. She started to recognize how much she had blamed herself over the years for the way that Leif constantly criticized her. She began to understand that her compassion for Leif, who had lost his beloved brother in a car accident in his teens amid numerous other losses, was keeping her from facing up to the harm his abusiveness had done to her over the years. Perhaps most important, she could no longer deny the fact that Leif's cruel and frequent put-downs, of her and of Jethro, had wounded every heart in the family, though in different ways.

As painful as these realizations were, they placed Wanda on a path toward healing her connections with her children, so that she grew closer to them than she had felt since they were very young. As she learned not to blame herself for Leif's self-centeredness and verbal assaults, she gained the ability to stop blaming her children for the toll his behavior had taken on them.

These stories show some of the many paths to emotional injury, and to healing and reconciliation, that are walked by children whose mother is abused. They offer us glimpses of the alienation that abusers can cause between mothers and their children, and between siblings, and of the potential for those separations to be healed, so that loved ones can find their way back to one another. The dynamics that these families struggle with will resonate as you read on.

Children are aware of the abuse that is being perpetrated in their homes, even if they are rarely or never the direct target. They cannot fail, for example, to hear the hurtful words that crackle through the home, the insults and belittling toward their mother:

"You are so fucking stupid!"

"You shut up or you'll regret it!"

"You fat bitch!"

"These children are going to grow up to be as messed up as you are!"

Children learn to recognize ominous tones of voice and intimidating body language. They feel sharp pains when they see their mother humiliated or degraded. They are filled with an urgent desire to rescue her, but at the same time can feel paralyzed by fear, so they are left feeling guilty standing by and not intervening. Their innocence can slip away in the process.

If their mother's partner is physically violent, they may shrink into corners trying to make themselves invisible, praying for someone to come to lead everyone to safety. Or, if they are old enough, they may jump into the fray themselves and try to stop the fighting, hoping to be the peacekeeping force. If they happen not to be where an assault occurs, they still hear the screams and threats, the crashing of thrown objects, or the blows. Or they observe overturned chairs scattered across the kitchen and see their mother crying. The next morning they notice a bruise on Mom, or they can tell by the bags under her eyes that she hasn't slept. There are so many different signs of violence that it is next to impossible for children to miss them all.

Whether abuse in the home is emotional, physical, or both, children know that it's happening and feel its impact. Studies have demonstrated that children see and hear much more of the man's abusive or violent behavior than either parent realizes. And they take it all in. There is a tremendous amount you can do to help your children cope and heal, but first you have to accept that they have been affected. (And though the effects are not your fault—responsibility lies with the abuser, not with the target of the abuse—it is up to you to guide their healing, because no one else can.)

Many forms of partner abuse spill over onto the children, but some are hard to put a name to. What do you call it when a man, furious at his wife, peels out of the driveway in the family car, so that the mother has to drag her three children across town on a hot bus to their doctor's appointment? What label do we use when children develop a strong attachment to their mother's best friend, who is like an aunt to them, and the father abruptly decrees one day that she is no longer allowed in the house because he does not like her, so the children cannot see her? What do we say of the impact on children when a mother gets the news that she is pregnant with a fourth child, her second unwanted pregnancy, because her partner refuses to use birth control and won't take no for an answer when he wants sex?

If children don't see or hear the abusive man's mistreatment of their mother, they feel the aftershocks. They see her pain, they feel her withdrawal, they hear whisperings among their older siblings about what happened.

The critical question therefore is not *whether they know you are being mistreated*—they do—but *how they are affected* by what they know. Are they suffering emotionally, and if so, what are their feelings like? What meanings and interpretations are they placing on the events that unfold before them? What lessons are they learning—and mislearning—about how to treat their loved ones, how to resolve tensions, and how to survive traumatic experiences? These are issues that this book is here to help you work through with your children.

You may also be concerned, as many mothers are, about how your partner treats your children directly. If your intuition—or your direct observations—tell you that your children are in any way unsafe with their father, you will find sections in the chapters ahead that will help you to sort out the risks. Research tells us that men who abuse women are six times more likely than other men to abuse children. Many of the mothers I speak with are especially concerned about the emotional abuse the children are enduring from their father, through hurtful put-downs, ignoring them in ways that make them feel worthless, humiliating them in front of other people, and using them as weapons in controlling or hurting the mother. So you may be looking for ways to help your children heal from what he has done to *them,* not just to you, and for strategies for protecting them from him in the years ahead.

The fact that you are choosing to read this book indicates that you are a caring parent, eager to learn ways to help your children. I find that women who are living with abuse rarely get the credit they deserve for how hard they work to understand their children's difficulties, to give them assistance, and to protect them from exposure to the abusive man's behavior. In fact, I hope that one thing you get from reading this book is the reassurance that you are already doing a great deal for your children, that steps you have already taken to shield your children from your partner's aggression, or to bring them soothing and healing love and affection, have already made an important difference in their lives. Many, perhaps even most, of the approaches you are already using to assist your children are sound. Rather than asking you to develop a radically different approach, I hope to guide you to expand the range of what you try, to draw in more support from your surrounding community, and to experiment with some new ways of being with your children. I wish to build upon the strengths of your mothering rather than pick apart the weaknesses, or supposed weaknesses (the way your partner probably does).

Many of the pages ahead, particularly in the early chapters, offer insight into what your children are going through. As you read these sections, which can be disturbing at times, you may find yourself asking, "But what is the solution to all this?" Many, many suggestions will follow, so hang in there through the hard parts; in fact, almost every chapter ends with a section called "What Can I Do?" that lists specific actions you can take and explains how to carry them out. But remember also that simply by deepening your understanding of your children's emotional landscape, you are already growing in your ability to be a healing force for them. The better you grasp the realities they face, the more patience you will have for them, the better you will respond to their emotional distress, the more skillfully you will intervene in their misbehavior, and the less you will blame them—or yourself—for the problems in your family.

As you read this book, it is important to strive to treat *yourself* with compassion, just as you attempt to show compassion to your children. You will need to take an honest look at some errors you have made in the past, but also forgive yourself for them. You will need to examine which of your coping mechanisms have been healthy and which have been less so, but remember that you have been doing your best so far, even if now you want and need to do even better. Mothers who live with abusive partners cope with their worries for their children in a number of ways. You may, for example, have persuaded yourself that the children are a separate issue, not connected to how your partner treats you, telling yourself, "He only does those things to me, not to them, and I can deal with it." Or you may have developed strategies to insulate your children, perhaps finding ways to stave off fights with him until after they've fallen asleep, or giving in to him when he's angry so they won't be exposed to the vicious reactions he has when you stand up to him. Some days you may cope by simply trying not to think about the effects he's having on the children, because you have thought and thought about it and still haven't been able to figure out how to make his abuse stop or how to get help for them. Perhaps you are thinking about ending your relationship, or have attempted to leave in the past; getting away from the abusive man can often bring a big improvement in the children's lives but sometimes it doesn't, depending on many factors that we'll examine in the chapters ahead.

None of these ways of coping is entirely good or entirely bad. You will hear neither criticism nor judgment from me in this book, as I do not want to contribute to the mountain of invalidation that your partner has no doubt already dumped on you. And unlike friends or professionals you may have talked to, I will neither encourage you to stay with your partner nor tell you to leave him (although I will ask you to look carefully at the pros and cons for your children of either option). You will do best if you respect yourself for the steps you have taken in the past to survive, while also continuing to reach for strategies that will liberate you and your children in the long term.

Abuse commonly leaves a woman feeling isolated. You may feel distant from people around you because you don't feel able to tell them about the mistreatment you are enduring, from being embarrassed or afraid to tell or because you don't want to turn people against your partner. Perhaps your partner cuts you off from other people by accusing you of cheating on him or by making it difficult for you to go certain places or see people you care about. This leads to one of the most critical messages of this book:

If you want to be able to protect your children from your angry or controlling partner, it is very important to expand your own base of support.

Even if it seems impossible to reach out right away, look for any avenue you can find in the weeks and months ahead to talk on an abuse hotline, speak to a neighbor, get on the Internet at your town library, or meet a friend for a quick lunch. You can have much greater success putting the insights and advice from this book into practice if you expand the resources and support available to you. (For further suggestions, see Resources, "Child Protective Services Issues," page 349.)

Finally, I want to reassure you that the chapters ahead will address the issues that are most burning for you. Mothers who live with abuse often find that confusion is a daily experience, and that there are many perplexing issues to sort out in order to figure out how best to assist their children. Therefore, I have set out to answer the questions that abused women most commonly ask me about their children, including:

Can my partner abuse me and still be a good father?

Why are my children so defiant with me—and so well behaved with him?

Is my son going to turn out like him?

How much should I tell my children about the abuse?

Will my daughter get involved with men like her father?

Should I leave him for the good of my children?

How do I get the court and the child protection workers to stop talking to me like I'm the one with the problem?

How can I help my children heal?

As we explore these questions and many related ones, you will learn how to help your children open up about their feelings, how to make a "safety plan" with them, how to choose a good therapist or support group for them, ways to assess how likely your partner is to abuse the children, and a range of other concrete, practical skills that will help you to build—or rebuild—the kind of family life you are craving.

A set of crucial messages is woven through the insights—which are sometimes painful—and the guidance that I offer in this book. Since I am eager to have you take these points to heart, and hold them inside you as you take on the challenging work that lies ahead, I want to summarize them right from the start:

- You *can* make a difference, a big one in fact, in how life goes for your children.
- One of the best ways to help your children is to get good help for yourself.
- Children see what is going on around them, even when you think they don't, and they learn (and mislearn) from what they see.
- Neither you nor your children deserve verbal abuse, disrespect, coercive control, or intimidation.
- Facing your children's distress can be painful for you, but you will be glad you did it.
- Children need at least one parent who can validate the effects the abuse is having on them.
- In order to understand the impact your partner is having on your children, you will have to look squarely at how he is treating and affecting *you*.
- You are the most important person in your children's lives.

- If they get access to the right support and resources, children can heal.
- If you and your children have been driven apart, you can grow close again.
- It isn't too late.

Raising children well is perhaps the single most difficult task in the human lifespan. To do so while being undermined, denigrated, or bullied by your partner is harder still. It is my fervent hope that the chapters ahead will help you feel understood and supported in the challenges you face. I also hope that my words will give you confidence that you can be your children's bedrock, bringing them feelings of security and self-esteem, and creating an environment in which they can heal and flourish. And above all I hope that the options I share in these pages will help you to find a path for yourself and your children toward a life that is free from abuse and full of kindness, affection, appropriate discipline, and love. I believe you can do it.

Part I

The Abusive
Man and
Your Children

Chapter Two

The Abusive Mindset and Children

"He pressured me into having natural childbirth, and then called me a 'wimp' when I broke down and accepted an epidural."

"He expects the children to take care of his feelings, instead of the other way around."

"He's vicious to me sometimes, but our children think he's great."

"He tells everyone he loves being a dad, but his patience wears thin really quickly when it gets difficult."

Your angry or controlling partner is a daily presence in your children's lives and minds. Their emotional experiences, their perceptions of you as a mother, and their view of the world are all being shaped by the messages he sends them and the example his behavior sets. They struggle, just as you do, to figure out how to feel about him. Do I love him? Do I hate him? Can I trust him? Is he going to turn his abusive behavior toward me one day? Will he change?

They also grapple with questions about him as a role model. Is there something wrong with what he is doing, or is his behavior Mom's fault—or our fault? Should I try to be like him, or not? Do I need to learn how to abuse power the way he does in order to avoid becoming his victim, or the victim of someone like him?

Your partner's mistreatment of you, whether it occurs daily or intermittently, raises questions for your children about you as well. Is Mommy as bad as he sometimes says she is? Is it okay for us to talk to Mom the way he talks to her? Is Mommy going to be able to protect us from his verbal (or physical) rampages? Does Mommy really care about us? (I know that you care deeply about your children or you wouldn't be reading this book, but your abusive partner may create confusion for your children about whether you are there for them or not, in ways that we will see.)

Over time, you can help your children resolve these pressing and perplexing questions for themselves. Your leadership is critical to them. But to lay the groundwork of insight and empathy that your children are looking for from you, we need to begin at the beginning, examining the nature and dynamics of an abusive man's problem. If you have read my book *Why Does He Do That?*, you will recognize the characteristics of abusers as I discuss them. But this time I will be focusing on how his problem affects the lives of your children and impinges upon you as a mother.

Abusive men vary a great deal in how negatively they affect the children, although they always have some degree of hurtful impact. You may find that your partner creates only a few of the problems I describe below, or many of them. This chapter will help you to recognize and name certain difficulties that may be arising in your family, which is the first step toward finding solutions.

Control

What do the following actions have in common?

- Your partner yells at you to shut up.
- You are trying to make a point in an argument, and he snarls, "You are such a stupid idiot, you obviously just don't listen."
- You say hello to a friend from work on the street and your partner immediately jumps into interrogating you about whether you are attracted to him.
- Your partner sulks if he doesn't get his way, or gives you the silent treatment, until you give in.

The common thread is *control*. Your partner is interfering with your freedom to express your opinions, to stand up to him, or to have freedom to care about other people. The explosive outbursts that he subjects you to, the cutting remarks, the accusations, the periods of silent treatment, all share at their core his desire to control you.

Along with those behaviors comes a set of attitudes to justify what he does; he believes that he has the right to have the last word in a conflict, that his way is the only way—especially when the stakes are high—and that if you resist being controlled by him your defiance proves that there's something wrong with *you*. If you stand up for yourself at the wrong time—and it may always be the wrong time—you pay a stiff price; he retaliates with name calling, ridicule, or physical intimidation.

Think back over incidents in which your partner has hurt you emotionally or frightened you, and ask yourself, "What was he trying to control about me in that situation?" You will find that you can come up with an answer for most incidents; once you understand that his goal is to control you, the behavior of your abusive partner rapidly starts to make more sense.

The abusive man's control of his partner touches the lives of children in many ways, sometimes beginning before they are even born. Some of my clients in abuser groups, for example, have histories of refusing to use birth control so they cause their partners unwanted pregnancies. The birth process itself can be an arena for the man's control. One woman recounted to me, for example, how her partner yelled at her for being grouchy while she was in labor and called her a "bitch" at the hospital, adding, "Look at you, you're a mess." A client of mine who was a fanatical believer in natural childbirth called his wife a "quitter" when she finally couldn't take the pain anymore and accepted an epidural during her long and difficult labor with her first child. A man's behavior during pregnancy and childbirth is a preview of what his parenting style is going to be like, and of the troubles that lie ahead.

Research has shown that women who have intimidating partners are far more likely than other women to feel that they have to change their approach to parenting when their partner is around. If the woman knows that the man demands stricter discipline, then she becomes harsher and more rigid than she really wants to be. If, on the other hand, he insists that she not impose discipline, she becomes a loose and permissive parent under his gaze. In short, he makes it hard for her to stick to what she really believes is best for her children.

If this problem feels familiar, you may now find yourself asking, "But isn't this my own fault for putting up with it? Shouldn't I just stop letting him push me around as a mother?"

The answer is, "It depends." You should try to be more assertive with your partner *if that makes things go better for you and your children.* But here lies precisely the bind many women find themselves in: Some abusive men respond by making things *worse* for the family when they are challenged. If, for example, you tell your partner to please stop undermining you with the children, and he retaliates by loudly calling you a "stupid bitch" in their presence, the way out for you is far from clear. So begin by not blaming yourself for his control of your parenting.

Other clients of mine make the mother herself pay for sticking up for the children. Jim Ptacek's important study *Battered Women in the Courtroom* (Northeastern University Press) found that nearly a quarter of women who go before a judge to seek a protective order are there because the man has threatened or assaulted the woman *about her parenting,* usually specifically related to her refusing to bow to his decrees. Dictatorial control over the whole family is widespread among abusive men. One way of formulating the view that many abusive men have about child-rearing is:

He considers the children *the woman's* domain of responsibility but *his* domain of *authority.*

In other words, he feels that the mother should do the bulk of the childcare, but he should have the right to make the most important decisions about how they will be raised.

Take a moment to examine the question of whether your rights as a mother are being denied by your partner, using the list below as a guide. You have the right to *fully equal say* over how your children are to be raised, including:

- What styles of discipline they will experience.
- What their daily routines will be.
- What freedoms they will be permitted.
- How they are allowed to express their emotions.
- What people they can spend time with, including your friends and relatives.
- What schools and religious institutions they will attend.
- What types of extracurricular activities they can participate in.

- How to approach every other aspect of the complex and highly demanding process of deciding how best to help children flourish.

If your partner is disrespecting or overruling you as a mother, or is bullying your parenting decisions, that isn't good fathering. If he exhibits a dictatorial "head of the household" mentality, even occasionally, that's unhealthy for your children and unfair to you. So to the extent you safely can—depending on how severely retaliatory your partner is—start working to recover your voice over child-rearing decisions, and reach out for support to help yourself get stronger.

Entitlement

Does your partner expect you to live up to a high and unreasonable set of demands and expectations? Yet at the same time does he act angry or victimized when you demand anything of *him?* Is he selfishly focused on his own needs, even if he was generous early in your relationship or is generous with other people? Do you feel that no matter how hard you try, nothing you do for him seems to be good enough, and he always acts as if you owe him even more? The answers to these questions reveal a man's level of *entitlement,* which is the fundamental outlook that drives men's abuse of women. It is your partner's entitlement, not your faults or failures, that is causing him to be chronically critical of you and dissatisfied.

Parenting children while living with a highly entitled man can be exhausting. I once asked the partner of one of my clients how many children she had, and she replied, "Five—four young ones plus him. He creates more of a burden than they do, to tell you the truth, because he always wants more."

If your partner is very entitled, you may notice that your energy and attention keep being drawn away from your children and onto him. Does he, for example, become irritable when he feels that you are too focused on the young ones and "ignoring" him? Does he say, "You care more about the children than you do about me"? These kinds of statements reveal his belief that his needs should come ahead of the children's, and that the arrival of children into the home should not reduce the catering he receives. Matthew, whom we met in chapter 1, illustrated this attitude when he accused Grace of using her pregnancy as an excuse to be lazy.

QUESTION #1:
Why do some men begin their abuse, or escalate it, during pregnancy?

A man's selfish focus on his own needs is sometimes revealed most sharply during his partner's pregnancy. When a woman is carrying a child, she has to focus on doing what is good for her and for the growing fetus. She needs to eat well, get rest, and keep her back and legs strong. She strives to avoid stress and conflict, since they can have a negative impact on her health or the baby's. She may feel ill, particularly in the early months, and have unpredictable and deep mood swings. These are all normal aspects of pregnancy.

The more entitled a man is, the greater difficulty he has accepting these changes in the woman's life. One of my clients, for example, responded to his girlfriend's vomiting in the morning by scolding her for not fixing him breakfast. Abusive men often exhibit this kind of refusal to look beyond their own comfort or convenience.

In social circles, the pregnant woman tends to become the center of attention. Friends and family check on how she's feeling, ask if the baby is kicking, bring the mother food and drink, and give her advice (often more than she wants). The abusive man doesn't take well to seeing everyone's energy directed toward his partner; *he* wants to be in the spotlight.

Effective child-rearing relies on a parent's ability to put the children's needs ahead of his or her own. But an angry and controlling man commonly expects the children to meet *his* needs, reversing the proper roles. If your partner is of this style, check for signs that your children may be becoming burdened with a sense of responsibility to take care of him. By emphasizing and modeling for them that children are not responsible for taking care of adults, you can help make sure they do not take on a "parentified" role toward their father—or toward you. This in turn will help them not lose touch with their own needs and desires and start to feel unsure about who they are.

Start to notice whether your partner's demands are frequently drawing you away from being able to fully attend to your children, or if his entitled attitude is interfering with your family life in other ways.

Disrespect

Disrespect and abuse are almost synonymous. You don't abuse someone you respect, and you don't respect someone you abuse. I have almost never had a client who didn't exhibit various kinds of contempt, superiority, and demeaning behavior toward his wife or girlfriend—it comes with the territory of abuse, and in many ways *is* the abuse.

Unfortunately, it is next to impossible for children to remain unaware of their father's core attitude toward their mother. If he is condescending and arrogant, if derision and disgust rumble in his voice and contort his facial expressions when he addresses you, your children can't really miss it. They hear him interrupt you over and over again or see him laugh at you; they sense that he sees you as beneath him, and they observe that he doesn't consider your feelings or opinions worth listening to.

And he is a key role model for them, whether he is their father or not, and they may learn from him how to treat you and each other. If he views you as hysterical, over time they may come to have a similar attitude. If they hear him call you a bitch, they may learn to do the same. They may start to express their annoyance toward you with the same condescending ring to their voices that he has. (And if your partner is a physical abuser, your children, particularly your sons, can be at risk to physically assault you themselves or hit their sisters and younger siblings, as several research studies have demonstrated.)

If you are chronically facing contemptuous or defiant behavior from your children, the root problem may be in your partner. In the chapters ahead, I discuss various strategies for overcoming the attitudes and behaviors that the abusive man models for the family, so you can guide your children toward an outlook of mutual respect and caring.

Manipulation

Consider the dynamics of the following scenarios from cases I've been involved in:

• An abusive man talks privately to his nine-year-old daughter in his room, with tears streaming down his cheeks, about how mean Mommy is to him. He also says to her, "Your brother told me he thinks your new haircut looks stupid, but I think it's nice."

• Because of her alcoholism, a woman has lost custody of her children to the state, which has placed them in foster care. During a period when she is sober and on the road to getting her children back, her abusive husband keeps buying beer and keeping it in the refrigerator—even though he doesn't drink himself—

"just in case friends come over, so I can have something to offer them."

• A client of mine agrees to stay home with the children one evening so his wife can go out with friends, but around dinnertime a big argument breaks out and he storms out of the house without the children, forcing her to cancel her plans. He later admits to me in session that he provoked the confrontation because he wanted to go out himself.

• A divorced abusive man tells his teenage son that if he leaves his mother's house and comes to live with him, he'll buy him his own car.

Most abusive men do not rely entirely on outright verbal abuse, threats, or physical intimidation. They find that they can gain more power by using subtler tactics of *manipulation* that are much harder to name or identify. These can involve quite a range of elements, a few of which include:

• Lying to people or misleading them to get them to do what he wants them to do, or to turn them against each other.
• Concealing his real motives to convince people that he is trying to help them, when he is actually fixed on furthering his own interests.
• Playing on people's longings or other vulnerabilities, buying their allegiance.
• Getting people to feel sorry for him regarding situations that are largely of his own making.

Most of my clients, for example, cultivate a positive public image. They do favors for friends and neighbors, they joke and laugh, they play up to people in positions of influence, working to develop allies who can support their denial or back up their abusiveness.

I find that the abusive man with children concerns himself particularly with how people view him as a father. He may make himself a prominent presence at sporting events and awards ceremonies, yet be pretty scarce when it's time to change diapers or rise out of bed when a child calls for help in the middle of the night. He may praise his children for the benefit of the neighbor's ears, yet at home always find fault with them, tearing down their self-confidence and self-esteem.

What are children to make of their father's popularity? One likely outcome is that they will think, "No one else seems to notice anything wrong with him, so the problem must be with one of us." This impression can be reinforced by the blaming words he yells at you or at them around the house: "You pushed me too far, it's your own damned fault, if you weren't so stupid this wouldn't happen."

Your partner's manipulations can even color *your own view* of his parenting. When I ask the partners of my clients whether there are any problems in how the man treats the children, they commonly answer, "Oh, no, he's mean to me, but he's nice to them. He's a really good father." But when I follow up with specific and detailed questions, I find the great majority of the time that my clients are indeed causing problems in the family. I ask such questions as:

> *Does he make you look bad in front of the children?*
> *Does he undermine your parenting?*
> *Does he make it seem like he's going to be there for the children and then fail to come through for them?*
> *Does his anger sometimes scare them?*
> *Does he favor any child over others?*

The woman is often surprised by her own answers, as she had never thought about household tensions in these terms. You may find that you have in fact been noticing destructive effects that your partner has on the atmosphere of your home, but you have been blocking them from consciousness because his periods of charm and manipulation toward the children (and toward you) get you confused about who he is.

Not every abusive man manipulates the children or sows tensions among family members—at least not deliberately. But if you look closely, beyond the surface impressions that he creates, you may find that your children, and your relationships with them, are suffering more than you were aware of, and that there are steps you need to take to keep your children from being manipulated.

Intimidation

Most abusive men become physically intimidating at some point. This pattern typically involves some degree of physical violence: punching walls, smashing objects, poking or grabbing you, blocking your path, threatening you, driving in a terrifying way with you in the car. (You may not have thought of these kinds of behaviors as "violent" before, but they are.) He may also intimidate you in subtler ways, by towering over you during arguments, getting frighteningly loud, turning bright red with rage, or making veiled threats such as, "You're really pushing me too far," or "You don't want to find out what I'm capable of." On the other hand, he may outright assault you, as a great number of abusive men do, with slaps, punches, choking, kicking, or other attacks that can be terrifying or cause serious injury.

Children pick up on the threats, whether implied or explicitly stated, that are communicated by the abusive man's explosive outbursts and aggressive body language, and your flinching or frightened reactions. The research on children's exposure to partner abuse shows that they are aware of much more of their father's violence than the parents think they are, and can sometimes describe incidents in detail that both Mom and Dad didn't think the child even saw. These experiences are scary for children. They worry that their mother will get hurt, perhaps so severely that she won't be able to look after them. They lie awake in bed staring into the dark or wake up later from nightmares. And they worry that someday he will turn his violent behavior toward them; although I have sometimes heard mothers say, "Oh, my children know that he would never hurt them, no matter what he does to me," the reality is that they *don't* know that, and can't.

I understand how difficult it can be to accept the reality of your children's fear or terror when your head is already swirling with your own. But they need you to notice. And, as we will see, they need you to find ways to have open discussions with them about how scary certain incidents can be for them.

Isolation

Some abusive men treat their partners like personal possessions that can be shown off on certain occasions and kept under lock and key the rest of the time. Do you find that your partner keeps a close eye on you? Has his behavior driven away any of your friends or relatives, or made it difficult for you to see loved ones and keep in touch? Has he claimed that these rifts are for your own good, or for the good of the family ("They get too much in our business," or "Your family tries to control you, you need to break free from them," or "We always have a fight after you see them; they aren't good for you")? When an abusive man impedes his partner's social connections, his goal is to make her dependent on him and always available to him. He wants her to always be focusing on meeting his needs, free from any distractions—such as having her own life—that might get in the way. And on some level he's afraid that if she has close and healthy contacts with other people, she will find the strength to get free from his bullying and demands. (And he might be right.)

If your partner uses isolation tactics with you, take a moment to examine whether he is also cutting your children off socially. If you are afraid to see certain friends because he turns hostile if he finds out, or if you feel you have to stay at home all day because of how angry he gets if you aren't there when he calls to talk to you, your children can miss important life experiences. If he refuses to provide any money for the children to be involved in activities, that intensifies the problem. They may not get to have a broad range of people in their lives, they may miss out on chances to have fun, to get exposed to stimulating ideas, or to feel part of their community. You and your children can get on each other's nerves if you feel cooped up in the house together, and they may start to take their frustrations out on you, since they have no way of understanding that Dad is the cause of the restrictions they live with.

Isolation can be the glue that holds all the other aspects of abuse together. It is difficult for women and their children to heal from abuse, and find a way to make it stop, unless they can get help and support. So if you are feeling cut off from other people or experiences, one of your highest priorities needs to be to search for ways to reach out and expand your freedom, for your own sake and for your children. Here are some steps to consider:

• First, pay attention to whether the isolation is being imposed on you by your partner, and by your fears of how he will react if you go out or talk to people, or if, on the other hand, your isolation is self-imposed. You can solve the problem either way, but first you have to notice where it's coming from.

• Unless your partner is frightening to you, try asserting your need to be out more. Explain that your children need more social contact and experiences, and that you and they need a break from being in the house together. Put your foot down with him as much as you safely can.

- Call a hotline for abused women to talk about the isolation and get emotional support. (See Resources, page 337.)

- Open up with your friends and family about the fact that he makes it hard for you to see them, and strategize with them about ways to increase your contact.

- Involve your children in activities in the community as much as possible, such as lessons or sports teams, which will have the additional benefit of giving you a good excuse to go places with them.

The Importance of Your Leadership

I want to step back now for a moment from these various examples of ways in which an abusive man can cause turmoil for a mother and her children. You are probably finding, as you read, that your partner exhibits some of these weaknesses but not others. You may also be thinking about ways in which his unhealthy parenting qualities are offset by his better aspects, such as times when he is kind to the children, takes an interest in getting to know them, or supports you in the challenges of being a mother. Perhaps your partner hasn't abused you during your pregnancies. Maybe he has made the effort to attend school conferences and doctor appointments. You may struggle with the question of how to balance these pros and cons, a question that weighs on many abused mothers. But what matters most for now is to begin reflecting on the ways in which your children's distresses, or conflicts you have with them, may be rooted in your partner's abusiveness. From there, you can develop a course of action to help your children heal from what they have heard, seen, and felt.

QUESTION #2:
Can he abuse me and still be
a good father?

Even an abusive man who treats children reasonably well, and who doesn't damage the mother's ability to care for her children, still provides a role model for children of men abusing women, and creates an unhealthy atmosphere in the home. A good father does not abuse his children's mother. The abusive man teaches children that abusing a woman is excusable, that men can blame women for their own actions, and that disrespect is normal. Therefore, your children need you to be their guide and leader to the fullest extent possible. You are the person in the best position to help them choose the road toward love, kindness, nonviolence, and respect for all people—including you. I have seen so many abused women manage, even in extraordinarily painful or unsafe circumstances, to be their children's anchor in the storm, to keep their children whole and hopeful. The chapters ahead will, I believe, help you on your way toward that goal.

Key Points to Remember

- Abusiveness toward women involves a predictable constellation of attitudes, values, and behaviors on the part of the abusive man.
- Each of the characteristics typical of abusive men has important potential implications for children in the home. Every child who has frequent contact with a man who abuses women will be affected by that relationship.
- A good father does not abuse his children's mother. A man's abuse of a mother proves in itself that he is not

thinking or caring adequately about what is good for the children.

- Being conscious of your partner's abusiveness, as hard as that may be to face, will make you a more effective parent and healing resource for your children.
- Your children, both daughters and sons, need you to be their primary leader and positive role model, since a man who abuses women cannot fill that role.
- You are the most important person in your children's life. You can make a tremendous difference to them. You are their mother.

Chapter Three

Abusive Men as Parents

"He won't listen to what the children have to say. He just lays down the law and that's it."

"He turns into SuperDad when we're around other people."

"I don't feel like he really knows our children. I wish he would take more of an interest in them."

"He can be so nice to them sometimes, but on a different day he'll be so selfish I can hardly believe it. The children keep getting their feelings hurt by him."

"I would rather have him hurt me than hurt them. That's the worst."

Before we can enter children's emotional world and begin developing ways to help them work through the abuse they have heard and seen, we need to spend some time considering a few other areas in which your partner may cause discomfort or confusion for your children. These issues focus on his *direct interactions* with your children. As with the areas explored in chapter 2, you are likely to find that he exhibits some of these weaknesses but not all of them.

By the time you are finished with this chapter, you will have a thorough basis on which to assess which challenges are the most pressing ones that you and your children are currently facing. You will then be able to use the remainder of this book to help you design responses that will move your family toward healing and strength.

What Good Parenting Requires

Raising children is an extraordinarily demanding task, as any caring, involved parent knows. To do it well demands a wealth of knowledge, patience, energy, and flexibility. Here are just a few of the strengths and abilities that a parent is called upon to use in meeting children's needs and providing leadership for them:

- To focus on them for long periods of time, paying attention to what they say in words and what they communicate through other signals.
- To put the children's needs ahead of your own most of the time, which often means having to delay the meeting of your own needs, perhaps for years.
- To listen respectfully to children's opinions and complaints and make careful adjustments in your parenting approach based on what your children are expressing about themselves, while still remaining in authority and relying on your own judgment as the ultimate guide.
- To see each child as an individual who needs a unique parenting style, rather than making the mistake of thinking that one approach or philosophy can fit all children.
- To accept that your children will love other adults in addition to you, and handle the jealous or competitive feelings that may come up for you without dumping them on the child.

- To accept that your children will grow and gradually become independent from you.
- To balance your responsibility to keep your children safe with their need for independence.
- To accept that your children are their own people, not carbon copies of you.

No parent can succeed in all of these areas all the time. We struggle with our own anger and frustrations, and we collide with demons inside us, often ones that are still lurking from the worst aspects of how we ourselves were raised. Since we can't lay aside all of our own needs for twenty years while our children grow up, we feel the tension of how to find time and space to feel close to other adults, to have some fun, to get some exercise, to spend some time quietly thinking or reading or listening to music.

Given that these challenges can be overwhelming for any of us, imagine what it means for an abusive man to attempt to raise children, or even be around them frequently. He may genuinely like children, he may even be excited about the prospect of fatherhood—I have certainly had clients of whom these things were true—but the real-life demands of parenthood tend to bump hard against the selfish and domineering characteristics that lie at the core of his problem. As we saw in chapter 2, the abuser is a man who is highly controlling, who expects his needs to be at the top of the agenda, who thinks he is superior to his partner and often to his children as well, and who thinks he is right about everything. So although abusive men vary in how destructive they are to children, a set of themes inevitably appears to some degree in their parenting. Bringing these areas into sharp focus can deepen your insight into your children's emotional struggles.

Authoritarianism

My clients can often be heard describing their philosophies of child-rearing in terms such as these:

"If your children aren't a little afraid of you, they won't respect you."

"My wife lets the children talk back to her, but I'm not taking any of that lip from them."

"Just like armies need generals, a household needs a strong man at the command post. You have to make sure everyone understands that you're in charge."

"I'll let our kids and my wife argue for a while, but when enough is enough I have to step in and sort things out."

The thinking that lies behind an abusive man's intermittent (or constant) dictatorial control over his partner can form the underpinning of a rigid and dogmatic style with children as well. The partners of my clients frequently report being upset that the abusive man:

- Is unwilling to hear the children out about important issues, so they get silenced just as she does.
- Insists on sticking to bad parenting decisions long after it has become evident that they aren't working or aren't fair.
- Gives overly harsh punishments for misbehaviors that are typical in children.

As dozens of women have said to me, "When it comes to the children, it's his way or the highway."

Psychologists and parent educators have identified three general styles that describe most approaches to raising children. The first is *permissive parenting*. In this style, the parent does not tend to set clear or consistent limits on the children's actions, or to impose predictable consequences for misbehavior. Children are given more freedom than they are developmentally ready to handle, and the parent hopes that everything will just turn out okay. The parent tends to plead for cooperation rather than demand it, and over time the children figure out that no one is really in charge. They therefore wind up feeling insecure, and may be lacking in respect for the permissive parent. The parent gets increasingly frustrated by the children's defiance, so he or she periodically erupts in angry shouting or other inappropriate behavior with the children, and then returns to being somewhat passive and powerless. The permissive parent is often someone who lacks self-respect. (However, when abusive men are permissive parents, the cause tends to lie more in irresponsibility, or in a desire to manipulate the children's loyalties against the mother.)

The second style is *authoritarian parenting*. Here the parent exercises too much control over the children rather than too little, and the children's voices get silenced. The parent does impose consequences for misbehavior, but in a way that is too harsh so that lasting pain results for the child. The consequences tend to be erratic, so that a small transgression may lead to a huge punishment depending on the parent's mood. The authoritarian parent tends to overreact to feeling defied by children in any way, coming down on them with a loud "Bad dog!" kind of tone that can both intimidate them and make them feel dehumanized. Over time, children who are subjected to authoritarian parenting are likely to become either overly compliant automatons or wild and uncontrollable, unresponsive to any attempts to discipline them. The authoritarian parent is often someone who lacks respect for the children.

The third style, and the only approach that psychologists find brings consistently good results, is *authoritative parenting*. (It sounds almost the same as authoritarian parenting, but it's quite different.) This Mom or Dad is clearly in charge of the children, but in a way that allows the children to have a voice and takes their feelings and opinions seriously. Children are treated with respect, even when they are being disciplined by the parent, but the parent also respects herself or himself, insisting on being spoken to politely by the children and maintaining the role as the authority. The children are given freedom and responsibility appropriate to their age. The parent is flexible, making adjustments to take the children's needs into account and being willing to change decisions or parenting approaches when they aren't working. The rules are clear and explicit, and consequences are not harsh but are certain, so children can't weasel out of them. Children feel safe and secure, knowing that the parent is in charge and that they can push against him or her without the parent breaking (like the permissive parent) or lashing back at them (like the authoritarian parent). Children raised in this atmosphere learn over time to self-regulate so that they become less dependent on adults to keep them in line, and are less likely to become unquestioning followers who are subject to blindly going along with a bad set of peer influences.

The detailed descriptions of these three styles are primarily to help you analyze your partner's approach to your children, but can also help you think about your own style and how you might improve it. Many of the suggestions I offer in the chapters ahead encourage you to reach for the "authoritative parenting" style, while your partner may keep pushing you toward permissiveness or authoritarianism. Your cultural background, and that of your partner, will of course be a strong influence on the values you each have regarding appropriate parenting, and each culture has its strengths and weaknesses with respect to how well children are treated.

A fair number of my abusive clients flip back and forth between permissive and authoritarian parenting, so that the children have no idea what to expect from their father. Mothers sometimes say to me, "Every day is different. The children and I wait in suspense to see which version of Dad is coming through the door,

and whether the evening is going to be okay or is going to be hell."
(For the alcoholic or drug-addicted abuser, these ups and downs
can be partly connected to whether he has been using or not.)

My clients sometimes reveal a distorted definition of what it
means for children to "respect" parents; they confuse respect with
fear, and believe that if children aren't intimidated by their fathers
they won't take parental guidance seriously. But the reality is that
children do not benefit from being afraid of their parents. If children follow your lead because they're scared of you, later in life
they are likely to do an about-face and reject your example with
great resentment, sometimes intentionally becoming everything
they know you will most hate. Or, even worse, they may fall in with
other people who control them through fear just as their parent
did—perhaps becoming involved with an abusive partner, or joining a gang, cult, or militia. In order to have a more promising future, your children need to follow your leadership for a different
set of reasons:

- Because they feel safe and secure with you.
- Because they admire the way you live your life and want
  to be like you.
- Because they see that your way of doing things leads to
  good results.

These are examples of genuine respect for a parent, while fearing
you is not.

While authoritarian parenting is hard on any child, its destructive power grows when children are simultaneously being exposed
to the man's emotional or physical abuse of their mother. Therefore, children who have endured these kinds of experiences need
help sorting out the mutually reinforcing negative messages, including victim blaming, that they have absorbed. (And an abusive
man who decides to work seriously on changing, as some do, needs

to understand that he must become less controlling with his children, not just with his partner, if they are to heal and avoid following in his abusive footsteps.)

Underinvolvement

A few years ago, I was doing an intake interview with a man named Arthur, who was joining one of my abuser groups. I asked him the names and birth dates of his children, and he replied that he had two boys, ages fourteen and eleven, but that he didn't know the older one's birthday though he was "pretty sure" it was in August. Arthur went on to tell me that he was divorced, and that he had won custody of the older boy! He insisted his son was better off living with him, but when I asked why he didn't know the boy's birthday, he said, "Oh, when my wife and I were together, I pretty much left stuff like that up to her, so there wasn't really any reason for me to know it."

My clients use various excuses for their lack of attention to their children. One is, "I work hard all day, and when I get home I need time to rest and relax." I respond by saying, "You can't end a day of parenting responsibility by punching a clock—your partner certainly doesn't get to do that. Children have to be attended to until they fall asleep." And in reality the work doesn't even end then, since their clothes have to be laundered, lunches prepared for the next day, permission slips filled out, and a never-ending list of other tasks that call for attention. I then go on to say, "I doubt that your partner gets to spend two or three hours a day with *her* feet up, declaring that it's all been too hard for her and you need to bring her something to drink, a newspaper, and a warm dinner."

The debate doesn't end here, however, because my clients don't have an accurate concept of what is involved in running a household with children, so they brazenly declare to me that their wives or girlfriends sit on their backsides all day in front of soap operas. "I know it's true," the man will insist to me, "because she tells me what she watches." When I ask for more details, he usually tells me that she catches one or two favorite shows a day as a break. Now, *he* gets a lunch break, plus a couple of other breaks, but he still considers her a slacker for needing any rest at all. (And it often turns out that she keeps doing work, such as ironing, even while she's watching her program.)

The imbalance looks even greater when we consider the fact that the single-breadwinner household is largely a thing of the past. When I ask a client about his partner's weekly schedule, I generally find out that she is working part-time or full-time outside the house *on top of* doing the bulk of housework and childcare the rest of the time, which makes his excuses for not helping even weaker.

(I do occasionally have cases where the woman genuinely isn't accomplishing much during the day, but it usually turns out that she is suffering from depression, due largely or entirely to the fact that she is being abused.)

In short, the abusive man may want the status of father and the pleasures of having children, but he tends to lose interest rapidly when it comes to the hardships and sacrifices. He may be enthusiastically and proudly present when the baby emerges from the birth canal, he may jump to give the baby that exciting first bite of solid food six months later, or to be there for the drop-off on the child's first day of school. But he'll be much harder to find the third time somebody has to get up to feed or calm the baby in one night; or when a daughter or son needs some patient help with challenging homework; or when the transportation to school becomes a daily grind instead of an exciting event. At these times, his entitlement comes creeping in and he slips back toward his selfish and self-centered habits.

Dad's lack of availability to the children sometimes has the sad effect of *increasing* his value in their eyes, the way any scarce commodity becomes more desirable. Most of the time he may be critical and invalidating toward them, or ignore them, so when he turns attentive or kind the children feel grateful and enchanted by his power. If this dynamic is present in your family, you may need to gently help your children become aware of how their starvation for Dad's attention is setting them up to be manipulated.

Neglect and Irresponsibility

Allow me now to take a few of the characteristics that make up men who abuse or control women, and mix them together.

- Self-centeredness, so he often isn't paying very good attention.
- Disrespect, so he doesn't necessarily take children seriously when they make cries of fear or distress (such as waking from a nightmare).
- Arrogance, so he thinks his own judgment about what is safe or wise for children is the only measure he needs to use.
- Manipulativeness, so he wants to win the children over to his side by impressing them with how fun, casual, and risk-taking he is capable of being.

The result? A recipe for children to have their needs overlooked, and to periodically be placed in danger. Certain scenarios along these lines repeatedly turn up in the cases I'm involved in, some more common while couples are still together and others more frequent post-separation. These include:

- Allowing the children to watch movies or play video games that are inappropriately sexual or violent.
- Exposing the children to pornography by carelessly leaving it where they can get access to it.
- Taking the children in the car without proper seat restraints, sometimes combined with scary driving or alcohol consumption.

- Allowing teenagers to go wherever they want with anyone they choose, placing no restrictions on the hours they keep, and ignoring obvious signs of drug or alcohol abuse.
- Ignoring other signs of potential danger, such as allowing children to go down ski trails that are too advanced for them or allowing them to play too close to traffic.
- Bringing his friends who abuse substances, abuse women, or chronically get in trouble with the police over to the house and exposing the children to them.
- Abusing their mother in front of them or where they can hear it.

If your partner is controlling or abusive toward you, try not to leave your children in his care. If you have to rely on him for childcare while you work, or on an occasional evening when you desperately need a break, make sure that you speak with them about how the time went, and take seriously any concerns or upset that they have about his parenting, or any unexplained injuries. Try also to get an idea of what kind of material they saw on television or video. Your children need to know they can count on you to keep them safe. Dozens of abused women have told me over the years how regretful they feel that they didn't tune in sooner to their children's subtle—or not so subtle—cries for help.

Undermining of the Mother

Take a moment to answer whether you agree or disagree with the following statements:

My children act as though they don't respect me.

                                    YES_____   NO_____

My children ignore limits I attempt to set for them.

                                    YES_____   NO_____

My partner is rude or domineering to me in front of the children.

YES_____ NO_____

My partner overrules or undercuts my parenting decisions.

YES_____ NO_____

My partner doesn't think I'm a very good mother, especially when it comes to big or tense issues.

YES_____ NO_____

To control my children, I have to threaten to tell their father what they did.

YES_____ NO_____

My children listen to their father more than they listen to me.

YES_____ NO_____

If you find yourself answering yes to some of these questions, there is a good chance that your partner's conduct is undermining your authority with the children.

Abuse undermines a woman's parental authority by its very nature, because children learn from the abusive man's example that disrespecting you is acceptable. In addition, your partner may deliberately undermine you as a way to increase his power and control in the home. Chapter 7 examines this problem in detail, with many suggested solutions.

Wanting Children (and You) to Be Just Like Him

Does your partner seem aggravated or affronted when you refuse to be a carbon copy of him? Does he view any way in which you are different from him as a way that you are inferior to him (for example, his taste in music is "good" and yours is "bad")? Does he turn rapidly irritable when your opinions on friends, politics, or other subjects don't line up with his? In short, does he seem bothered that you are your own person, and not simply an extension of him or a loyal follower of his leadership? These are all behaviors that I call *identity control*. They are products of the abusive man's superiority and his lack of respect for personal boundaries.

When an abusive man has this problem, it may spill over into his child-rearing, so that he has trouble accepting his children as independent human beings with their own thoughts and feelings. He may even view them as personal possessions, which he has the right to mold and control as he chooses. Children living in this atmosphere can come out feeling suffocated by Dad, yet at the same time try hard to shape themselves into a form that will please him. If this dynamic appears in your family, your children will have an intensified need for you to be someone who can support the development of their separate identities, as I discuss further on.

Believing He Knows It All

Men usually come into parenting with less knowledge and experience than women do. They typically do less baby-sitting during their teenage years, take less responsibility for the care of their younger siblings, and receive less advice from their parents about bringing up the next generation. So to be effective parents they need to be willing to learn from their partners, accepting guidance and feedback as they work to become more skilled.

But unfortunately, the abusive man doesn't like to admit that his partner is better prepared for raising children, much less to look to her for leadership. I have clients who speak with the authority of a king about how children should be raised but turn out to have abysmal parenting judgment and little familiarity even with their own children. Arrogance and ignorance in these men go hand in glove. If you are finding that your partner has a frustrating degree of closed-mindedness when you attempt to educate or influence his parenting, this is why. You may not be able to make him listen to you, but you can at least hold onto the reality that it's his problem, not yours.

Child Abuse

There is no concern as great for an abused mother as her worries about whether her partner will harm her children as he has her. This section will help you sort out how great the risk is that the abusive man will hit, violate, or be emotionally cruel to your sons or daughters, and the following section will guide you in the steps to take if he does.

There is a substantial overlap between the particular style of abusiveness a man uses toward his partner and the forms in which he mistreats children; both research studies and my clinical experience indicate that around 40 percent of abusive men carry their behavior pattern over onto other family members. So if your partner screams and swears at you, be alert to whether he is verbally abusive to your children as well. If he finds fault with every aspect of your character and barrages you with impossible demands, notice whether he is tearing the children down and making them feel that nothing they do is ever good enough. And if he threatens you, hits you, or shoves you around, check with them periodically to make sure he isn't physically abusing them as well.

QUESTION #3:
How can I tell whether he is going to abuse my children?

Physical Abuse

The research on child abuse provides some warning signs you can watch for in a man whose violent tendencies are likely to carry over onto the children, including:

- If he is highly controlling or domineering toward you, and especially if he uses violence, threats, or other physically scary behavior.
- If he abuses drugs or alcohol.
- If he has rigid attitudes about how children should behave and how strictly or harshly they should be punished.
- If he was abused himself growing up.
- If he threatens to hurt the children (which is abuse in itself).

If your children report to you that your partner has hit or frightened them, take their reports seriously and begin strategizing ways to keep them safe, such as leaving with the children for a period of time, demanding that he stop hitting the children (if you safely can), or calling child protective services (see chapter 10).

If your partner hurts your children accidentally in the course of threatening or assaulting you, that's child abuse, too. He might hit a child with a blow that was meant for you, or shove a child out of his way to get his hands on you, or knock you down while a child is in your arms. One of your children might intervene physically to try to stop a fight and get injured in the process. If any of these kinds of injury happen to your child, your partner is responsible, not you or the child. At the same time, it falls to you to find a way to protect them from him, which may mean having to call the police, a therapist, or a child protective worker for assistance. We will look at the options below.

Psychological Abuse

Among the most frequent sources of pain for the abused mothers I speak with is watching their children be emotionally torn down by their father, through such behaviors as:

Put-downs: He criticizes the children in a harsh and insensitive way, belittling their athletic abilities, calling them "stupid," "bonehead," and similar names, ridiculing their anger or hurt feelings. Daughters can be particular targets of body insults such as "fatso" and "smelly," and may develop a preoccupation about their body image as a result. The father is often oblivious to how deeply his words are cutting the child, although he also may deliberately target the subjects that are most sensitive for them or humiliate them in public. Sometimes the abuse of the woman and the child come in the same sweep, as in insults such as, "You're just as dumb and overemotional as your mother is."

Ignoring: Some women report to me that the abusive man treats one (or more) of the children as if he or she barely exists, or behaves in other openly rejecting ways. I had a case recently where the mother's live-in boyfriend literally would not speak to her twelve-year-old son for weeks, looking right past him as if he were a phantom, because the boy had stuck up for his mother against her partner's bullying of her. The silence can be scary for children, as well as emotionally injurious, because they may see it as a warning sign that their father will soon be exploding.

Making and breaking promises: Dozens of mothers have shared their upset with me over watching their children repeatedly disappointed by promises to spend time with them, take them on special outings, or bring them certain presents that their fathers failed to keep. In a similar vein, I often hear reports of abusive men ruining special days in their children's lives, such as birthdays or important holidays.

Sexual Abuse

Men who abuse women have considerably higher rates than other men of violating children's boundaries. However, rather than becoming alarmed about this possibility, which will cause stress for you, it's best instead to work to prevent sexual abuse before it happens. Teach your children about their rights to privacy and about the importance of not keeping secrets from you, and take seriously anything they do complain of regarding even subtle boundary violations. Without any direct confrontation, you can demonstrate to your partner that you intend to be alert to your children's safety. We will examine these issues in detail in chapter 5, including warning signs of those abusive men who are most likely to be invasive with children.

What Can I Do?

Most chapters in this book end with a section like this one, giving practical advice for how you can promote your children's well-being in the face of the challenges I have described. These ideas will get more plentiful in the chapters ahead, as I begin to explain more about children's emotional reactions, but here are some ideas you can already begin to apply:

Work to overcome any denial you have about how your partner treats you. If you are not being altogether honest with yourself about the level of control or cruelty that your partner is subjecting you to, you could fall into underestimating the impact on your children. If, for example, you tend to blame yourself when he gets irrationally angry, you may catch yourself telling your children that it's their fault when he screams at *them*. If you keep telling yourself that he really isn't so bad—while your inner voice is telling you something different—then you could slip into thinking that your children are overreacting to their father or playing the victim. If these examples ring a bell for you, try to face more squarely how he is affecting you, and in turn you will be able to support and protect your children more solidly.

Believe your children. If your partner is controlling, scary, or overly angry toward you, it's unlikely that your children are exaggerating or inventing their reports of how he treats them. They need you to believe and support them, avoiding the kinds of mistakes that we saw Breanna make in chapter 1. Children tend to reveal the truth about their home experience not only through their words, but in their behavior and emotional reactions.

Understand that the solution may not be immediately clear. Part of what makes abused mothers feel tempted to discount their children's complaints about Dad, or to overlook their behavioral reactions, is the thought, "If what they are saying is true, I have to do something about it, but I don't know what to do." Trust that solutions will come to you over time, with the help of the pages ahead. Many avenues toward healing exist. In the meantime, your children need you to take their concerns seriously. In fact, validating what they are feeling is every bit as important as finding a way to make your partner's destructive behaviors stop.

Help your children to feel held by you. I am speaking not so much of hugging or cuddling your children, although physical affection is very important, but of making your child feel *emotionally* held. Think of your heart as having arms, and of wanting your children to feel those loving arms wrapped around them all the time, even when they are far from you. Keep asking yourself, "What can I do that will make the children feel that I am a safe harbor for them?"

If your partner is violent to your children, consider involving the police or child protective services. Consider also reaching out for help to a program for abused women or to a therapist, but be aware that those professionals may be mandated to report your partner's child abuse to child protective services if you give them your name. If you are struggling with how to respond, begin by talking to a hotline without telling who you are, and ask them to help you think through your options.

Take pride in your strengths as a mother, and build on them. Don't believe what your partner may tell you about what a bad parent you are. If he knew so well what was good for children, he wouldn't be abusing you. Look for help and feedback from other sources, such as books on parenting, family centers, and children's medical providers. (See also the Resources section in this book.) *Every* parent needs to work on improving his or her parenting— but don't look to your abusive partner for guidance on how to do it. And remember, there is much you do well as a mother already.

Don't hit your children. Give up spanking and any other form of violence toward your children. I understand how tempting the use of physical discipline can be, and in many cultures it is widely accepted, but an extensive collection of research demonstrates that children who are hit suffer emotionally and ultimately show *more* behavior problems, not fewer.

For children who are exposed to an abusive man, avoiding violence toward them becomes even more important. Hitting children sends them the message that people who love you can hurt you, that violence is your own fault, that aggression is justifiable as long as "it's for your own good." As you will see in chapter 4, these are unhealthy values that children already tend to be absorbing from witnessing their father's abusive behavior, and that you do not want to reinforce in any way. Your behavior needs to demonstrate for your children that no one has the right to use violence toward them, including—or especially—their own loved ones. In addition, being hit by you may reawaken memories they have of times that your partner assaulted or threatened you, or scared the children with his aggressive explosions around the house.

Get help and support for yourself. One of the best things you can do for your children is to take good care of yourself. Join a support group for abused women, which you can learn about by dialing information or by calling (800) 799-SAFE. Support groups are available for free across the United States and Canada, and you are welcome to participate whether your partner's aggressiveness includes physical violence or not. Reach out for help in other ways, whether from friends, clergy, a therapist, or a supportive and insightful book. If you have developed a substance abuse problem, perhaps as a way of coping with being abused, take the step now of getting into a recovery program and work toward being clean and sober. You deserve to be treated well and to be nurtured and assisted. The more help you can draw upon, the more you will have to offer your children. And the better you treat yourself, the better you will treat them.

Look for ways to challenge your partner's abusiveness. If you safely can, put pressure on your partner to participate in a specialized program for abusive men (not an anger management program, as such services are not appropriate for men who abuse women). If he is physically violent or threatening, consider calling the police.

Key Points to Remember

- The profile of a man who abuses women includes characteristics that tend to lead to weaknesses in how he treats children and how he treats you as a mother.
- Responsible fathers don't abuse or dominate mothers.
- Don't assume that your partner won't do the kinds of things to your children that he does to you. He may.
- You can find ways to keep your children safe and assist them in healing from frightening or hurtful experiences they may have undergone. Solutions that are not immediately apparent will gradually emerge if you don't give up.

Chapter Four

Understanding Your Children's Inner World

"My children are doing fine. They don't even realize how he treats me, because he only does it when they're not around."

"My daughter used to be so outgoing with other children. Now she always clings to me, or else she plays by herself."

"My son talks to me just the way his father does. I swear, he's turning out just like him."

"Our children just don't talk about what they are feeling. I wish I knew more about what's going on with them."

Mothers who have angry, controlling, or violent partners come to my lectures and ply me with urgent queries about their children. Many of the myriad issues they raise can be boiled down to this:

"What are my children feeling and thinking? What is going on inside them? How are they really? Are they going to be okay?"

This chapter will help you grasp the complex and conflicting currents running through your children's hearts and minds, and offers tools to help you get your children to let you into their inner world. The deeper you delve into their experience, the more you will be able to make them feel that you are holding them through their confusion and distress, so that they can feel confident that they—and you—will make it through.

Living with an abusive partner can convert life into a series of crises—or one never-ending crisis—so that you may feel that attempting to deal with your children's distress will overwhelm you. But if you take these challenges on one at a time, remembering to be patient and forgiving with yourself, you will discover what an important resource you can be for your children, and you will benefit as well.

Key Concepts in Children's Experiences

Concept #1:
Your Children Are Aware of the Abuse

Some mothers assert to me that their children don't know about their father's behavior because they haven't been present during his eruptions. But researchers have found that children of abused women usually know considerable details about their father's demeaning or bullying behavior, and they experience a swirl of thoughts and feelings about the events they have heard and seen or have learned about from their siblings.

QUESTION #4:
My children don't seem to be affected by
my partner's abusive behavior. Are they?

How do children find out about their father's abuse of Mom?

• *They see the incidents.* Children directly witness many of the acts of abuse that occur in their homes. Researchers tell us, for example, that three-quarters of children living with violent men are physically present for at least one assault. Some mothers report that weeks or months after a scary abusive event, their children suddenly mention details of what happened that the mother had no idea the child had witnessed. They watch through doorways or cracks, they stand at the top of staircases, they hide behind furniture. Sometimes they are right out in the open, but the mother is so upset by her partner's rage or violence that she never registers the child's presence.

• *They hear the incidents.* Yelling, threats, objects flung onto the floor, slaps—the sounds of any of these reverberate loudly through a home, as does the sound of Dad screeching away in the car after his explosion. If they are in bed, the yelling or other loud noises wake them up. They may race to seek the companionship of their siblings and to make sure that the younger ones are okay. Or they may not have fallen asleep in the first place; children who grow up exposed to abuse become hyperalert to signs that Dad's tension is building, and may lie awake on tenterhooks praying for their parents to fall asleep without incident.

• *They hear about events from each other.* Siblings talk privately about scary or upsetting incidents that they witness. Word can travel fast through the family. Older children don't always use good judgment about what younger ones should be told.

• *They see the impact on the home.* Children may notice overturned chairs, smashed plates or glasses, holes in walls, broken toys, clothing strewn around. Abusive men never clean up their own messes after acting out aggressively, and the mother may be too shaken to do anything but lock herself in a room and cry herself to sleep.

- *They see the impact on you.* Children have an intuitive grasp of reactions in you that outsiders might not notice. They notice that you are shaky or unsteady, unusually short-tempered or distant. You may stay in bed later than normal. Children's minds can do detective work, as they reconstruct for themselves what must have occurred. If the abuse involves physical violence, they may see bruises or scratches, or notice that your makeup is heavy.

Between incidents, children may notice that you have a strong startle response, such as flinching when someone makes an abrupt movement. They may see how strong your emotional reaction is to abuse or violence in a movie you are watching together. Few adults realize just how sensitive and observant children can be when they suspect that one of their parents is suffering or is not safe.

- *They feel the atmosphere.* Children have powerful radar for cruelty and intimidation. Even if your partner has never hit you, they can tell that he frightens you and puts you down. Their perceptions of your feelings may resonate with ways that he sometimes makes *them* feel, which helps them put the pieces together.

Proceed on the assumption that your children are aware of a great deal of your partner's abuse toward you, and that they need help handling their upset feelings and their confused questions about it. Don't pretend that everything is okay; you may hope that doing so will help them not to worry, but actually it just adds to their distress because they know there is a problem. There is no need to avoid the issue, because you are capable of bringing your children the emotional assistance they need.

Concept #2:
Children's Interpretations Can Matter as Much as Their Experiences

In order to get behind the eyes of children, especially young ones, and to glimpse their world as they see it, we sometimes need to let go of our adult ways of understanding events. Here are examples of statements children sometimes make about the abuse in their homes:

"If the police come to our house, they will put us all in jail."

"Mommy was crying because I didn't do what Daddy told me to do, and then he yelled at her and called her a bad name. She's very angry at me for making Daddy yell at her like that."

"Mommy's boyfriend called her 'stupid idiot' right before he shoved her against the wall. He calls me that name a lot, so he's probably going to hurt me soon like he hurt her."

"I heard that if your dad hits your mom the people come and take you away to live with a different family, and you don't get to live with Mom anymore."

Children have their own ways of making sense out of what they see and hear, and the mental leaps they take can be surprising to adults. Their perceptions are further distorted if they hear their father make threats or false statements to their mother, or if he lies to them directly. For example, physical abusers sometimes tell children that the police will take all family members to jail if they come to the house, in order to frighten them out of calling for help during an assault.

Thus the first step to understanding your children's experiences is to encourage them to tell you what they know and feel about events, and to try to draw out the meanings that they assign to what they have witnessed. Then you can validate and support their feelings, offer them reassurance for their fears, and correct any misconceptions they have. Remember, though, not to offer them false reassurances, such as, "Daddy would never do that to you," because if you turn out to be wrong, they will have trouble trusting you the next time.

Concept #3:
Your Children Are Frightened

Fear washes over children when they hear Mom getting screamed at or threatened, when Dad erupts periodically in extreme and irrational rages, or when Mom gets assaulted. They worry that you will get badly hurt, and they feel compassion for your pain. They long desperately for the power to make the incident stop. And they worry that he will turn his aggression in their direction the next time, especially if he has in the past.

Most children of abused women hide how scared they feel. They don't want to add to your burden, so they try to handle their feelings inside themselves or by talking to each other. They may also fear that they will be punished, either by the abuser or by you, if they show how upset they are by the way you get treated. Some children cope with their anxiety by channeling it into overeating, refusing to eat, or into other kinds of frenetic or distracted activity. Others lose themselves in fantasy worlds. Their fear can reveal itself through nail biting, teeth grinding, or outbreaks of acne or eczema. Another clue can be the development of phobias or compulsions, in which the child becomes unusually afraid of monsters, has to wash his or her hands constantly, or develops an irrational fear of strangers. Some children receive a diagnosis of attention deficit or hyperactivity disorder, obsessive-compulsive disorder, or oppositional defiant disorder, when they should more correctly be viewed as trauma survivors, shaken by fear and anxiety, who need safety and healing more than medication.

Children's emotions from upsetting incidents remain inside them, and can be triggered by things that happen in the present, or by scenes they watch on television or in movies. If there are times when you feel confused by the strong reactions your children have emotionally, consider the possibility that something has brought an earlier traumatic experience to the surface.

Concept #4:
Children Believe They Are to Blame

A typical scenario in the home of an angry or controlling man might go something like this:

Tracy and Eric are arguing because Tracy needs more help with the endless work of running the house, cooking the meals, and looking after the children, which she is trying to handle on top of working part-time. "Or, if you can't do that, at least clean up your own goddamn messes," she says in exasperation. Eric shoots back furiously that Tracy is a "lazy, nagging bitch," and he starts kicking the children's toys, which were scattered on the living room floor. "You don't control these fucking kids!" he yells. "And then you blame me when this house is a mess!" The children know instantly the signs of Dad's escalation, and the older one, Justin, feels an impulse to run between Mom and Dad but is afraid he will get hurt. As Justin hesitates, Dad suddenly shoves Mom down on the couch and storms out of the house. The children stand in shock, staring at Tracy. She sits crying and rubbing her hurt elbow. Then she becomes aware of the children gaping at her, and in her humiliation she barks at them, "Come on, kids, clean up your mess." It turns out that a couple of the toys are broken from Eric kicking them, and the younger girl and boy begin to cry when they see the pieces.

What is going through the minds of these children? The younger ones are flooded with guilt, thinking, "Dad was furious because we didn't clean up our toys, and he shoved Mom. We made her get hurt." These thoughts translate into the feeling, "We're bad." Meanwhile Justin, the older one, is berating himself bitterly. "Why did I just stand there instead of getting in Dad's way? Why do I have to be such a damn chicken?"

In short, the children feel guilty because they think they *caused* the abuse, or because they believe they *should have prevented* the abuse, or both.

The connections need not be as logical as they were in Eric and Tracy's story. Children can feel that they are to blame even if the argument had nothing to do with them. They live with a vague sense that somehow it's their fault, perhaps because they misbehaved days earlier or perhaps for no reason at all, simply because children's minds don't grasp cause and effect clearly, especially with respect to traumatic experiences.

Some children react to their guilt by becoming exaggeratedly perfect, hoping in that way to prove that they aren't bad, and trying to avoid any misbehavior that could lead Dad to hurt Mom. In a recent case where I was the custody evaluator, the father in the family was an emotional abuser who insulted, demeaned, and minutely controlled family members, to the point of requiring them to cook food in water that had already been used, timing them in the shower, and forbidding them to lock their doors when changing clothes. School personnel told me that the older daughter, Gina, was an outstanding student who got along well with everybody and helped other students resolve their conflicts. She was accepted into a prestigious New England college. Looking at the surface, Gina's mother might believe that she had not been affected by the abuse, unlike her younger sister, who was suicidal. But when I called Gina at her college dorm, she eloquently poured out to me (for two hours) the pain her father's dictatorial oppression had caused her. She cried repeatedly and told me that she was seeing the college counseling staff to help her cope.

Guilt can manifest itself in an opposite form, where the child abandons efforts to prove his or her worthiness and sinks into a self-accepted identity as a "bad kid," getting into trouble constantly and perhaps being unkind to other children. This transition often happens as adolescence begins. The "bad kid" sometimes believes, usually unconsciously, "If I can attract all the negative attention to myself, maybe that will get Dad to stop hurting Mom."

Although children so often feel that they have caused Mom to get hurt, they don't necessarily know what they did wrong. They may therefore constrict themselves, trying to shrink out of sight to avoid setting Dad off.

You can help relieve this weight by saying to your children as clearly as you can: "You didn't cause the fight. It isn't your fault in any way that Dad was mean to me. He's responsible for his own actions and his own problems. The adults have the job of making things go better, not the children." They may need frequent reminders of this kind.

Concept #5:
Your Children Want to Talk About the Abuse, But They Feel That They Can't

In Betsy McAlister Groves's book *Children Who See Too Much* (see Resources, "Children's Healing," page 343), she tells about a group of five-year-olds at a preschool who witnessed a bloody attack out the window of their bus on the way home one day. The next morning when the children arrived back at school, their teachers waited nervously to see how the children would react to the event and what kinds of questions they would ask. But to their amazement, *not a single child said a word about the assault,* and they all went about their usual business. After a couple of hours of this odd silence, the teachers decided to sit the children down and ask them what they had seen on the way home. Instantly, the floodgates opened.

Children poured out their feelings, talking about the incident for a long time. They wanted help understanding how the victim might have felt, they were eager to know whether the perpetrator had been caught and what would happen to him, and they expressed worry that they themselves might be in danger from him.

The adults could easily have misread the children's initial quiet that morning as meaning that they were not disturbed by the attack or had not really noticed it. They could also have concluded that the children preferred not to talk about it, perhaps to avoid the pain of remembering what had happened.

Why would children conceal their desire to share their thoughts and feelings when they were in such deep distress? The answer lies in certain assumptions children make, including:

"If the grown-ups aren't saying anything about what happened, that means we aren't supposed to talk about it." Your children may form this same belief if hours or days have passed since they saw Dad demean you or hit you and no one has mentioned it. They think, "Mom and Dad are acting like nothing happened, so that must be what they want us to do, too." Children can conclude that abuse is a shameful subject that can't be broached.

"The grown-ups can't handle our feelings about the scary event—it's too much for them." Children are aware that adults have their own fragilities, and they may think that certain subjects are too upsetting for us. Your children may drop hints about their concerns rather than raising them directly, as a way of probing to see if you can deal with their feelings. If your son says to you, "Did Daddy scare you last night?," and your response is, "Oh, don't be silly, he was just a little angry, that's all," the boy concludes that he's entering an area that is too sensitive, and he knows to stay away from the topic. On the other hand, if you respond instead by asking, "What did you see Daddy do that looked scary? How did that make you feel?," you show that you aren't afraid to address his feel-

ings. (And if he presses you on the question of whether *you* were scared, tell him the truth. He can tell that you were, and he needs the reality of his perceptions validated.)

"Talking about it won't help." Children may have received messages from adults or from other children that it's best to avoid unpleasant subjects. Although most children know intuitively that they feel better when they talk feelings out and get answers to their burning questions, the voices that say, "Just don't think about it" may succeed in silencing them. You may need, therefore, to give your children an explicit invitation to talk about traumatic issues, to open the door. If you let them know it's okay to talk, they often will choose to do so. (See also the excellent parenting guide *How to Talk So Kids Will Listen and Listen So Kids Will Talk,* listed in the Resources section, page 348.)

When Secrecy Is Imposed

Some children are scared to talk about their father's abusive behavior toward Mom. They may have even heard overt threats from the abusive man to silence them, such as:

> *"If you tell anyone what happened, the state (child protective services) will come and put you in a home, and you won't get to see me or Mommy anymore."*

> *"The police will come and put me in jail if they find out and I'll never be able to come home again."*

> *"I will kill Mommy if you tell."*

> *"You will be severely punished if you talk about this to anyone."*

These kinds of threats appear to be more common among physically violent abusers, and among those who violate the children's sexual boundaries.

Your children may also be afraid of *your* reaction if they don't maintain secrecy; children sometimes tell researchers that their mothers would be mad at them if they talked to anyone outside the family about their father's violence. If your partner assaults you in scary ways, you may feel tempted to tell your children to keep it secret out of fear that child protective services will come and take them away from you. But requiring your children to maintain silence about traumatic experiences can leave them with lasting scars. In chapter 10, "Dealing with Child Protective Services," we will explore some ways that you can escape this difficult bind.

In order to free your children from any bonds of secret keeping, remind them periodically that they are free to talk to you about *anything,* and that no one has the right to make them keep secrets from you. Tell them that they also do not need to keep secrets from their relatives, schoolteachers, or other trusted adults. The freer your children feel to tell the truth of their experiences, the safer they will be in the long run.

Having reviewed these important underlying concepts, I will now describe some of the signs that indicate that your children are experiencing distress from your partner's abusiveness toward you. These lists will help you to assess how your children are doing, and to see in what areas they may be in particular need of assistance and healing. These symptoms tend to vary with a child's age, temperament, and sex, and with the particular style of abuse that the father exposes them to. You can expect to find, therefore, that your son or daughter is struggling more in some areas than in others.

Behavioral Effects

If you are having a difficult time understanding or managing your children's behavior, you are not alone; researchers have found that a range of behavioral problems is substantially more common in children of abused women than in other children, and that they can respond to their inner turmoil in some very challenging ways. Here are some of the signs you might particularly watch for:

Behavioral Symptoms of Exposure to an Abusive Man

- Bullying, insulting, and physical aggressiveness toward peers.
- Withdrawal from social contact, poor peer relationships.
- Fear or upset about separation, especially from Mom.
- Oppositional and defiant behaviors with authority figures, especially Mom.
- Developmental regression (e.g., bed-wetting or daytime "accidents").
- Hyperactivity, anxiety, obsessiveness, or compulsiveness.
- Learning and attentional problems at school.
- Eating problems (e.g., overeating or refusing to eat).
- Failure to thrive in infants.
- Sleeping problems (nightmares, awakening easily, trouble falling asleep).
- Violence toward siblings, especially male to female and older child toward younger child.
- Running away from home.

Primarily in pre-teens and teenagers
- Substance abuse.
- Poor peer choices.
- Violence or verbal abuse toward dating partners, and/or perpetrating sexual assault.

- Violence or verbal abuse *from* dating partners, and/or sexual victimization.
- Violence toward Mom.
- Physically or verbally intervening to protect Mom.
- Imitating the abuser's behaviors toward Mom.

Emotional Effects

Some children turn much of their emotional pain and confusion outward, into challenging or disruptive behavior, while others tend to act out less but develop more noticeable emotional effects. Here are some distress signals your children may be sending that can alert you that they are having a hard time:

Emotional Symptoms of Exposure to an Abusive Man

- Fear, anxiety, nervousness.
- Depression, sadness, suicidal desires.
- Insecurity.
- Guilt, self-blame, shame.
- Anger, resentment, bitterness.
- Embarrassment or shame toward peers (e.g., reluctance to have friends over to the house).
- Feeling responsible to protect Mom.
- Feeling responsible to protect siblings, especially younger ones.
- Worrying about the safety of relatives and friends (generalized anxiety).

- Blame and resentment toward siblings.
- Blame and resentment toward Mom.
- Fantasies of standing up to, assaulting, or killing the abuser.
- Desire to have the kind of power the abuser has ("identifying with the aggressor").
- Fear of ordinary arguments because of feeling that they may turn frightening.
- Uncertainty about what is real.

There are a few points to keep in mind that can help you communicate more effectively with your children about their emotions:

Contradictory feelings can go together. Children can, for example, simultaneously hate the abusive man and wish to be like him. They can hate his cruelty while longing to have the kind of power he has—partly because they wish they could stand up to him and to people like him. Similarly, children can absorb negative attitudes toward you from their father, while still feeling an urgent desire to protect you. They can have fantasies of hurting the abusive man—researchers find that a large percentage of children exposed to domestic violence do—yet feel guilty about those aggressive thoughts and long to feel closer to their father. Recognizing these powerful crosscurrents in your children's emotional world can help you feel less confused and impatient about their moods, and strengthens your ability to name their feelings for them.

Children need space to feel what they feel. When a mother becomes aware of her children's emotional pain, she naturally wishes she could take the hurt away. You may feel tempted to say things like, "Don't be sad, don't be afraid, everything is going to be all right." But your children need you to be there with them *through* their pain rather than trying to chase it away, while also holding out for them the hope that their circumstances will improve. Strive to acknowledge and accept their range and depth of emotional reactions.

Children need their sense of reality validated. In a case that a colleague of mine handled a couple of years ago, a child of about seven watched in horror as her father killed her mother's beloved pet rabbit. Days later the traumatized girl asked her father why he killed the pet, and he said, "I didn't *kill* the bunny, Devon, it died because it was *sick*. I just took it away to bury it."

When adults deny scary, tragic, or dramatic events, the child witnesses can feel that their grip on reality is slipping. Have your children experienced any of the following?

- Their father has denied events that they saw or heard.
- After severe incidents, your partner and/or you have acted as if nothing happened and have made no further mention of what transpired.
- The children have been criticized or ridiculed by the abusive man, by their siblings, or by you for feeling frightened, angry, or confused after incidents, or for being afraid of their father.
- Police have come to the house and left without taking action, or made choices that confused the children, such as arresting you instead of the abuser.

Children need to know that they aren't crazy, that the abusive man's behavior—and perhaps sometimes yours as well—has indeed been scary and unacceptable, and that there is good reason for them to be upset by what they have heard or seen. Be sure to validate their sense of what is real. Don't blame yourself for your partner's actions, but do accept responsibility for your own, as this will help your children to feel safe with you.

Effects on Learning and Cognition

Are any of your children having difficulty in school? Are they learning slowly, becoming easily distracted, or seeming at times to disconnect from the world around them? Unhealed traumatic experiences can alter how the brain functions, as researchers are increasingly discovering. Consider where any of these mental effects are appearing in your children:

Learning and Cognitive Symptoms of Exposure to an Abusive Man

- Attention deficits (including symptoms that may be incorrectly attributed to Attention Deficit Disorder).
- Hyperactivity that interferes with learning and attention.
- Learning delays.
- Delays in language acquisition.
- Poor academic performance.
- Missing school often from claiming to be sick, truancy.
- Falling asleep in school (often due to being kept awake by abusive incidents).

If your child exhibits learning problems, think about whether you can partner with school personnel to bring assistance to your child. Consider talking to his or her teachers, or to a school counselor, about your partner's problem. You may feel embarrassed to reveal personal issues to school staff, but the potential benefit to your child is considerable. When teachers know that children are exposed to abuse at home, they can react more patiently to misbehavior, provide specialized learning programs, including an educational evaluation if needed, and increase the emotional support and affection they offer the child.

There are some situations, however, in which you might *not* want to tell school personnel about the abuse:

1. *Your partner is scary or violent, and you are afraid of how he will react if he finds out that you spoke to the school staff about him.* You can emphasize your safety concerns to teachers and ask them to keep confidential the information you share with them. However, the risk still exists that he could find out if a teacher forgets and confronts him about the abuse, or if school personnel feel obligated to make a child welfare report. If you have this concern, discuss your situation confidentially with an advocate for abused women (see Resources starting on page 337). Ask a school counselor or administrator what kinds of circumstances the school reports to the state and what kinds it doesn't, so you can use your best judgment about how much to reveal to your child's teachers.

2. *You are afraid that if the school files a report with child protective services, they will take your children away.* Again, this is an important concern, and one you should talk about with an advocate at the nearest program for abused women—ideally without giving your name or the names of your children. If you are a low-income woman, an immigrant, or a woman of color (such as an African-American, tribal, Latina, or Asian-American woman), you do run the risk of encountering a biased or alarmist reaction from child protective services. See chapter 10 for more information about dealing with the child protective system, bearing in mind that in some cases abused women have found that state intervention actually ends up *benefiting* them, and that the children do not usually get removed from the home.

3. *You live in a small town or a rural area where everyone knows everyone else.* Privacy for you and your children is important. But balance this concern against the possible benefits to you and your children of having school personnel understand the situation at home.

If you decide that you can't speak openly with the school about the abuse, there are still ways that you can advocate for your child's educational needs, including requesting special testing. For more information, see the Resources section, "Educational Advocacy," page 354.

Helping your child to heal emotionally will in turn help him or her to think more clearly and pay better attention. All of the suggestions and insights contained in this book can have the additional benefit of helping to overcome school or learning difficulties.

Effects on Children's Beliefs and Values

The abusive man is a role model for children who grow up in frequent contact with him; children absorb attitudes and behaviors from the influential adults in their lives. It may seem strange that children would take on their father's ways of thinking when they can see how destructive he is, but there are a number of reasons why they sometimes do:

- Children can find it hard to discern which of Dad's values are connected to his abusiveness and which aren't, so they don't know which ones to accept and which to reject.
- Children who are very upset emotionally are more vulnerable to accepting destructive attitudes, because their distress makes it harder for them to think critically and increases their craving for adult approval.
- Children don't necessarily realize just how destructive the abusive man is because he manipulates their perceptions and periodically showers them with kindness or gifts.

- Dad's unhealthy modeling can be reinforced by messages the children are exposed to from television, video games, rock videos and rock lyrics, or pornography that they gain access to.

Notice whether any of the following beliefs are starting to develop in your children, so you can take steps to replace them with healthier attitudes:

"It's acceptable for men to bully, intimidate, or demean women." This message is contained in your partner's behavior, and can be further reinforced if they hear him saying things such as:

"There's only so much a man can take!"

"I already told you I was sorry; what more do you want from me?"

"I'm just trying to get my point across and get you to listen to me!"

Researchers have found that boys who are exposed to an abusive man often grow up to mistreat women themselves. I have noticed in my work with violent teenage boys that they often use precisely the same excuses and justifications that they have heard their fathers and stepfathers use.

"Women are to blame for the abuse they suffer." Your children's values can be influenced by overhearing your partner blame you for his disrespectful acts:

"You pushed me too far!"

"You don't know when to shut up!"

"If you weren't so fucking stupid this would never have happened."

Girls can absorb Dad's modeling nearly as much as boys. A girl learns from Dad's actions and justifications that if a future partner abuses her, it's her own fault, so she should focus on changing herself. (I point out to my clients, "Your conduct is teaching your daughters that it's acceptable for a man to abuse them. Are you sure you want to do that?" For some abusive men, their behavior starts to feel less excusable when they picture it happening to their own daughters.)

"The abusive man is not responsible for his actions." The son of one of my clients got in trouble for fighting at school, and the boy's explanation was, "I beat that kid up because he was being such an idiot." I pointed out to the father that his son's behavior was a product of hearing his father blame his actions on other people.

"Males are superior to females." Boys who grow up hearing their male role model use words like "bitch," "whore," "nag," "fat," and "ugly," or see him hit or intimidate their mother, are being conditioned to look down on females. They may learn to bond with other males, including their fathers, through sharing jokes and glances that demean women. Girls in the family find it hard to maintain their self-esteem in the anti-female atmosphere that their father is engendering.

"Anger causes violence." Anger doesn't cause violence in relationships; entitled, disrespectful, and violent attitudes do. But children who live with abusive fathers have trouble making this distinction, and so may learn to use rage as an excuse for aggression. Equally important, they can start to suppress their own anger out of fear of becoming violent like their father, which leaves them with nowhere to go with the rage that they naturally experience in response to the cruelty they have witnessed.

"People who love you get to hurt you." This message is implied by the abuser's actions, and can be reinforced if the children overhear him saying things like, "I only act this way because of how

much I care about you." Absorbing this belief can increase your children's risk of being victimized.

In order to counter the model provided by the abusive man and by certain parts of our society, a mother is called upon to actively teach her children alternative values and to equip them to think critically about the messages they are soaking up. Chapter 15 includes a section called "Teaching Critical Thinking" that offers a detailed set of steps you can take with your children toward building healthy attitudes and beliefs (see page 292). You are their crucial leader toward a healthy outlook on intimate relationships, mutual respect, and human kindness. Seek ways to weave teaching and guidance about these values into your daily interactions with your children.

Mothers have a range of feelings in reaction to the above lists. As you read along, you have perhaps been thinking some or all of the following:

> *"A lot of these things seem familiar. Now I get why my children are so hard to deal with these days."*

> *"It feels so good to read the descriptions of what is going on in our family—it lets me know that someone understands what it's like."*

> *"Maybe I'm not the cause of all of my children's problems. Maybe he's at the root of quite a bit of what's going on."*

> *"It's my fault for choosing a partner like this one."*

> *"I guess I'm a bad mother if I don't leave my partner."*

Do your best not to be hard on yourself about your children's distress. You didn't choose to be with a man "like this one"; when you got involved with him, he seemed nothing like the controlling, demeaning person you are now struggling with. Leaving him immediately won't necessarily solve your children's difficulties, as we will see in chapter 9; there are many factors to balance in deciding what to do about your relationship. In the meantime, you will be less able to help your children if you become overwhelmed by guilt feelings toward them.

So rather than pointing the finger at yourself, use the information I offer in this chapter to:

- Increase your patience and compassion for your children.
- Help you to get through times of feeling that something is wrong with them or that they are just impossible children.
- Help you stop blaming yourself for your children's difficulties.

With their mother's help, children can heal. There is an extensive collection of ways in which you can bring healing to your children's lives, of which we have looked at only a handful so far.

Children's Feelings Toward the Abusive Man

Your children's inner world is likely to include unsettling conflicted feelings toward Dad, which you can help them identify, express, and sort out. Here are some of the turbulent emotions they may struggle with:

- Deep anger and bitterness about his bullying, selfishness, and cruelty, in conflict with feelings of awe regarding his power and charm, and the wish to emulate him in those aspects.

- Resentment about his hurtful treatment of Mom, in conflict with finding that if they join him in laughing at Mom or disrespecting her, they get in good with him, which helps them feel safe and builds their self-esteem—at least superficially.
- Bitterness about his coldness and lack of availability, in conflict with feeling drawn hungrily to the times when he does focus on them and show them kindness, precisely because those opportunities tend to be rare.
- Fantasizing about overpowering him or driving him away, in conflict with worrying about him, especially if he is the style of abuser who presents himself as a victim.

Children may figure out over time that as long as Dad is getting what he wants, home is a reasonably peaceful place, but that as soon as he doesn't receive the catering he demands or someone in the family stands up to him, the conditions change instantly to emotional or physical danger for Mom or for everyone. In this atmosphere they may work hard to keep Dad happy, and may blame Mom or each other anytime he gets upset, since they fear that someone is going to pay for his displeasure.

Many of the mothers I've worked with over the years have gone through periods when one or more of the children is defending or excusing the father's abusive acts and blaming Mom for his unkindness. This is of course a painful twist of events, but try to remind yourself that this stage will pass. Children who side with their abusive fathers do so to try to calm down their own whirling confusion of emotions, and to try to get Dad to be nicer to them. Particularly if Dad sometimes gets scary, children may be eager to be in good with him in order to feel safe. Keep working on improving your relationships with your children and helping them heal, and you are likely to find that this painful phase doesn't last.

I have worked with many families in which one or more of the children maintain an inspiring degree of courage and integrity, choosing to distance themselves from the abusive man no matter what the consequences and sometimes openly allying with Mom. In my experience, these children have healthier emotional and behavioral outcomes in the long run, but in the short term they have to endure the stress and anxiety that comes with defying the powerful abuser. (The abusive man, in turn, blames the mother for the fact that the child is alienated from him, refusing to see how his own behavior has driven his son or daughter away.) Notice the courageous stands your children take, including their outspoken or hidden forms of resistance. Give them praise and support for their efforts to protect their rights, maintain their identities, and stand up for themselves and each other—and for you. If you can shore up their strong aspects, you help them to avoid breaking in the weaker spots.

Children's Resilience

QUESTION #5:
Can my children heal from what they have been put through by him?

Emotional wounds do not have to last a lifetime. The resilient side of young people inspires me and gives me renewed hope and energy over and over again, as it comes through in the stories abused women tell me. Here are some of the heartening changes they have shared with me:

> *"My children and I are much closer than we used to be. We've worked through a lot of what happened and now we understand each other much better."*

> *"Jenny and Oscar used to fight like cats and dogs. They are so much nicer to each other these days."*

"Maria's therapist has made a huge difference in her life. I don't know where we'd be without him."

"The abused women's program in my town has a group for children, and all four of mine go to it. They do some really serious talking about what it's like to see abuse or violence, but they also have fun together playing and eating. My kids look forward to it, believe it or not."

"We are all doing so much better since I finally got my boyfriend to move out, and there's actually calm in the house. It's like a new life."

Children are poignantly fragile, but they are also enormously strong. Certainly they are vulnerable compared to adults, and because they have wide-open hearts they can be torn up emotionally. Yet coexisting with their delicate tenderness is an almost unstoppable force propelling them to find enjoyment in life, to tap into renewed sources of energy, to love and trust people again in the face of loss or betrayal. Children crave humane interaction, they long for emotional wellness, and they seek out—often unconsciously—opportunities for healing and reconciliation. In the face of challenges, they find ways to have fun, to take care of themselves, to forget the worst moments.

I will talk in detail in chapter 14 about children's healing, but there are central points that you can begin reflecting on now, including:

- Your children need to be as emotionally close to you as possible in order to recover well from traumatic experiences.
- They need to be as close as possible to any siblings they have.
- They need room to express and release their feelings, in-

cluding hours of crying and non-destructive tantrums, laughter, and expressions of fear and anxiety.

- They need their strengths praised and drawn upon, including as much time as possible spent doing what they most love and enjoy, whatever that may be (with the exception of addictive behaviors, such as exposure to video, which are important to reduce for reasons we will examine).

- They need to know that you can protect them, and yourself, from your controlling or scary partner. It may take some time to prove to them, and to yourself, that you can do this, but don't give up.

- The more your children sense that you empathize with their darkest hours, the more able they feel to keep moving toward the light.

What Can I Do?

This chapter has presented a great deal of information, including some parts that are painful to digest. So take a moment now to gather your strength, using some of the following messages to yourself as affirmations to hold onto:

"My children are counting on me. I can come through for them."

"They need me to take good care of myself. What is good for me is ultimately good for them."

"I deserve to live in a better atmosphere just as much as my children do. We are in this together."

"My children can heal, and so can I."

"We all deserve kindness, support, and assistance."

"We are going to make it."

———

Fortifying yourself with this kind of internal encouragement, you can move ahead to consider specific actions you can take.

Try to stop blaming your children, and yourself, for how hard things are for them. As we have seen, behavioral and emotional challenges are common for children who are exposed to an abusive man in their daily lives, or who have had such exposure in the past. They aren't bad kids, and you aren't a bad mom.

Let your children know that it's okay to talk about emotional or physical abuse they have heard or seen. Open up the subject yourself by asking them if they are upset "about what happened the other night," or by naming feelings for them, as in, "It must have been scary for you when Mommy and Daddy were yelling and Daddy knocked the things off the table." Tell them that whatever they feel they can share with you, and that if they have questions or fears, you can help them to understand things and feel safer. If they deny that anything occurred, take that as a signal that they aren't ready to talk about it—or perhaps even think about it—yet. They still need to know that *you* aren't afraid to deal with the issues.

Tell them that abuse is wrong. Children don't want to hear negative statements about their father as a person, such as "He's a bully," or "He's so selfish," and such pronouncements won't help them make sense of the events they've witnessed. But it is important for them to hear that his *actions* are wrong, such as, "Daddy shouldn't get so loud, I know that scares you," or "It's never okay for him to break things when he's mad." Explain to them that he has a problem that he needs to get help with, rather than implying that he is a bad person.

Model accepting responsibility for your own mistakes. Apologize to your children when you treat them badly or speak inappropriately to them, and tell them you will work on doing better. Doing so will help your children trust you more and feel closer to you. Equally important, it will help them think critically about the abuse, because they will start to notice that their father almost never takes responsibility for his actions in the way you do—though he may make very superficial-sounding apologies—and doesn't work seriously on improving his behavior.

Help your children not worry about you. Tell them, "Mommy is going to be okay," or "I'll get through this, I can take care of myself," even if some days you don't truly feel so sure. At the same time, give them some space to express their concerns about you; they need you to hear how upset they get when they see you emotionally or physically hurt. When you are having a hard time emotionally, be honest about that fact with your children—they can tell, so pretending that everything is fine won't help and in fact will just worry them further. At the same time, do your best to sound strong, so they can see that you will get through it.

Avoid relying on your children for emotional support. Give them small, digestible amounts of information about your partner's behavior and about your feelings, and leave out the most upsetting or scary aspects altogether.

Make safety plans with your children. While it's important to avoid burdening your children with adult responsibilities, you do want them to feel that they aren't powerless. So plan steps with them that they can take to keep themselves and each other safe, or to get help for you when they think you may be in danger. You will find a guide in chapter 15 under "Safety Planning with Children," page 303.

Accept the range of feelings your children have toward your partner. Some women I work with have a hard time allowing their children to express anger, bitterness, or fear about their father. Perhaps partly out of your own guilty feelings, you may be tempted to defend him or to tell the children that they are overreacting and being too negative about him. Or you may struggle with the opposite reaction, chafing when you have to listen to your children's warm or idealized feelings toward their father. But children need to be able to work through their ambivalence toward Dad, and they need one parent who doesn't draw them into the parental conflict or the abuse. So reach for the strength to support them in both sets of feelings.

Tell your children that the abuse isn't their fault. They need to know that they didn't cause you to be abused and couldn't have prevented it, and they may need to be reminded of this every so often.

Tell your children that the abuse isn't your fault either. Your children need to know that the abusive man is responsible for his own actions, and that he shouldn't be blaming you—or them—for what he does. These understandings are important to relieve their guilt, and to keep them from following in his footsteps.

If your children are old enough to date, be attentive to who their partners are. Girls whose fathers abuse their mothers are prone to get involved with domineering, manipulative, or violent boyfriends, especially if they have lived around the abuse for many years. Talk to your children about the warning signs of an abusive partner (see chapter 5 of *Why Does He Do That?*) and spend some time getting to know anyone they date. If your child gets involved in a bad relationship, read the excellent book *What Parents Need to Know About Dating Violence* (see Resources, page 339).

Try to reduce your children's exposure to violent or anti-female television shows, movies, video games, toys, and song lyrics. Repeated studies have found that the more time children spend watching video screens, the more aggressive and violent they tend to be. These effects are likely to be even greater for children who are exposed to an abusive man. Keep violent toys out of the home, monitor the lyrics of your children's favorite music, and make rules about what you will allow them to watch and listen to (even through headphones) in your home.

Seek help for yourself, your children, and your partner (if he is willing to get help), and let your children know that you are doing so. Children long to believe that the scary or hurtful atmosphere in their home is going to improve, and to know that at least one adult is taking steps to bring about the necessary changes. Begin with a call to the nearest program for abused women.

Keep pouring love into your children. There is nothing they need more from you than caring, affection, and kindness. And for children who are pre-verbal, including infants, your love is even more important, since they are not yet able to process their feelings with you by talking them through.

Key Points to Remember

- Children know that something is wrong in the home, and that you are being treated in hurtful and intimidating ways.
- Each child will be affected in a slightly—or greatly— different way from other children living in similar circumstances.
- Your children's problems are normal reactions to living in the unhealthy atmosphere that abuse creates; don't assume there is anything wrong with them. Show them that you believe in their goodness, even when they exhibit behaviors that remind you of him.
- The range of feelings, both positive and negative, that your abusive partner causes in you can be a helpful guide to the kinds of feelings your children are likely to be struggling with.
- Children need you to be able to listen to them and take in their feelings on a deep level.
- Your children can heal and move toward safety and freedom, and so can you.

Chapter Five

Protecting Your Children's Boundaries

"He makes comments about our daughters' bodies that I think are inappropriate, and it makes the girls uncomfortable."

"He doesn't allow our children, or me, any privacy. He listens in on phone calls, he opens letters addressed to other people, he barges into bedrooms without knocking. He's so invasive."

"He asked our teen son the other day whether he's 'gotten any' yet. I couldn't believe it."

"He demands to know the children's thoughts or emotions in a way that feels strange at times. It seems like he doesn't want them to be able to get away from him even inside their own minds."

In *Why Does He Do That?* I write about a day in the life of a family that was being controlled and manipulated by an abusive man. The parents were named Tom and Helen Turner. They had a thirteen-year-old daughter, Alex, and a son Randy, eleven. They were rushing off to their cousins' house for a party, when the following transpired:

When they were almost out the door, Tom noticed Alex's outfit for the first time, which he considered overly revealing. He barked, "You go right back upstairs, young lady, and put on something decent. You aren't going to the party looking like a prostitute."

Tears sprang into Alex's eyes, as she had been excited about what she was going to wear and had planned the outfit for days. "But Mom and I picked my clothes out together," she protested with a helpless whine in her voice. "She said I looked fine."

Tom glared at his wife, Helen, then laid down the law. "If you aren't changed in two minutes, we're leaving and you're staying here!" Alex ran crying upstairs to change.

Although there had been several tense moments as the family was preparing for the party, and Tom had been demeaning and bullying toward Helen, once they arrived at their cousins' house he acted happy and outgoing, so no one could have guessed the side of him that the family had just been strafed by. However, if the relatives had looked a little more closely, they might have been able to pick up on some of his manipulative style and lack of respect.

There were a handful of people at the party whom they hadn't met before, to whom Tom introduced Alex as his "girlfriend." He considered it a charming joke, but Alex squirmed and laughed awkwardly each time he said it. At one point he commented to some relatives on Alex's appearance, saying, "She's developing into quite an attractive young lady, isn't she?" Alex was near enough to hear what her father had said and she felt humiliated, especially since she was self-conscious about her developing breasts. Tom noticed her discomfort and said, "What, can't you take a compliment?" and a ripple of laughter went around the room. He then gave Alex a hug and kissed her on the head, telling his amused audience, "She's a great kid, isn't she?" His daughter forced a smile.

That night Tom barged into Alex's room after dinner.

"Dad!" protested Alex, "I'm changing! Please!" But Tom didn't leave and launched right into saying, "I only need to talk to you for a minute. I won't look—not that there's really anything to see yet, anyhow," and gave a chuckle.

Alex moved behind her closet door as much as she could. Tom went on, "I just want to tell you how proud I am of you for bringing home the kind of report card you did. I knew you could do it. I'm glad you listened to me and buckled down some. Your performance before was really making me feel bad, and I have enough on my mind without another thing to worry about. Good girl."

Below, I will take you step by step through Tom's behavior toward his daughter to show how the different pieces of his invasiveness fit together. But first let's take a brief step back to talk about the connection between abuse and boundaries.

Abuse Is a Boundary Problem

When I use the word *boundary,* I am referring to the limits we have around our bodies and our minds to protect our safety, our integrity, and our privacy. Our boundaries can be thought of as fences with gates in them. At certain times we decide to open the gates and allow chosen people to pass through; at other moments the way is blocked, and we have a right to have the limits respected. Certain people we prefer never to let in, and places exist within us that may be open to no one.

Some boundaries we can reasonably consider inherent, in that they are accepted by most cultures as natural and unassailable; they are just *there,* without us having to erect them. The outside of our bodies, our skin, is one such limit; no one should touch us without our consent or against our wishes. Certain parts of our bodies, such as our sexual regions (which many children learn to call "my privates"), have even firmer limits around them that no one should cross without a clear invitation from us, and that no adult should cross with a child or adolescent even if the young person appears to be a willing participant. Another inherent boundary is the right to cover our bodies in front of other people whenever we feel the need, and to be away from invading eyes when we want to change clothes. Even when we are dressed, we have the right not to be looked at in ways that feel invasive; for example, no one should sit and stare at you while you attempt to think, work, or rest because the power of their gaze will take over your mental space and you will be unable to focus on the activity you wanted to engage in. In other words, eyes can intrude upon minds as well as bodies.

Other boundaries are less universal, and are chosen by an individual based on what he or she finds necessary for physical or emotional well-being. You might find that you hate being tickled—many people do—or that you don't care for tight hugs because they make you feel suffocated. You may become enraged when someone tells you what you are feeling, so you proclaim firmly that you are the only one who gets to define what is happening in your heart. These kinds of physical and emotional boundaries may be specific to you, but you nonetheless have every right to expect and demand that they be respected.

When a person's inherent boundaries, or their individually specific ones, are violated, any or all of the following effects can appear:

- Feeling invaded and unsafe.
- Feeling degraded or dirty.
- Feeling confused, including having trouble distinguishing what is voluntary from what isn't (e.g., "Did I like

that, or didn't I? Did I want to be doing that, or was I pressured into it?").

- Feeling lonely, abandoned, not seen, or not understood.
- Having trouble trusting people (which may intensify over time).
- Feeling angry or enraged, becoming extremely defiant.

When children or adults experience severe or repeated violations of their boundaries, the above effects can become deep and chronic. In addition, the violations can cause them to lose part of their ability to handle the gates in their fences well. They may find, for example, that they sometimes let people in who turn out not to be trustworthy, or whom they didn't really want to allow to pass through in the first place. At the same time, they may shut good people out, only to regret later the missed opportunities for emotional or physical closeness. Or the gates may stop working at all, so they simply shut everybody out, leading to an isolated existence of mistrust, or let everybody in, leading to an existence of being exploited, with intimacy coming to feel like an unpleasant obligation.

These insights lead us back to a central point:

Abuse by a husband or boyfriend almost always includes some aspects of disrespecting the woman's boundaries.

Any form of physical abuse, for example, even if it involves so-called "lower-level" (though still serious) forms of violence such as poking, grabbing, or shoving, takes away your control over the limits around your body and leaves you feeling invaded. Researchers find that one-third or more of abused women have experienced at least one sexual assault by their husband or boyfriend. Certain powerfully demeaning forms of verbal abuse, such as calling a woman degrading sexual names, can make the woman feel sexually violated even though no actual contact has taken place. I have had a number of clients who listen in on their partner's phone calls, read her mail, or snoop into her diaries. Some abusive men reach deliberately for whatever behavior the woman has most strongly attempted to set limits around. These are all examples of boundary violations.

Since disrespect for personal boundaries is built into the conduct of an abusive man, at least to some extent, it is reasonable to be concerned about whether he will be emotionally, physically, or sexually invasive with children. This chapter describes dynamics you can monitor and steps you can take to protect your children's privacy and integrity.

Back to Tom

Using the above concepts as a lens, let's put Tom's style with his daughter under a microscope. His first move with Alex is to require her to change out of an outfit that he finds too sexy. At first glance this decision might seem motivated by appropriate parental protectiveness. But consider the effect of Tom's statement that Alex is dressed "like a prostitute"; he has just created, for his whole family, a mental image of his thirteen-year-old daughter having sex with men for money. Are these the actions of a man who is protecting his daughter from sexualization? His words have just sexualized her more than her outfit ever could have.

Next we see Tom introduce Alex as his "girlfriend" at the party. Is this just a cute joke? No, and here's why not. First, Tom is an adult, and adults nowadays generally have sex with their partners. So he is introducing an image of sexual contact between father and daughter, and drawing attention to Alex as a sexual being rather than the young teenager that she is. She naturally becomes aware of the eyes around her at this point. Tom makes Alex feel even more exposed by commenting to the amused onlookers that she is developing into an "attractive young lady." Alex is left feeling boundaryless in public, like a dream of discovering oneself naked at school. He then draws everyone's attention to her discomfort, taunting her, "Can't you take a compliment?"

Tom closes the scene with a twist that could reasonably be termed "crazy-making," by telling everyone what a great girl Alex is and giving her a hug and kiss, as if his invasive behavior should be seen as proving what a caring and appreciative father he is. As the target of this inversion, Alex may well find herself struggling to understand where the line falls between caring for someone and trampling their boundaries.

At home, Tom makes another boundary-crossing comment to Alex, referring to her breast development ("Not that there's anything to see yet") that lets her know that he's watching. He adds emotional invasiveness as well, trying to make her feel guilty about the distress her poor school performance has been causing him. We can reasonably assume that Alex ends this day feeling that she has little control over what parts of her Tom has access to, physically and emotionally.

Fortunately, not all men who abuse women bulldoze their way through their daughters' or sons' personal limits the way Tom does—although there are some who are worse than he is, as I discuss later in this chapter.

Boundary Violations Usually Start Small

Have you noticed any of the following problems in your partner's interactions with your children?

- He tickles them too long, not stopping when they want him to stop, so that the experience becomes uncomfortable for them.

- Physical horseplay between him and the children sometimes gets too rough because he doesn't contain himself
  properly, so that someone ends up getting hurt or frightened. He then switches over into anger or defensiveness,
  saying, "Come on, it was just a game."

- He teases them about issues that he knows are sensitive
  ones for them, or says hurtful things that he insists are
  "just jokes," perhaps sometimes including comments that
  you have specifically asked him not to make.

- He asks the children too many questions about their activities, thoughts, or feelings, and pressures or ridicules
  them when they don't want to tell him certain things or
  don't respond.

- He controls the children's emotional world by telling them
  that they have certain feelings that they really don't, by
  denying feelings that they do have, or by insisting on talking with them about issues that they feel private or embarrassed about, sometimes in front of other people.

While these behaviors may seem minor, your children may experience them as injurious; adults tend to have thicker skins, so we
can forget the openness and vulnerability of a child. Equally important, abusive men tend to escalate their boundary violations toward children over time, so that what is subtle today may become
overt a year or two down the road. It's important to sit up and take
notice if your children's limits are being disrespected, without waiting for worse invasions to occur.

Boys Can Be at Risk, Too

Abusive men sometimes target their sons as well as their daughters for invasive behavior. For example, many of my clients involve

their sons in inappropriate sexual discussions about females, which can leave a boy feeling embarrassed or uncomfortable. Some men press their sons to become sexually active and ask invasive questions about their sexuality. In one case of mine, the father admitted openly to me that he had taken his fifteen-year-old son to a prostitute because he felt it was time for the boy to lose his virginity. This cannot help but have been a humiliating and sexually unpleasant experience for the boy, since he was pressured into sexual contact that he was not ready for, that lacked any genuine caring, and that involved his father.

As with girls, violations of boys can come in various forms. For example, one client of mine became frustrated that his eight-year-old son was constantly losing pencils, and one day told his son, "You need to guard your pencils as if they were as important to you as *these*"—and he grabbed the boy's testicles. This man was, unfortunately, completely closed to understanding that he had sexually violated his son, and to imagining what the young boy must have felt. If you see indications that your partner is not respecting your son's limits, take those behaviors as seriously as you would for a girl.

The Incest Perpetrator

I will turn soon to reviewing strategies you can use to protect your children's privacy and integrity, but first I need to shed light on one more difficult subject: the more severe forms of boundary violation that constitute outright sexual abuse. Research studies, combined with writings by clinicians who specialize in counseling incest victims and perpetrators, paint the following picture of the man who may be a risk to sexually abuse his partner's children:

- He is abusive to you, and especially if his abuse includes elements of physical violence, intimidation, or severe invasiveness.

- He is highly entitled, becoming irate or retaliatory if he feels you are not adequately catering to his needs.

- He pays little attention to the child during his or her infancy.

- He perceives the child as an owned object.

- He reverses roles with the child, where he expects the child to take care of his needs and feelings rather than the other way around.

- He violates the child's emotional or physical boundaries.

- He is very manipulative toward the child or toward you.

- He drives wedges between you and the child, or isolates the child from siblings or from other social contacts.

- He targets one child for especially favored or especially harsh treatment, or both.

- He exposes the children to pornography, perhaps "accidentally."

- He abuses substances.

- He was a victim of child sexual abuse himself.

- He jealously guards one child from being sexualized by other people, while disrespecting her boundaries himself.

Research studies also suggest that the risk of incest is somewhat greater, though not dramatically so, from a man who is not biologically related to the child, such as a stepfather or Mom's boyfriend.

According to various studies, there is a considerable overlap between men who abuse women and those who sexually violate children. I have already described how abusiveness is, in itself, a type of boundary problem. Moreover, incest perpetrators are known for their entitled attitudes, their hypercontrol over family members, their manipulativeness, and their tactics for driving wedges between mothers and children, so that children won't disclose the abuse. (Children's fear of their father, especially if they have seen him use violence against their mother, can be an additional obstacle to revealing his violations.)

There are other similarities between these two groups of offenders, including:

- Conditioning or requiring family members to keep the abuse secret.
- Making a range of excuses to persuade himself and other people that he isn't responsible for his own actions or that he "lost control," including blaming the victim for "seducing" him, just as the abuser says that his partner "provoked" him.
- Justifying his actions as having been for the victim's own good, as with the incest perpetrator who said to me, "I didn't want her learning about sex out on the street, so I wanted to teach her at home."
- Confusing love and abuse, as with a client of mine who described his sexual abuse of his young son as if it had been a positive form of mutual intimacy.
- Chronic lying and dishonesty, especially to cover or excuse the abuse.
- Experiencing domination as sexually exciting, sometimes combined with having trouble feeling sexual in situations that *don't* involve domination.
- Seeing family members as personal possessions.

Underlying all of these parallels is the mentality of *exploitativeness;* that is to say, a belief, usually unconscious, that it is acceptable to use other people for your own purposes, without regard for their feelings or needs, or for the damage you may be causing them.

My goal is not to alarm you; even though men who abuse women have higher rates of perpetrating incest than other men, there is still only a small minority who do. Rather, I want to equip you with the knowledge of what warning signs to watch for in your partner's behavior and attitudes and in your children's reactions to him, so you can make sure your children stay both sexually safe and free from other forms of boundary violation.

What Can I Do?

While the abusive man is always responsible for his own actions, there are steps you can take to lessen the risk that your children's boundaries will be violated, and to increase the likelihood that if your partner does make them feel uncomfortable or invaded in any way, they will reveal the problem to you quickly and seek your support and protection. Invasive men are less likely to escalate their inappropriate behavior if they sense that they are being watched carefully, and that they are not succeeding in training children to keep secrets. Communicating well with your children about these issues will help ensure that they won't be victimized outside the home either; research shows that children exposed to abusive men are more vulnerable to being taken advantage of sexually by other people, not just by their father.

Teach good boundaries and model them. Explain to your children that their bodies belong to them, and that no one has the right to touch them in any way that they don't like. Don't require them to kiss or hug relatives or friends at any time, and let them know that they have the right to refuse affection or closeness *with you* whenever they want. Teach your children to ask for privacy in the bath-

room and while changing clothes, and interrupt any invasive behaviors they use with each other, such as unwanted touching.

Don't use any form of physical discipline with your children, including spanking, so that they will have a clear sense from an early
age that adults are not supposed to cross their physical limits in any
way. If you want your children to recognize boundary violations
and disclose them when they happen, you have to be absolutely
strict about respecting their physical integrity *yourself,* even in ways
that may be difficult for you.

Explain the difference between "good secrets" and "bad secrets."
Go over the following with your children: "A good secret is one
that is fun to keep, such as knowing what someone's birthday sur-
prise is going to be. Also, a good secret is one you keep only for
a few days or a couple of weeks, and then it's time to tell. A bad
secret, on the other hand, makes you sad or upset, such as when
someone hurts you and then says you shouldn't tell your mother
about it. And with the bad secret, the person tells you to keep the
secret for good, not just for a few days." Explain further that it is
never okay for an adult—or even another child—to make them
keep a bad secret. As an example, point out to them that Mommy
has no secrets that she expects them to keep about anything.

(There's one exception to this rule, however: If Dad is a physically violent or threatening style of abuser, mothers and children
may sometimes have to keep secrets from *him* to protect their own
safety. If this is true in your situation, make sure to discuss this distinction explicitly with your children.)

Explain that they don't have to keep secrets to protect other
people. This is important because sexual abusers will sometimes
tell children that their mother, or a sibling, will get hurt if they reveal the violations.

Explain about "good touch" and "bad touch." Help children
identify the private parts of their bodies, including genitals, rear
end, and the insides of their mouths, and that no one—not even

a parent—is to touch them there except briefly for washing or putting on medicine. If any way that they are being touched makes them feel bad, they should tell Mommy, even if the person says not to tell. Model the point for them by adding, "Even if *I* touch you in a way that doesn't feel good, I want you to be sure to talk to me about it, and I won't do it again."

Keep your children as socially connected as possible. Work hard to foster your children's friendships, to have them involved in activities such as athletics, music, or drama, and to have them spend time with other adults who care about them. Children who are not isolated are less likely to keep secrets about boundary violations. If your partner is determined to isolate you and your children, this may be an uphill climb, but do whatever you can. (I review some strategies for combatting isolation at the end of chapter 2.) Some well-meaning parents overly restrict their children's social contacts in the hopes of preventing sexual abuse, when the result may actually be to make children more vulnerable, both at home and outside.

Believe your children. Children almost never lie to their parents about boundary violations, including sexual abuse. It's true that very young children can sometimes misinterpret innocent forms of touch; but given the tendency of men who abuse women to disrespect children's boundaries, it's better to err on the side of caution and take protective steps when they report worrisome incidents.

Try to react to disclosures, or to boundary violations that you witness yourself, in ways that are supportive, educational, and calm. Explain to your child that Dad's behavior was inappropriate and that the child has a right to have his or her boundaries respected. Praise the child for raising the issue, and say that you always want to know when these kinds of problems occur. Ask the child if it's okay to talk to Dad about it. If the child consents, talk to your partner about the behavior that you are uncomfortable with, say that you see it as a boundary issue, and see if he is willing to agree not to repeat what he did. Be as clear as you safely can be with your partner about which parenting behaviors are acceptable to you and which are not. Then keep an eye on what happens, since abusive men do not always feel obligated to keep their agreements.

If the child does not want you to talk to your partner about the issue, he or she probably has valid concerns about retaliation for having told. In this case, you may have to protect your child through other means, such as:

- Not leaving the child alone with your partner, making excuses to always be present yourself at bedtimes, bath times, and other moments of vulnerability.
- Teaching your child how to get away from the invasive behavior (if that is realistic for your child's age, maturity, and temperament).
- Separating from living with your partner (I discuss the pros and cons of this choice in chapter 9).

Because many forms of boundary violation are somewhat subtle, your child may need some help putting his or her discomfort into words and developing language to name the inappropriate behavior. He or she may also feel guilty for criticizing Dad. You can help relieve this burden by saying, "I'm not talking badly about Daddy, I'm just helping you to understand why this particular thing that he did isn't okay. It wouldn't be okay if I did it either, or anyone else."

Avoid acting mad or upset (even if you really are—most parents do feel angry upon learning that their children's boundaries have been violated). If children are afraid that you will be too angry at Dad or will stop liking him, the next time they experience his invasiveness they may not tell you. They may also stop talking about it in order to protect *you,* because they don't like to see you so upset. And finally, they tend to misinterpret strong emotions as meaning that you are angry at *them,* even if you try to make it clear that you aren't. So use descriptive language, such as, "I don't like it that he kept staring at you when you told him to stop," but try to keep your tone as calm and even-keeled as possible.

If your child discloses overt sexual abuse to you, such as that Dad touched his or her private areas in a sexual way, got him or her to touch Dad sexually, or penetrated any part of his or her body (including the mouth) in a sexual way, separating from your partner will of course be the only option, at least in the short term. (You are unlikely to be able to stop such serious behavior through confronting your partner, although he may well promise not to re-peat it.) I recommend that you read *A Mother's Nightmare—Incest,* which will help you get through this distressing experience in the most constructive way possible, and allow you to be the best re-source for your child's healing (see Resources, page 347).

Finally, avoid any response that could make your child feel to blame, such as, "Why didn't you tell me sooner?" You may feel guilty that the violations have happened—this again is a normal parental response—but be careful not to turn that guilt back on your son or daughter.

Be verbally and physically affectionate with your children. The more your children get their needs for praise, attention, and cud-dling met by you, the less vulnerable they will be to being taken advantage of by others. A man who violates children's boundaries sometimes lures children with affection or attention that they are hungry for. Also, the more thoughtful, caring touching they receive from you, the better they will recognize inappropriate or invasive touch when it occurs.

Keep the most open lines of communication possible with your children. One of the best forms of protection for children is their knowledge that they can talk to you about *anything* they need to, and that you will respond in an open and sensitive way. Keep working on your ability to have successful conversations with your children about difficult issues of any kind.

Key Points to Remember

- Abuse involves, by nature, some level of boundary violation.
- Men who abuse women disrespect children's emotional, physical, or sexual boundaries more commonly than other men do.
- Your children need good information about their own limits, and need you to model respect for their boundaries.
- Good communication between mothers and children is one key to keeping children protected.
- You can successfully protect your children's boundaries, and in the process you will discover ways to better protect your own.

Part II

The Abusive Man and Family Dynamics

Chapter Six

A Weekend with the Abbott Family

Nick, twelve, and Robin, nine, awoke with excitement on a snowy Friday morning during their February school vacation week. For over a week they had been anticipating their family ski trip, and the day had finally come. To make the prospect even sweeter, five inches of new snow had fallen during the night, and now the clouds were thinning and the sun was poking its rays onto the sparkling powder. Kristen, their thirty-six-year-old mother, had succeeded in persuading her husband, Wayne, thirty-five, to put in for a day off from work—almost unheard of for him—and was calling in sick to her own job. They were going to have a family day, for the first time in months. The children were thrilled that Dad was joining them; he was not often available, nor was he a great skiing enthusiast. Kristen added to the festive atmosphere of the day by whipping up pancakes.

After breakfast Kristen asked her son to help her with the dishes, and in an instant the tone of the morning took a dramatic downward turn. Nick felt put-upon and reacted with sharp anger.

"Why do I have to do the dishes? That's stupid! Have Robin help you with them if you can't handle it yourself, I've got to get my gear together." He started to stomp out of the kitchen, and Kristen yelled at him to come back and do what he was asked.

At this point the children's father stepped into the fray. "Now, Kristen," he said, his voice radiating condescension as if he were talking to a two-year-old about eating crayons, "Nick is a twelve-year-old boy, I don't think he needs to be washing dishes. I'm sure you can handle it. Nick, get your equipment out quickly and then help me shovel the walks." Kristen glared furiously at her husband.

Nick, feeling triumphant, sneered at his mother. "Why didn't you just listen to me when I told you this was stupid, Ma?" His father smiled at him and rolled his eyes as if to say, "She's impossible, isn't she?" and they both strolled off. Kristen glared furiously at Wayne, then turned to Robin and told her to help clean up.

Wayne headed outside to clear snow, but he was increasingly angry that Kristen had glared at him, and soon stormed back into the kitchen to confront her. "What the hell were you giving me that dirty look for?" he hissed, keeping his voice low but harsh. "You think I'm going to put up with that shit from you? I don't have to just stand there and let you turn my son into a mama's boy."

Kristen said anxiously, "Wayne, the children can hear you. Please stop yelling." This defiance was the last straw for Wayne. "*I'm* yelling? You're the one that screeches, Kristen, not me. You're always angry with someone about something. Listen, I'm not going on any damn ski trip with *you*. You just go ahead and raise that boy the way you want to—he'll turn out a mess like you!" He turned on his heel, stomped up the stairs, and slammed the door of the TV room behind him.

Half an hour later, Wayne still hadn't appeared. Robin climbed the stairs and called to him, "Dad, it's getting late. Can we go?" His voice came snarling back through the closed door, "Leave me alone! Don't bother me!" After another half hour had passed, it was plain to see that the trip was off.

Nick and Robin launched desperately into trying to salvage the day. Nick said, "If Dad doesn't want to go, then the hell with him. Let's just get out of here." But Kristen knew that she and the children would pay for it later if they left him at home sulking, so she told Nick no, their father would be too upset. "Jesus," he sputtered, "you just let Dad push you around, like you're spineless. Act like a grown-up, for crying out loud."

Robin felt crushed as it sank in that they really weren't going, and she flashed angrily at her mother. "Why did you have to go and pick a fight with Dad on this day of all days? You know what his temper is like, you know how he gets! You've wrecked our day!" The children flew out slamming the door, leaving Kristen feeling run over from all sides.

A few minutes later Robin began to have second thoughts, as a weight of guilt settled over her about how bad her mother must have been feeling. She found Nick in the neighbor's yard, where he was looking for his friends, and tried to persuade him that they should go together to apologize to her. Nick replied with a dismissive laugh, "You've got to be kidding. I'm not going to say I'm sorry for telling it like it is. You want to suck up to her, go ahead." Robin went nervously back into the house and said to her mother, "Can I make you a tea?"

A couple of hours later, Wayne finally emerged. He silently got himself a sandwich and then went outdoors, where he ended up joining Nick and his friends in a snowball fight. Nick's friends were impressed by how childlike and entertaining his father could be—they even felt a little envious. Then Wayne got quietly into his car and drove off without saying good-bye to Kristen or Robin. Later it turned out he had gone into the office, not returning until dinnertime.

That evening, when the children were upstairs getting ready for bed, Kristen asked Wayne if he could help her get the ski stuff out of the car. He leaped back into anger. "I'm not the one who had to start something this morning with yelling and dirty looks and criticizing people. I'm not emptying the fucking car. I went and worked this afternoon, you know, while you sat around on your butt all day. I'm not a mule, you know."

The argument escalated rapidly, with Kristen yelling and pacing around while Wayne followed her, mocking her angry statements and telling her she needed a psychologist. "Get yourself some medication, you're acting totally crazy, with the children right upstairs. Get a grip on yourself!" These taunts made Kristen even madder. She felt set up to get hysterical but didn't know how to describe what Wayne was doing or defend herself against it, so she yelled, "You bastard!"

Wayne had again reached his breaking point—or at least, that was his excuse to himself. He swept his arm across a table that had houseplants on it, scattering leaves, dirt, and smashed pots across the living room floor. Kristen screamed and Wayne bolted out of the house, not returning until the children were asleep. He then disappeared to work all weekend.

On Monday, Nick got in trouble at school for tripping a smaller student in the hallway, which he did because he enjoyed the laughter it provoked from his friends. A notice was sent home from the assistant principal of the middle school informing Nick's parents that he had been repeatedly involved with aggressive behavior toward classmates and mouthing off to teachers, and that he was risking suspension.

The same day, Robin, who was a well-behaved and bright student, complained to her elementary school teacher of cramps in her legs and was sent to the nurse's office. After lying down for a half hour Robin was still in pain, and the nurse decided that she should see a doctor. The school called Kristen at work to come pick up Robin. As Kristen left the office, her boss grumbled with annoyance about how often she ended up missing work for one reason or another.

The pediatrician was unable to identify any cause of Robin's leg pains. He pointed out that Robin had had many ailments over the past two years, including stomachaches, knee pain, and headaches. The doctor took Kristen aside and said, "Is there anything going on at home that we need to talk about? Children sometimes respond this way to stress or upset." Kristen was caught off guard by the question, but she had known the doctor for several years and felt considerable trust in him. "My husband and I are fighting a lot these days. Maybe she's upset by it."

The doctor gently probed further. "Are you ever afraid at home? Are you feeling controlled or intimidated?"

Kristen took a deep breath. "Mostly it's just put-downs. But, yeah, I guess I get scared sometimes. He really lost it this weekend." The doctor spoke compassionately and kindly to Kristen about the tough situation she was in, and gave her a pamphlet from a program for abused women.

Wayne arrived home in high spirits that night. He had met a deadline at work, and the bad feelings he had from Friday's confrontations with Kristen had subsided. He had also been feeling sexual that afternoon, so he wanted to paper over their tensions. As the family headed to the dinner table, he gave Kristen a hug and said, "Hey, I'm sorry about what happened, but let's put it behind us." Kristen recoiled slightly and looked at the ground, not smiling. The children noticed her reaction. At dinner Wayne was jovial and entertaining, and his silly antics made the children laugh. Kristen felt awkward and somber, disconnected from the rest of the family. After dinner, Dad announced that he was taking everyone out for ice cream sundaes. The children were thrilled to see the fun and generous side of their father make one of its rare appearances.

Kristen went up to Nick's room to make sure his homework was done. Nick took the moment to say, "What do you have against

Dad? He tries hard to make things go better around here; I don't
see why you can't meet him halfway. He can be really nice." Kristen hesitated for a moment. Then she decided the time had come
to stop avoiding the issue with Nick, who was increasingly turning against her. "Nick, I know how hard it can be to feel caught
in the middle of all this. I know you would like to help us work
things out, but you can't. The grown-ups have to take care of
themselves. But I'm going to get help for us, so you don't have to
keep going through this."

Meanwhile, Wayne found their daughter in the TV room. "Listen, Robin," he said, "I just wanted to apologize for how grouchy
Mom has been lately. I don't know why she flies off the handle like
that. She hurts my feelings, too." Then he slowly walked away
looking victimized.

Around two in the morning, Robin woke up yelping from a
nightmare. She ran into her parents' bedroom and asked if she
could sleep with them, to which Kristen said, "Of course, honey.
Are you okay?" Wayne propped himself up on his elbow and
snapped, "Jesus, Kristen, you treat her like she's a two-year-old.
She's not a baby. Robin, you're not sleeping with your parents
when you're in the fourth grade! Get right back in bed!"

"I'm only in *third* grade, Daddy," pleaded Robin, but her father
ignored her.

Robin returned to her bedroom and lay there trembling. Kristen started out of bed to go to her, but Wayne reached out and
grabbed her arm. "The way you pamper that girl, she's never going
to grow up! Stay here and let her be!" Kristen pulled her arm out
of Wayne's grasp but lay back in bed, afraid to see how he would
react if she defied him.

About ten minutes later, Kristen could tell by Wayne's breath-
ing that he had fallen asleep, and she tiptoed down to Robin's bedroom, closing the door behind her. As soon as her daughter felt

her next to her, she burst into tears. "What *took* you so long, Mom?" she wailed.

Robin confided to her teacher that day that her brother often teased her, imitated her, and called her names, and sometimes shoved her or punched her arm. The teacher responded, "It's really hard having an older brother, isn't it? Sibling stuff can be hard, but deep down you'll always love each other." Robin said, "Sometimes I don't even want to be at home. And my dad is kind of the same way as my brother."

The teacher realized that her first response had been insensitive, and apologized to Robin for making light of her anxiety. "I'll talk to your mother about what you've told me, okay? We'll see what we can do about it. Everyone should feel safe at home, and it sounds like you don't."

That afternoon, Kristen received a phone call from Robin's teacher. Emboldened by her positive experience in the doctor's office, she plunged ahead and spoke frankly about Wayne's abusiveness. They scheduled a time to meet in person in a few days. Kristen was realizing that Wayne's behavior was affecting her children more than she had thought, but she was also starting to feel for the first time that maybe she didn't have to manage this situation all on her own. Maybe other people could understand what she was up against and help her figure out what to do.

Over the next two chapters, I will take you back through the Abbotts' story one step at a time, drawing out what can be learned from the rocky path their days took. In the process, you will learn ways to guide your family along a different route, breaking free from abuse and manipulation and reclaiming life for yourself and your children.

Chapter Seven

Defending Your Role as Mother

"I don't seem to know how to manage my children's behavior very well. They walk all over me."

"Things come out of their mouths sometimes that sound exactly like his abuse. I swear I can hear him talking through them."

"My husband's a lot better at keeping the kids in line. I'd be in a real fix if he weren't around."

"I think I've been good to my children, but sometimes they seem so bitter toward me. I don't get it, and it hurts."

An abusive man can send shock waves through every fiber of a family. Each interaction, every relationship, every heart can be affected by the chronic mistreatment you are the target of. The next two chapters explore how your partner's behavior can distort family life, and what you can do to get your family back on track and keep it that way.

Because of how hard it can be to put your finger on the family dynamics that an abusive man can create, you may find that you often blame yourself or resent your children for the hard times in your home. Thoughts such as these may go through your mind:

> *"I just don't know how to control these kids. They'll listen to their father but not to me."*
>
> *"I guess I'm just too lax with them. I should be stricter."*
>
> *"My children verbally abuse me—they're turning out just like their father."*

You may have moments of such frustration that you wonder if maybe you aren't a good mother. Your partner may compound these doubts by criticizing your parenting harshly or dressing you down in front of your children. And perhaps you have also felt judged by relatives, schoolteachers, or other people in your life for your children's difficulties or for your conflicts with them.

The pages ahead will help you to name and identify some of the challenges that your partner's actions may be causing in your life as a mother. Through these insights, you can move away from blaming yourself and feeling incompetent, and toward intervening effectively to change direction.

How Abuse Undermines Your Authority

Your partner's abuse or control of you can undercut your ability to take a proper parental role as your children's authoritative leader. This undermining happens in two ways. The first has to do with the *inherent undermining effects of abuse;* even if your partner is not intending to weaken your authority as a parent, his behavior can have that result by its nature. The second has to do with *deliberate undermining by the abuser;* a majority of my clients make their partners' parenting lives difficult on purpose, and we will look at why and how they do.

Undermining That Is Inherent to Partner Abuse

When a man chronically mistreats his partner, his actions send messages to the children and serve as a behavioral model. These negative influences tend to outweigh any constructive teaching he may give them in words, because children learn most powerfully by example. This point is illustrated in a training video on domestic abuse, in which a man named Ty describes how his father used to tell him that males should never hit females, *even though Ty's father used to beat his mother.* And it was his father's actions, not his words, that had a lasting impact; Ty grew up to be an abuser of women himself.

QUESTION #6: Why don't my children respect my authority?

What do children learn—*mis*learn, really—about their mother's authority from seeing and hearing their father ridicule her, shout her down, ignore her, or intimidate her?

- "Dad doesn't respect Mom, and since we love him and look up to him, that must mean that Mom isn't worthy of our respect either."
- "When Dad doesn't want to hear what Mom has to say, he tells her to shut up, walks away and ignores her, or throws things around the house. So that's what we should do when we feel bothered by her."

- "Dad gets furious if Mom asks him to take care of things that he doesn't feel like dealing with. That means that we have the right to do the same thing, so we tell her off when she bugs us to clean our rooms, do our homework, or walk the dog."
- "If Mom ever complains about the way Dad is talking to her or treating her, he makes it clear that she is ridiculous for believing that he's doing anything wrong. So if she ever says to us that she doesn't like how we're talking to her, we know to just make fun of her for complaining, the same way he does."

Let's begin by examining the lessons that Nick, the twelve-year-old Abbott boy, has learned from his father, Wayne. Early in the day, following breakfast, we saw Nick change in a flash from a cheerful boy full of enthusiasm for the family ski trip into a surly, resentful, superior young man. What had occurred? Simply this: His mother had asked him to meet his responsibilities by helping wash the dishes. But Nick had absorbed his father's attitude that males shouldn't have to contribute to domestic work except when they feel like it. Remember how Wayne reacted when his wife asked him to help unpack the car? Nick has learned from his father to feel *entitled* not to help, and to openly defy or ridicule his mother if she doesn't back down.

As Nick gets further into his teens, he may become physically aggressive toward his mother when he is angry at her, since violence—at least toward objects—is part of the behavior that Wayne models. Several studies have found that adolescents whose fathers assault their mothers often start to hit her themselves.

As we saw in chapter 4, children can absorb a range of destructive messages from their abusive father. Some of those values are especially damaging to a mother's authority, such as:

"Males should make the rules and females should obey them."

"Males are entitled to make all kinds of demands on females, but females who make any demands at all on males are 'nags' or 'bitches.' "

"Males have the right to become intimidating when they are really angry."

In this atmosphere, it is understandable if you have to struggle to maintain your authority, especially over your sons. We will look below at strategies you can use to reestablish and maintain your proper maternal role.

The Dynamics of the Aftermath of Abuse

Witnessing an incident of abuse can leave children feeling vulnerable, unsteady, and emotionally raw. Over the ensuing hours or days, they may be searching for ways to make sense out of what they've heard or seen. Because of how confused and needy they feel during this period, they can be easily influenced, particularly if someone offers them a way to relieve their pain.

When Wayne Abbott littered the floor with the plants he knocked off the table, Kristen was left reeling. For the following two or three days she felt shaky and drawn up inside herself. Robin and Nick saw her go through this dark tunnel but they didn't really understand her reactions. What they were aware of was simply that she was distant and short-tempered. Wayne, on the other hand, didn't have to struggle with feelings of entrapment, fear, and confusion—life is very different for the abuser than for the target of the abuse—so he was soon able to pull himself together and turn on the charm. Nick and Robin thirstily drank in their father's generosity, and it seemed to them that their mother must be the cause of the tensions. Sure, in day-to-day life she was the kinder, more patient, more attentive parent, but what was going on *right then* was what counted; they were reeling from the abuse they had just witnessed, and so were highly impressionable.

Children can be further influenced by overhearing their father's justifications:

> *"You know perfectly well how much it pisses me off when you do that, but you had to go ahead and do it anyhow, so how do you expect me to react?"*

> *"I was just trying to make you listen to me because you don't listen."*

> *"You take everything the wrong way and blow it all out of proportion. It's your own fucking fault."*

Finally, the pain and confusion your children go through after witnessing abuse leaves them hungry for you to console them and help them feel secure. But you may be overwhelmed yourself, feeling shaken up, humiliated, or enraged. If you can't fully be there for them—and it isn't your fault if you can't—they may feel abandoned at a crucial moment, and those feelings may come out in defiance or rudeness toward you.

One solution to this problem is to talk to your children as soon as you feel able to after an incident. If you were emotionally unavailable for some period of time in the immediate aftermath, make sure they know that you are there for them now, and that they can talk to you about what things have been like for them. Don't blame yourself for not being able to be SuperMom right after being abused, but do make sure that your children know they can count on you.

One Escape Route for the Children— But Not the Best

Children find injustice sharply painful, and feel a debilitating powerlessness when they observe mistreatment that they cannot stop. One way in which they sometimes can escape the heartbreak of witnessing cruelty is to convince themselves that no injustice has actually been done; in other words, to see the abuse as necessary or deserved, and to see the victim as inferior. So if your child can just decide that Mom is to blame for Dad's viciousness, or that she's crazy or absurd, then—poof!—life has just gotten a bit more bearable.

The abuser may actively encourage the children to take this way out, manipulating them into blaming their mother and looking down on her. A child can then gain the additional reward of getting in good with Dad, which can mean being on the protected list, safe from his insults, rages, or violence.

In order to keep your authority from being further eroded by this dynamic, discuss the question of personal responsibility explicitly with your children. Explain to them that their father has to take complete ownership of his actions and cannot blame you—or them—for his explosions.

How an Abuser May Deliberately Undermine Your Authority

When Kristen Abbott and her son, Nick, wound up in a tense exchange over the dishes, Wayne took steps that planted corrosive seeds in the children's relationships with their mother. The first was that he *overruled* Kristen. He spoke in a dictatorial tone, placing himself above her on the decision-making ladder, and he released Nick from obeying her. The unspoken lesson this interaction communicated to the children is unmistakable: "The real parental power lies with Dad. Mom is simply his deputy, only having power to the extent that he delegates it to her."

Once the children realize that this kind of hierarchy is in place, the mother can lose direct control over them and be relegated to warning, "Wait until your father comes home and I tell him what you did."

After Wayne undercut Kristen's authority, Nick was openly rude to his mother, and he received an approving smile from his father. From Nick's perspective, a critical event had just taken place: *His father rewarded him for treating his mother contemptuously.* Dad's facial expression also carried another important message: *"You and I are males together, Nick, and we run the show around here over these females."* He thereby bonded with Nick, manipulating him to join his dad's privileged team.

Finally, some angry and controlling men *teach children overtly to disrespect their mother.* Wayne demonstrated this approach in his nighttime conversation with Robin, subtly painting her mother as unstable and incompetent. I have had clients who tell the children that their mother is alcoholic or that she sleeps around. He may portray her as mentally ill—and periodically drive her to hysteria in front of them to prove his point. He may also whisper to them that she is a bad mother or that she doesn't love them, which can shake their trust in her. I have worked with children of abused women who say to me, "Mom doesn't have any idea what she's doing. Everything would fall apart if we didn't have Dad to hold things together." This is the outlook the abuser has conditioned the children to adopt.

Undermining the children's mother is destructive parenting. If you can safely confront your partner directly about eroding your authority, look for ways to do so. There is no excuse for what he's doing, and the problems his actions will lead to—or may have already led to—are obvious.

Interfering with Your Parenting

Parenting involves many aspects besides authority. In this section we look at both direct and indirect ways that your partner may pose obstacles to your efforts to care for your children, which may be at the root of some of your current struggles.

Direct Interference

A few nights after the scary incident in which Wayne Abbott smashed the plants on the floor, we saw nine-year-old Robin enter her parents' bedroom trembling from a nightmare. Her father's response was not only to order the girl back to her own room, but to forbid her mother to accompany her through the darkness, grabbing Kristen's arm and barking his stern instructions. Kristen was thus barred from caring for her child at a moment of dire need.

Why didn't Kristen just go to her daughter's room anyhow, in defiance of Wayne's prohibition? A number of factors weighed on her:

- By grabbing her arm, Wayne put Kristen on notice that he could overpower her physically. He had acted out violently just a few nights earlier, so his threatening body language was frightening to her.
- Wayne had a history of making Kristen's life miserable with mental abuse for days at a time when he felt defied. She had to consider the emotional price she would pay if she didn't bend to his will.
- Kristen knew from past experience that Wayne would also make the children pay, not just her, if she didn't obey him.

This last bind was illustrated for me by a client named Xavier, whom I worked with a few years ago. When he was angry at his four-year-old son, Arturo, he used to pull hard on his ear, which would make the boy squeal with pain. The mother, Rosa, was extremely distressed by this violence and mustered up the courage to tell Xavier never to do that to the boy again. Xavier responded with fury that Rosa would try to "tell him how to be a father" like that, and he retaliated by locking the young boy in his room for three hours and not permitting Rosa to go to him. This experience left Rosa in a terrible bind: When Xavier was abusing Arturo, she was forced to be silent, for fear that the boy would get hurt even worse if she attempted to intervene. Rosa had no choice but to look for a way to escape the relationship if she possibly could.

Dozens of women have told me of serious interference in their parenting from their abusive partners. The most common complaint is of being prevented from picking up a crying infant or from comforting a hurt or frightened child. One woman described the abusive man refusing to drive her and her baby to the hospital after their infant daughter had mysteriously fainted. Another woman told me that my client had locked their ten-year-old son out in the snow and then told her, "If you go to him, I'm locking you out there, too." She was afraid to leave the house, because that would have left him indoors alone with their five-year-old daughter, in his enraged and threatening state.

Take a moment to consider whether your partner's interference sometimes prevents you from caring for your children in the way you would choose to. If so, your rights as a mother are being violated, and you deserve assistance in seeking ways to recover them.

Indirect Interference

Your partner may make your life as a mother difficult simply from the effects his mistreatment has on you. It's difficult to feel fully connected to your children when you are in emotional pain. Abuse can leave a woman depressed, making it hard to play energetically with children. Your frayed nerves may make you snappy at times. If you aren't always able to give your children the quality of attention you wish you could, your own emotional injuries may be getting in the way. Your partner's failure to contribute adequately to household responsibilities may also be leaving you exhausted, so you feel that you have less energy to offer your children.

Consider a few examples of how your partner's abuse can affect your parenting:

Making you too strict: Does your partner take it out on you when he feels the children are being too loud or too rambunctious, or are having too much fun? If you allow your children some freedom, do you pay a price? If so, you may feel forced into being a much more restrictive parent than you think is good for your children.

Addiction: The bitter taste of chronic degradation or intimidation can cause a woman to develop self-destructive habits to escape the pain, including abuse of alcohol or drugs, or addictive use of the Internet (an increasingly common problem). Some women are pressured into substance abuse because the husband or boyfriend wants someone to share his addiction. Addictions that you develop are likely to have a bad impact on your parenting, and can put you at risk of losing custody of your children, as I discuss in chapter 10. If you are abusing substances, *get help;* as with the other challenges I describe in this book, you don't have to solve the problem of addiction by yourself. (Look under "Addictions" in the Resources section, page 350.)

You become the children's target: We saw Robin Abbott's reaction to her disappointment when her father canceled their ski trip: She turned angrily on her mother. Robin knows that she can't confront her *father;* there would be hell to pay if she did. Challenging him wouldn't do any good anyhow; abusers respond to grievances at best by ignoring them. Robin tries to get her mother to give in because she knows her father never will.

Double binds for you: An abused mother can get caught between a rock and a hard place in her children's eyes. If you stand up to their father, your children may get angry at you for causing him to explode, as Robin did with her mother. But if you *don't* stand up to him, you may find your children confronting you disparagingly, "Why do you just stand there and *allow* him to treat you like that? Don't take that from him!", similar to the things that Nick said to Kristen when she refused to go skiing without their dad. We saw another bind in Rosa's case, where she feels that efforts to protect her son could make things worse for him.

These examples illustrate why your own healing is inseparable from your children's healing. Make it a priority in your life to take good care of yourself, including seeking help regarding your partner's abusiveness. (You might pick up *When Love Goes Wrong* or *Why Does He Do That?* if you haven't read them yet—see the Resources section, page 338.)

Why Does He Want to Damage My Relationships with My Children?

Not all abusive men seek to weaken mother-child connections. I have had clients over the years who have neither insulted the woman's parenting abilities nor tried to pull her apart from her children, though they still cause stress for her as a mother in other ways, as we've seen.

But when a man does drive wedges, the mother can find herself wondering why on earth her partner wants to hurt her connection to the children. There can be several reasons:

He senses that your relationships with your children are a source of strength for you. He may be able to tell that you derive pride and self-confidence from being a good parent, and that your children provide you with love, affection, and companionship that could help you be less dependent on him.

He wants to control the home, and feels entitled to do so. The abusive man can't be the king of the castle in the way he desires unless he trains the children to see him as a higher authority than you.

He considers himself superior. As twisted as this may sound, an abusive man's attitude of superiority can lead him to believe that he is *a better influence* on his children than you are, so he tries to get the children to be more like *him*. My clients tend to particularly take this attitude toward raising their sons.

He wants to make sure the family doesn't unify against him. Abusive men lose some of their ability to bully the family when mothers and children stick up for each other and refuse to be divided, as sometimes happens. This last point is a complex and crucial one that we will return to in chapter 8.

What Can I Do?

Now for the good news: There are *many* actions you can take to strengthen your relationship with your children and protect or reestablish your maternal authority. But it is important to try to move forward quickly, as time is of the essence; the deeper the wedges your abusive partner drives between you and your children, the harder the road to recovery can be. At the same time, remember that emotional injuries take time to heal, so you may not see instant results from your efforts. Work hard on your relationships with your children, and greater trust and closeness will begin to emerge.

Try not to blame yourself for not being a perfect parent—*nobody* is a perfect parent—or for not being able to jump at once into all the suggestions that I offer below. Do the best you can, and then be compassionate with yourself. This approach will in turn help you show compassion to your children.

Here are important steps to consider:

Stop believing that your abusive partner is a good father. A good father does not abuse his children's mother, since doing so shows tremendous disregard for the children's feelings and needs.

Even if he is nice to the children most of the time and avoids deliberately involving them in his abuse of you, he is still being irresponsible and uncaring toward them through what he is doing to *you*.

Begin taking mental note of how his behavior affects your children and your relationships with them. To the extent that you can stop blaming yourself and your children for the high level of tension in your home, you have already taken a giant leap toward recovery for all of you.

Insist on complete respect from your children to the fullest extent that you can. The earlier you can catch the children in beginning to absorb a contemptuous or bullying attitude toward you, the better your chances of turning the tide. Be firm in requiring them to speak to you nicely, say "please" and "thank you," and listen when you speak to them. Don't permit sarcasm, sputtering noises of disgust, or insulting facial expressions. Any disrespect you allow to go by unchallenged will tend to mushroom, because the abuser creates a rich soil in which children's bad attitudes toward you can grow.

Impose consequences for disrespect. For example, when a child says imperiously, "Ma, I asked you five minutes ago to get my socks. How come they still aren't here?," respond by not bringing the socks at all. If you are spoken to like a servant, refuse to give them anything. Permit no swearing, interrupting, or other signs of disrespect toward you, and don't allow one child to undermine you with another. For guidance on successful approaches to discipline, read one or more of the books listed in the Resource section under "Parenting Issues," page 348.

I realize that when your abusive partner is around, it may be impossible for you to hold the line on these expectations because he undermines you or actively joins the children in mistreating you—after all, it's his example that they are following. But put your foot down as much as you can, and when he isn't around, be absolutely firm.

Insist on respect for females in general. Don't let your sons or your daughters make sexist comments, make fun of girls or women, or behave rudely or contemptuously toward any female in their lives, including their sisters. Try to keep magazines, videos, and CDs out of the house if they are hateful to females or degrade them sexually. Disrespect for females in general, if allowed, will soon come home to roost in the form of disrespect toward you specifically, and by boys toward their sisters.

Support your children to be assertive and to have a voice. Surviving abuse is a steady battle to keep yourself, and your children, from being silenced. So at the same time that you demand respect from your children, support them also in speaking up for themselves, including with you. Let them know that they are permitted to question your decisions, raise objections, or speak angrily to you—as long as they do so with respect. If you want your children to avoid internalizing your partner's behavior and attitudes, you have to teach them to think for themselves, and that means they are going to stand up to you, not just to other people.

If you can safely confront your partner's undermining of you, do so. Abusive men vary in how physically dangerous or verbally vicious they can be. If your experience tells you that you can stand up to him without paying a horrible price, demand that he stop undercutting your parental authority. Ask him to read sections from parenting books that explain the impact on children when parents aren't unified, or see if friends or school personnel are willing to talk to him about the importance of backing you up. If he gets the message that people around him believe that undermining you constitutes bad parenting on his part, there's some chance he will ease up. (But tread cautiously if your partner is physically violent or threatening, or performs acts of severe mental cruelty when he wishes to retaliate.)

QUESTION #7:
How much should I tell my children about the abuse?

Give your children a moderate amount of information about your partner's inappropriate behavior. Some abused mothers believe that it is better for their children to know nothing about the abuse, while others tell their children everything. A middle course between these two options is actually what works best. Women are often understandably reluctant to tell their children the truth of how their father behaves, wanting to let the children remain innocent and unburdened and not wanting to turn them against him. But children figure out what is going on, at least on an intuitive level, and they usually hear and see much more of the abuse than their mother realizes. They need information in order to make sense out of what they witness, and to help them not internalize the messages that Dad's behavior communicates to them. Perhaps most important, if you equip them with a digestible amount of knowledge regarding the realities of their father's abuse of you, he will find it harder to lie to them and manipulate them against you.

A while after an incident of abuse—when emotions have settled a little for you and for your children, perhaps in a day or two—engage your children in frank and direct discussions of what happened. Don't speak badly of their father, but describe to them concretely which of his behaviors were unacceptable, and ask them to talk about their feelings. Tell them that neither they nor you are at fault for the abusive man's actions. Reach for a close connection with them through this conversation, offering them support and understanding for their feelings.

Don't lie on your partner's behalf or cover for his behavior. You may feel that it's your responsibility to protect your children from awareness of their father's destructiveness by making excuses for him, taking the blame yourself for his actions, or lying to hide what he has done. It is natural to want to maintain your children's positive view of their father and to keep them from getting their feelings hurt by him. But covering for him backfires in the long term, precisely because it works; they *will* let him off the hook, and blame you or themselves for his actions, if that's what you train them to do. (Especially since that's what *he* trains them to do.) You will end up wishing you hadn't. Your children will be much safer as the years go by if you allow them to see the realities of who their father is, in both his best and worst aspects, so that they will know to protect themselves from him emotionally.

(You may have to lie to *him* to protect *them* sometimes—that is another matter altogether—but don't lie to them to protect him.)

Create as much structure as possible in your children's lives. The presence of an abusive man in the home tends to bring chaos and unpredictability, factors that have been directly tied to depression in children. As much as possible, try to provide a sense of structure and routine. Some valuable elements include regular mealtimes, set bedtimes, and attention given to transitions, so that children are given a few minutes' warning before it's time to switch to the next activity, leave home, or go to bed.

Be the best parent you can be. As challenging as it is, your children need to be able to rely on you to help them feel held and watched out for through what can feel to them like an emotional— or physical—war zone. Draw on every resource you can, including parenting books and training courses, parent support groups, and "parent centers" or "family centers" that may exist in your area. Be an authority with your children but not a distant one; stay close to them, listening well, respecting their feelings, and giving them support. When you have conflicts with your children, make it a priority to work through them rather than leaving them unresolved, as the abusive man can exploit festering tensions for his own purposes.

Combat isolation. Your children are more likely to stay well in the long term if you are well. So reach out for assistance. Call an abused women's hotline, visit a support group, or go to a therapist who specializes in abuse. Slip out to talk to a friend or relative, or sneak a handwritten note into the mail if that's all you can get away with. Take the leap of opening up to someone—anyone you can trust—about the mistreatment you are suffering from your partner and about your concerns regarding your children. Reaching out for help is a risk, but not doing so is a greater one.

Combat isolation for your children as well. Strive to involve them with an array of playmates, and encourage other caring adults, such as healthy relatives, to play an active role in your children's lives. Help them to see that there are other role models—including other males—who don't behave as your partner does.

Consider leaving your relationship, at least for a while, if you can do so safely. Under the right circumstances, leaving your abusive partner can bring important improvements to the lives of your children. But leaving can also involve risks. We'll examine the complexities of this option in chapter 9.

Many more suggestions are still to come in the pages ahead. Reach for sources of hope about the future, and seek assistance from both friends and professionals. If you are currently at a discouraging point, remember that there is still time for your parenting life to go well. I have seen abused mothers bring about remarkable turnarounds in their family life, when they gained access to good information and support. Better days lie ahead.

Key Points to Remember

- Abuse is, by nature, inherently undermining of a mother's parental authority.
- A majority of abusers undercut the mother in deliberate ways, adding to the intrinsic effects of abuse.

- Don't blame yourself for how difficult your relationships are with your children, but do take rapid steps to attend to the rifts and tensions that may be mounting.
- You and your children can have close, loving relationships in the long term.
- Your children's healing is linked to your own.

Chapter Eight

Maintaining Healthy Dynamics in Your Family

"He gives our youngest child so much more attention than he gives the older ones. I don't get why he has to treat them so differently—it really hurts them."

"I finally got my husband to move out of the house, which was such a relief, but now my teenage son has started to take over the role of abusing me. I can't believe this is happening."

"My children are fighting and hitting each other constantly."

"Since my boyfriend left, we've all started to grow closer again."

A mother named Ellen came to my counseling practice recently seeking guidance on how to help her three children. She explained to me that she was divorced from the children's father, Maurice, who had been dictatorial and verbally abusive to her during their marriage, and she now lived on a small farm that was also home to three horses. Her son and two daughters continued to see their father regularly, including most weekends and some evenings. She felt disturbed by a sense of division spreading through her family relationships, with the following manifestations:

• Her oldest child, a fourteen-year-old named Patrick, has always been his father's favorite and is still closely allied with Dad. But now he is also starting to distance himself further and further from Ellen emotionally, which he recently rationalized by saying, "I feel bad when I'm with you because you care more about your horses than about us. That's all you can talk or think about." Ellen was quite struck by Patrick's statement because she almost never discusses her horses when she is with him, or any other aspect of her own life; conversations between them focus mostly on Patrick. "But the thing is," she told me, "the children's *father* has always claimed that animals were more important to me than he was. And he was bitter that our divorce made it possible for me finally to have horses, since he had always stood in the way of my getting any while we were together."

• Her second child is an eleven-year-old girl named Rhonda. Ellen said sadly, "Maurice treats Rhonda like she doesn't exist. He'll come in the door and look right past her and start talking to Patrick, which really hurts her. I don't know what she did wrong in her father's eyes." But at least Rhonda is not impressed by her father the way Patrick is, and so isn't getting drawn into his mentality. "She sees Maurice for who he is—she's not fooled at all." Ellen then added, "Rhonda also confided in me that when the children are with their father, he says a lot of bad things about me, and gets them drawn into it. It makes her feel terrible."

• Patrick and Rhonda fight like cats and dogs, as they have since they were much younger. Patrick chronically puts his sister down, ignores her at times, and on a few occasions has shoved her or punched her.

• Ellen's youngest, an eight-year-old girl named Wendy, is a people-pleaser. "Wendy tries as hard as she can to be on good terms with everyone. She doesn't like arguing. She keeps a lot bottled up inside and has this nervous smile on her face a lot. I worry about her. She worships her dad, though, and seems to really enjoy her time over there."

- Every time Maurice gets angry at Ellen he uses the children to get at her. For example, he recently said to Wendy, "I'm not going to be able to take you to that carnival on Saturday like I promised you, because your mother took me to court for more child support so now I have to work Saturdays to earn extra money." Ellen explained to me that the real reason Maurice has to work Saturdays is that he is buying a boat, but he was furious about the increase in child support so he punished Ellen by hurting Wendy.

This chapter brings to light the kinds of disruptions to family dynamics that abusive men like Maurice can cause, and offers solutions for getting those connections back on track and functioning in a healthy way. Many men with abuse problems seek to drag the family down into a hole with them, rather than face their abusiveness and overcome it. But they often fail, as families manage to stick together and keep moving toward well-being and freedom.

Use of the Children as Weapons

Some abusive men—but fortunately not all—try to increase their power by using the children to hurt or control their partners, as we just saw Maurice do. These tactics can cause mothers considerable distress. Look at the list below, reflecting on whether your partner has ever used your children against you in any of these ways.

Use of the Children as Weapons of Abuse

- Turning children against their mother.
- Convincing them that the abuse is their mother's fault.
- Requiring them to monitor and report on their mother's behavior when he isn't around, or rewarding them for doing so.
- Involving the children in abusing their mother.
- Being psychologically cruel or physically abusive to the children to upset their mother.
- Endangering the children to upset her (such as by driving recklessly).
- Ignoring or neglecting the children when angry at her.
- Threatening to harm the children.
- Threatening to abandon the mother with no resources to provide for her children.
- Threatening to report the mother to child protective services (or actually doing so).
- Not paying child support, underpaying, or paying late.
- Threatening to abduct the children (or actually doing so).
- Threatening to kill the children.
- Threatening to take custody of the children (or actually doing so).

If you have sometimes been the target of tactics such as these, you may have felt trapped, not sure how to stand up for yourself without putting your children at risk.

How are your children affected by being drawn into their father's abuse in these ways, and how can you help?

They feel guilty. Children feel bad if they collude with the abuse, but they also feel afraid not to. Boys tend to feel attracted to their father's power, but then feel bad about themselves for becoming like him. You can assist your children by talking with them about the binds they find themselves in, and telling them you understand if sometimes they have to play along with their father. Help them recognize that they are manipulated or intimidated into participating in the abuse, so they can forgive themselves.

But at the same time, get them to start thinking about strategies they could use to *avoid* having to go along with the abuse, pointing out that they will feel better about themselves if they succeed. Ask them for their own ideas about how they could respond when they feel pressured by their father. Try role-playing things they could say or ways they could safely slide out of colluding.

They can become accustomed to abuse as a way of life. Children who are pulled in as pawns of abuse can start to feel that being cruel to people, laughing at them, or manipulating them are normal ways to behave. Respond by frequently holding out for them examples of kindness and generosity—including examples from their own conduct—and help them keep their faith in human nature alive.

They feel angry. In the families I work with, I find that the more the abusive man weaves the children into his destructive behavior patterns, the more resentful they become, especially toward authority figures. They may start to believe that no one has integrity or is worthy of respect. Give them room to express their anger and mistrust, including toward you, but insist that they do so respectfully.

They feel insecure. Children sense unconsciously that when they participate in mistreating their mother, they are sacrificing her as a dependable source of security. And though they may enjoy the sensation of being "in good" with Dad, they know on some level that he is not trustworthy—so they feel like they can't rely on anyone. Do everything you can to let your children know that you forgive them, and reassure them that they will not lose your love even if they sometimes do things that upset you.

How (and Why) Abusive Men Sow Divisions

You may have noticed that two themes repeatedly sprout up in my descriptions of family functioning with an abuser living in the home: (1) tensions are frequently high between mothers and children, and (2) similar resentments tend to mount between siblings. Let's take a look at some of the roots of these conflicts.

Favoritism

> ## QUESTION #8:
> ## Why does he treat some of our children so much better than others?

Favoritism is one of the most divisive forms of unhealthy parenting, and unfortunately turns up with alarming frequency among my clients. An abusive man may play favorites as a divide-and-conquer strategy to increase his power in the family, or because his sexism makes him give a higher status to male children, or because he is simply too lazy to build connections with those children with whom he has less in common.

When the abusive man gives a child special treatment, children can fall into unhealthy roles, beginning with the *favored child*. This role is filled more commonly by a boy than a girl; the abusive man tends to favor male children because of his negative attitudes toward females. The favored child finds that his special status gives him a thrilling link to Dad's power, almost like the king's minister, and brings a relieving sense of being protected from Dad's abusiveness. To be sure to stay in his father's good graces, he may distance himself from Mom or from any siblings who are "on her side."

The abusive man tends to do a negative type of "male bonding" with the favored son, where they make jokes together at the expense of females in the family or bond about their superiority to females in general. This boy is at particular risk to follow in his father's footsteps as an abuser of women unless his mother or other influential adults can help him change direction. In cases where the favored child is a girl, she can become as rude and superior toward her mother as a favored son does. At the same time, she learns to hate and erase *herself;* she is being drawn into the abusive man's mentality and domain, where there is no room for genuine self-esteem for a female.

The favored daughter also runs an increased risk of having her boundaries violated by the abusive man, as she is being conditioned to be very eager to please him. If your abusive partner lavishes a lopsided amount of attention, praise, and affection on one of your daughters, perhaps mixed with occasional harsh criticism, be sure to take the steps described in chapter 5 to monitor her safety in your home.

The *slighted child,* on the other hand, feels envious and resentful toward the favored child, seeing the special attention or privileges that he gets. She or he feels inadequate and wishes to be a more attractive, competent person who could win Dad's attention and approval. If the slighted child has been closely attached to Mom and perhaps protective of her, she or he may consider abandoning that position in hopes of pleasing Dad. Many children decide to stay loyal to Mom, however; later in this chapter we'll look at some of the factors that help keep mothers and children from being pulled apart.

A third role often emerges, where a child acts as the *peacemaker,* attempting to get along with everyone, to not take a side, and to help others resolve their conflicts. At the beginning of this chapter, we saw Ellen's youngest child, Wendy, adopting this stance. Like the role of favored or slighted child, the peacemaking role has both advantages and disadvantages, and comes with its own sources of stress.

These roles can shift over time. Children attempt different strategies to feel safe and secure, and go through periods of attempting to stand up to the abuser and reject his values. The favored child sometimes renounces his or her special status after a while, showing solidarity with siblings or with Mom. Unhealthy dynamics can fade over time, as mothers and children find ways to feel stronger in themselves and closer to each other. Later in this chapter we will look at some approaches you can use to counter the divisive effects of your partner's favoritism.

Driving Wedges Intentionally

We have seen a number of examples in this book of abusive fathers driving family members apart, such as Matthew, who pressured his wife not to breast-feed their son, and Greg, who manipulated his children so they would want to leave his ex-wife's home and come live with him. My clients use a range of such tactics to sow divisions, including:

- *Deliberately breaking confidences:* For example, a girl might say to her father, "I think Kayla is having a hard time with the fact that I have a boyfriend and she doesn't, and it's getting between us." He might respond by running to Kayla and saying, "Your sister says you're jealous of her," thereby widening a gap that his daughter was actually trying to figure out how to close.

- *Lying to family members about what others have said:* For example, I have had a number of clients who have said things to children along the lines of "Your mother said that taking care of you is too much trouble for her and she is going to put you up for adoption, but don't worry, I won't let her do that."

• *Imposing collective punishments:* If one child misbehaves, for example, the abusive man may declare that the trip to the movies is canceled for the whole family. When a parent punishes everyone for the actions of one person, family members develop deep resentment toward the child who misbehaved, who in turn will feel ashamed and bitter from having to carry the blame.

• *Feeding existing tensions:* For example, when a daughter talks to her father about her anger toward her mother, the father may make statements to fuel her anger and encourage her to see her mother as an impossible person, rather than proposing constructive solutions or pressing the child to work out her resentments with her mother through direct communication.

• *Getting family members to feel sorry for him:* In chapter 6, we saw Wayne's eyes well up with tears as he told his daughter Robin how badly her mother hurts his feelings. An abusive man who uses this tactic sometimes succeeds in getting the children preoccupied with how their mother has caused *his* suffering, inverting reality.

If your family feels fragmented or factionalized, divisive behaviors used by your partner may be part of the problem. In the pages ahead you will learn steps you can take if he is sowing divisions.

The Divisive Impact of Exposure to Abuse

Children who live in a home where their mother is abused tend to fight with each other a lot. Researchers David Hurley and Peter Jaffe wrote in the *Canadian Journal of Psychiatry* that relationships between siblings who are exposed to domestic violence "are marked by high levels of sibling rivalry and jealousy, with punishment, intimidation, exploitation, and scapegoating passed down the sibling hierarchy from eldest to youngest." Physical fighting increases as well, as these children are much more likely to use violence toward each other or toward their mothers than other children are.

QUESTION #9:
Why do our children fight with each other so much?

Even in homes where the father does not use favoritism or deliberately drive wedges, divisive cracks can form just from the atmosphere that abuse creates. Consider the following causes:

The behavior that the abusive man models: Siblings in any family tend to replicate their parents' behavior in how they treat each other. So when children repeatedly hear or see cruel put-downs, blaming of the victim, or physical intimidation, they practice these power moves on their siblings—and on Mom—and adopt the abusive man's excuses and justifications.

The impact on children of fear, hurt, and anxiety: Children who live on tenterhooks awaiting their dad's next explosion are bound to point fingers at one another: "You made Dad lose his temper"; "You should have shut up when he told you to shut up"; "You shouldn't have made a mess like that when you knew it was almost time for him to come home"; and so forth. Your own fear of him can lead you to blame your children in the same way.

The abuser is too powerful to confront: Family members discover over time that if they try to get Dad to realize the harm he has done, he responds by hurting people even more deeply than before. So you may find that you and your children channel your fear and anxiety toward one another, and accumulate mutual resentments in the process.

Scapegoating: The above dynamics taken together sometimes

lead one child—or the mother—to become the family scapegoat. If one of your children has become the "Bad Kid," or the "Troubled One," or the "Child Who Can't Do Anything Right," consider the possibility that he or she has become the carrier of the family's distress. To interrupt such use of one child as a dumping ground, it will be necessary for you to help all of your children—and yourself—become more aware of their own feelings about the abuse in the home, and find healthier ways to channel and heal those emotional injuries.

As you develop an awareness of where the tensions between your family members are sprouting from, you will become rapidly more able to help work conflicts out and maintain unity.

Why Your Children May Distance Themselves from You

Some partners of my clients have reported to me with great sadness that one or more of their children were pulling away from them emotionally. This kind of distancing is more common in boys, but happens with girls sometimes also. Boys are sometimes conditioned by the abuser to feel ashamed of their mother, and so may work hard to prove that they are not like her and don't need her emotionally. Both boys and girls may find that Dad is nasty to them if he sees them being affectionate with you or if they take your side at all. He may taunt his sons with terms like "mama's boy" to make them feel bad about craving closeness with you.

Your children may struggle with a set of complex and contradictory feelings toward you, just as they do with their father. They may feel let down by you because of times when the abuse drove you away from them. They may feel exhausted from years of arguing with you due to the abuser's success at brewing tensions. They may blame you for their father's behavior.

At the same time, *your children desperately need to feel close to you.* On some level they know this themselves. You are their indispensable source of consistent love and nurturing, of accepting them for who they are, of understanding their deep feelings, of believing in who they are capable of being. You are their positive adult role model, from whom they must learn how to be mature, responsible, non-abusive adults, capable of having intimate relationships that are healthy and kind. Underneath the emotional wounds and unresolved bad feelings, your children love you deeply and wish more than anything to be close to you and to feel protected by you.

Why the Abusive Man Sows Divisions

The abusive man may not have a consciously destructive plan—most of my clients are not coldly cruel or calculating—but on some level he is profoundly drawn to power, and he gains leverage over everyone in the family when he creates infighting. His goals may include:

Keeping family members from unifying against him. In families where siblings stay loyal to each other, and where mothers and children maintain solidarity, the abusive man has less power to control Mom and everyone else. I have worked with some families, for example, in which siblings actually pulled together to physically drive the abuser out of the home. Children in some families tell lies to protect their siblings from being harmed by the abuser, call the police during assaults, and encourage their mothers to get help.

Meeting his own emotional needs. By succeeding in getting children to ally with him, the abuser wins supportive companions. It is quite common for abused mothers to say to me, "He isn't really a father to our children in how he interacts with them. He's more like a buddy." In other words, he doesn't offer appropriate discipline or guidance, but has fun with the children and bonds with them against Mom.

Escaping responsibility. Amid all the chaos, the shifting allegiances and the bitter factions, and the scapegoating, Dad manages over and over again to slide out of being answerable for his actions.

Will He Succeed in Driving Us All Apart?

I hear a sharp anxiety in the voices of some of the mothers I speak with as they become aware of the cracks that are forming in the family structure. The question presses: "Is he going to succeed in getting my children to hate me? What should I do?"

While many abusive men cause tensions among family members, most do not succeed in driving them apart for the long term. Children gradually see through the fronts that their father puts on, or he finally shows them his true colors one day in a fit of rage, or one clear-thinking sibling manages to lead the others out of the fog. Mothers keep trying new ways to reach their children, and with enough efforts they are likely to strike upon an approach that works. Researchers have pointed out that abused mothers work hard to improve their approach to parenting as a way to compensate for the unhealthy dynamics fostered by the abuser, and those efforts make a big difference in some families.

Some abused mothers remain close and unified with their children throughout—I have worked with many families over the years of whom this was true—and there are siblings who find ways to keep their relationships loyal and supportive. The wonderful book *Childhood Experiences of Domestic Violence* by Caroline McGee is full of examples of children courageously standing by their siblings and their mothers, and of family members coming through for each other in touching and inspiring ways.

If mothers and children can avoid being manipulated, they are natural allies for each other, since they are being wounded by the same man. I have been involved in cases where family members pull together as a team, jointly crafting escape plans, developing code words to signal each other when Dad is heading for an explosion, lying to the abuser to cover for siblings or for Mom, hiding car keys, and cooperating to protect everyone's freedom and safety. I could not count the number of families in which mothers and children have stood by one another emotionally—even if they had to hide that solidarity from the abusive man—helping siblings when they are scared, telling each other, "It isn't your fault," giving hugs and offering kindness. Acts of courageous resistance come in many forms, some of them secretive, such as sneaking food up to a brother or sister whom the abuser has banished from the dinner table. Despite the divisions and tensions that arise, most families exposed to an abusive man have much to celebrate in the love that continues to flow across the obstacles, in the courageous ways in which mothers and children resist the abuse and stand up for themselves and each other, in the tireless efforts to find joy and kindness in life.

I have observed some recurring themes among those families that do manage to hold together well, fending off the abuser's splintering force:

- *Families that receive education about abuse, its tactics, and its effects.* Mothers and children find it easier to avoid pointing fingers at each other when they can recognize the abusive man's maneuvers, have names for his different controlling behaviors, and understand each other's reactions to him. Many programs for abused women now offer supportive and educational groups for children to help them identify and heal from the effects of witnessing abuse. You are educating yourself by reading this book, gaining insights that you will share with your children in many ways.

- *Mothers who develop especially strong parenting skills.* In addition to the many concrete suggestions I offer throughout this book, you can find a list of valuable parenting resources in the back of this book to help you learn new approaches to child-rearing, so that you can be the best mother you are capable of being in your challenging circumstances. The paramount goals are to give your children love, to combine flexibility with solid discipline, to shield your children as much as possible from your partner's behavior, and to talk with them directly about the abuse.

• *Mothers and children who get strong community support.* The more your relatives, friends, schools, and faith community are there for you and your children, the better the chance that the abusive man will fail in his efforts to drive you apart. In order to get this kind of support, though, you have to reach out.

• *An abusive man who is not a skilled manipulator.* If your partner is not particularly charming or clever, or is sloppy at covering up his motives and intentions, your children will find it easier to see through him. But even if he's slick, they can figure him out with time and education.

• *An abusive man who is not involved with the children a great deal.* For example, relationships between mothers and children often improve rapidly once the abusive man is no longer in the home, as long as his visits with the children are short, infrequent, or professionally supervised. Don't press your children to be close to their father; maintaining some distance from him is actually a sign that they are taking good care of themselves, and will benefit them in the long run.

What Can I Do?

You can help guide relationships within your family toward resilience and solidarity, and away from collusion and infighting. Following the guidelines below will make it harder for the abusive man to pull you and your children apart, creating the best chance for mutual support and healing in your family:

Be strict about treating your children equally. In order to counter the abusive man's tendency to play favorites, strive to give your children a secure sense that they each have equal rights and a central place in your heart. Treating them equally does not, however, mean treating them all the same; in fact, trying to give your children exactly equal shares of everything, or telling them that you love them all the same, can backfire in practice. Part of how you show how much you care about your children is by focusing on their unique needs, and on the particular love—not the identical love—that you feel for each one. The book *Siblings Without Rivalry,* by Faber and Mazlish, is a terrific guide toward these goals.

Unless your partner is too scary or retaliatory, challenge him about his favoritism. Give him material to read that will educate him about the long-term impact of treating children unequally, and point out the dynamics that you see resulting.

Help your children resolve their conflicts. Adults often make the mistake of either intervening *too little* in children's conflicts—not noticing that they are hurting each other emotionally and aren't finding constructive solutions—or intervening *too much,* jumping in to make a ruling about which child is right and which one is wrong, so that children don't learn how to work out their own disputes. Instead, children need parents to do the following:

* Give them some space to work it out on their own, but pay attention to what is going on. Don't jump in too quickly, but let them see that you're listening. Wait to get involved until it looks like the argument might turn physical, or one of them is making mean comments, one of them is being silenced, or an extended argument is not moving toward resolution.
* When it is time to step in, avoid telling the children the answer. Instead, help each child to describe his or her feelings and needs to the other, require them to listen well to what is being expressed, and ask them to come up with a solution that is fair and

respectful. Suggest possibilities rather than making a ruling. Don't take the situation over with your own authority unless there is no other way to protect the rights of one of the children from being trampled.

Be alert for signs that the family (including you) is starting to target one member for criticism, pity, or disrespect. If you see patterns of scapegoating developing, interrupt them quickly.

Don't use your children as confidantes. You may feel tempted to rely on your children for emotional support, especially if your partner is making it difficult for you to have close relationships with your friends or relatives. But children can become burdened when adults confide in them about painful or private issues. It is important, therefore, for you to seek ways to get emotional support and caretaking from other adults—including services for abused women—and let your children be children. This becomes even more necessary if your partner sometimes manipulates the children into feeling sorry for him, as we saw Wayne Abbott do; they need to have a solid parent whom they don't have to take care of, to counter his example.

Help your children express their feelings about incidents of abuse they have seen, heard, or learned about from siblings. If your sons and daughters can talk about their hurt feelings, their anger, their fear, or their worries about you, they are less likely to channel their distress into taking pieces out of each other. Not all children like to put their experiences into words, so you might ask them to draw a picture that shows what they felt about an incident, and use other approaches to help them express themselves, as chapter 14 examines in detail.

Teach your children to think critically. Your children need to develop the ability to analyze the tactics used by their father, and to recognize the underlying motivations for his actions. This awareness will help them avoid his manipulation and be more able to stay

loyal to one another. The best way to do this is by helping them to
think critically about situations that don't involve their father—so
they won't feel that you are trying to turn them against him—and
then allow them to figure him out for themselves. You will learn
more in chapter 15, under "Teaching Critical Thinking," page 292.

Promote a family ethic of mutual support and solidarity. Tell
your children from time to time that your family is one in which
siblings treat each other with kindness, offer support to each other
in hard times, and keep competition to a minimum. Start sen-
tences with, "In this family we . . . ," so your children learn to take
pride in being part of a household where children stick together.
If the abusive man starts to use divisive tactics, your children will
have an immediate impulse to recoil from his maneuvers, since
they've been taught to value staying by one another.

Expand your own voice within the family. A man's frequent criticism or undermining can gradually force a woman into a passive
role. Look for ways to take back your power in the family—while,
of course, being aware that an abusive man tends to retaliate when
the woman refuses to shrink into the background the way he wants
her to. Don't take unnecessary or foolish risks, but do keep re-
gaining your strength as much as you can—including in ways that
may be hidden from your partner.

Focus on hope and away from self-blame. Even if you put all of
the above ideas into practice, combatting the divisions in your
family may still be an ongoing struggle, depending on your particular situation. Some factors are beyond your control, including
how sophisticated your partner may be in his manipulations, what
vulnerabilities your children may have that he is able to exploit, and
the circumstances in your community—such as how popular and
admired your partner may be. You can overcome these obstacles,
but you will have to give yourself time and draw on multiple
sources of support.

Key Points to Remember

- The presence of an abusive man in the household affects how each family member gets along with all of the others.

- It isn't your fault if your children are exhibiting problems with infighting, verbal abusiveness, or violence toward each other—but it is up to you to address those problems because no one else can.

- Your children need your leadership to guide them back toward treating each other well and sharing love and support.

- You and your children have a common need for healing and solidarity. Help your children understand that what hurts one of them hurts the whole family, and what helps one of them brings benefit to all. Be a team.

- Take pride in the efforts you and the children are already making to share love, stand up for yourselves and each other, and build a life that breaks out of the mold the abusive man is trying to form. Celebrate the courage and kindness that is already present. Despite the harm your partner's behavior patterns may have caused, a current toward joy and health still flows in your family, and you will see it if you watch for it.

Chapter Nine

To Leave
or Not to
Leave

"My friends say my children would be better off if I got a divorce, but my minister says I shouldn't deprive them of a father. What should I do?"

"The children adore their father. They'd never forgive me if I made him move out."

"If I left, I would have to leave without my children, because he told me he would kill me if I ever took them away from him."

"He told me if I ever break up with him, he'll go for custody of the children, and his family has a lot of money to help him with the legal battle. I don't dare go."

You may go through periods in life when you feel surrounded by people, whether friends, relatives, or professionals involved with your family, who just don't seem to grasp how rugged and unpredictable the terrain of your life is. Perhaps they toss simple solutions at you for complex problems, or bristle with irritation when you hesitate to leap immediately into the course of action *they* think is best, or even lecture you as if you were a slightly impaired child. Confusing and contradictory messages may swirl around you, depending on who is talking, that sound something like:

"Just because he mistreats you, that doesn't mean he's a bad father."

"If you cared about your children, you would leave him. You're choosing him over them."

"It's harmful for children to grow up without a father—they'll be scarred for life if you get divorced."

"If you don't leave him, the child protective workers are going to put your children into foster care because they're being exposed to domestic violence."

"You can't just throw a relationship away without trying to work on it."

Caught in all these crosscurrents, how is a mother to figure out the most promising path to choose? The mixed and unrealistic messages can become unbearable, causing some women to shut down into a survival mode where they stop trying to find a way out and just focus on making it to the end of each day in one piece.

Several years ago I was helping a verbally abused woman struggle through a decision about whether to flee from her husband with her two-year-old daughter. Her husband Simon's threats were becoming terrifying, even though he had never hit her. He kept warning her, "You have six months left, Kim. You'd better shape up by then. I'm telling you, six months left." Kim's heart would race and she would beg Simon to tell her what he was threatening to do, but he wouldn't answer. He would just get a chilling sort of madman smile on his lips, and drum his fingers over and over again on the table like the background drumbeat in a horror movie, and say, "You don't want to find out. Don't try it." Kim was scared to death.

I began working with her on getting hooked up with a program for abused women, and making a plan for when and how she and her daughter would flee. Kim decided not to wait until her "deadline" expired, because she thought the outcome might be fatal, and instead made plans to leave within a few weeks, as soon as she could get the details worked out.

After three or four weeks had gone by, I received a call from Kim one afternoon with the surprising declaration that she had decided not to leave. Why this abrupt change in plans? Kim explained that her city's newspaper had printed a front-page story that morning on "research" showing that children who grow up without fathers face dismal futures of juvenile delinquency, substance abuse, poverty, and low self-esteem. "I can't do this to my daughter," she said. "I just have to stay here, whatever happens." I didn't hear from her again.

I obtained a copy of the article that Kim had read. Stunningly, the writer included not a single mention of domestic violence or any form of abuse, leaving invisible the mountain of research evidence showing the psychological harm to children of exposure to a man who terrorizes their mother.

Kim's experience captured poignantly for me the dilemmas facing a mother when she tries to decide whether, when, and how to leave her abusive partner, including the struggle of how best to balance her own needs and the needs of her child.

Facing Hard Questions About the Future

Many years ago, when I was new to the field of domestic abuse, I remember reading that for many women leaving an abusive man feels like jumping off a cliff. The unknowns are so many, and the abuser feels so powerful. For a woman with children, these fears can be even more dizzying. See if any of the following worries loom for you:

It feels like there's nothing and no one out there. Being the target of cruelty or violence can sometimes leave you feeling alone in the world, especially if people around you keep acting as though nothing is happening. You may have kept the abuse secret out of shame or embarrassment, or from fear that your partner would retaliate if he found out you told anyone. Perhaps even more important, a majority of abusive men make the woman's social life difficult by prohibiting her from talking to certain friends, chasing relatives away with rude or scary behavior, or driving the same kinds of wedges that he does inside the family.

There seems to be no way to survive economically. When you fantasize about leaving your relationship, the challenge of how to keep the family sheltered, clothed, and fed can seem insurmountable, and all the more so if your children are young. Abusive men commonly sabotage the woman's efforts to break away by leaving her with debts, refusing to pay child support, quitting jobs, starting expensive legal actions (such as litigation for custody or visitation), or simply vanishing. No caring mother wants to leap off into a future where she is unsure if she will be able to provide for her children. The greater the number of children a woman has, and the younger their ages, the greater the challenges she faces figuring out how to get away from an abuser.

He seems like he might react dangerously, or has made explicit threats. Depending on the style of abuse your partner uses, you may be peering over that cliff at what looks like a set of sharpened blades, because he has said ominously, "If you ever leave me, we'll all be dead," or "If I can't have you, no one will." Or he may make less violent but equally paralyzing threats, such as that he will report you to child protective services and get your children taken away from you, that he will sue for custody of the children in family court, or that he will have you committed to a mental hospital.

The children will be angry and/or heartbroken. Children are often highly attached to their abusive fathers, though not always for the healthiest of reasons, as we saw in chapters 3 and 4.

You are simply scared. Abuse can cause lasting traumatic effects in a woman. Some women develop generalized fears and phobias, not just fears of the abusive man. Others start to find it hard to trust anyone because of their partner's betrayal and dishonesty, and so feel anxious about relying on people or reaching out for help.

If any of these haunting preoccupations, or similar ones, are casting a shadow over your life, try to take some of the following actions:

- Call a hotline for abused women (see Resources in the back of this book) to have a confidential conversation about your options.
- Attend counseling sessions or a support group at a program for abused women—the hotline staff can tell you where to find these free resources as nearby as possible.
- Work with the staff on the hotline or at the abused women's program on creating a "strategic safety plan" for you to use both before and after any attempts you may make to end your relationship.
- Read *When Love Goes Wrong* by Ann Jones and Susan Schechter, particularly chapters 7 to 9, which guide a woman step-by-step in making a decision about leaving, and planning how to leave as safely as possible when she decides it's time to go, (see Resources, page 338).

Whether, when, and how to leave an abusive relationship is an intricate and highly personal decision that only you can make. If anyone in your life is pressing you to break up with your partner—or doing the opposite, leaning on you to stay with him or to "give him another chance"—try to explain that you are already under all the pressure you can stand from the abusive man himself, and that what you need from other people is patience, understanding, and teamwork. (I discuss these issues in detail in chapter 15 of *Why Does He Do That?*)

Here are just a few of the many thorny questions that women find themselves needing to sort through as they contemplate the future:

Am I in greater danger physically and emotionally if I stay with him, or if I try to leave him?

Are my children better off living with their father, or undergoing a familial breakup? What are the other costs and benefits to my children of leaving my partner (such as possibly having to move, perhaps being stalked by him, and other concerns)?

Is he capable of changing? (See chapter 14 of *Why Does He Do That?* for guidelines on how to assess this question.)

Is it worth being single, and giving up my dreams for our future together, in order to get away from his abuse?

Is it really that bad, or can I just deal with it?

No one should be attempting to answer these questions for you. At the same time, you should avoid trying to cope with this maelstrom on your own. What you need is not people who will tell you what to do, but rather ones who will help you think through these factors for yourself and encourage you to trust and rely on your own best thinking.

(Remember, though, that if you are having to ask yourself, "Is it really that bad?", that in itself is a strong clue that the answer may be "yes." Bear in mind also that a man's problem with abusiveness does not go away unless he deals with it directly, honestly, and courageously.)

The Pros and Cons of Your Children Leaving Your Abusive Partner

I wish I could tell you that breaking up your relationship is the best way to end your children's emotional difficulties and set them on the path to a brighter future. Many people who talk to abused mothers, including quite a number of professionals, mistakenly think that the problem is so simple and the solution so clear. The reality is that each situation is different, and each *abusive man* is distinct, with his own constellation of controlling and intimidating behaviors and entitled attitudes. How much your children can benefit if you leave your partner depends largely on how he reacts to being left, including whether he harasses you for years, attempts to kill you, or sues for custody of the children.

QUESTION #10:
Should I leave him for the good of my children?

Each child, in turn, has a unique set of feelings about his or her family and a specific set of needs. Some children thrive after getting the abuser out of the house, while others have tremendous difficulty adapting to the disruptions in life, or are fearful that the abuser will appear one night and hurt everyone, or are sick with worry that their father is going to commit suicide or drink himself to death.

As you struggle through the real-life decision about the future of your relationship, I encourage you to put your thoughts in writing. Make a list on a piece of paper of the pros and cons of staying and leaving. Dozens of abused women I have worked with over the years have made such lists and report that doing so has been a clarifying and empowering process for them. Below you will find a guide to key issues you will want to look at in weighing the advantages and disadvantages for your children. Additional concerns will no doubt occur to you.

We'll begin with some of the potential benefits to your children:

Not having to see or hear you being mistreated. As we saw in chapter 4, children are by nature deeply caring and empathic, and they suffer emotionally when they see another person abused, especially when it happens to someone they love. After you and your partner separate, the children's exposure to his behavior may be much less frequent and intense.

Getting relief from the fighting and tension. Living in an atmosphere of chronic anger and tension between parents wears children down, even in families in which there is no abuse or violence. Many children report feeling relieved when their parents finally split up because the calm is so welcome. Children who have been exposed to abuse value that peace even more because they could never be sure which fights would escalate to verbal abuse or scary behavior.

Setting an example for them of not tolerating abuse. Your children are looking to you to teach them values about how people should treat one another, including what type of kindness and respect intimate partners should show. When you choose to end your relationship with their father, you send them a message that you aren't willing to live with abuse and that they shouldn't accept mistreatment themselves. The example you set may influence how your sons will treat women when they grow up and how able your daughters will feel to stand up for themselves and protect their rights.

Your parenting will improve. Without the stress of daily exposure to verbal abuse, controlling behavior, and disrespect, you will be more able to be patient and loving with your children, to discipline them appropriately, and to share close or fun times with them. And you may get some relief from having abuse brought into the home through your children's imitations of their father's behavior.

Relief from fear and danger. As I discussed in chapter 4, children find it scary to be around an abusive man, especially if he sometimes becomes intimidating or violent. Sometimes the children even get hurt directly because they get hit or shoved by accident, because they try to intervene to stop the fight, or because the abuser decides to hurt them. These risks can decrease if the parents aren't under the same roof anymore. (However, there are also cases where the danger to the children is *worse* after separation than it was before, as I discuss below.)

Not having to be verbally or physically (or sexually) abused by him themselves. Getting away from the abusive man often means that children escape abuse that they were being subjected to directly, since so many abusers spill some aspects of their destructive behavior over onto other family members. (I have to give another caveat, however: If the abusive man is awarded unsupervised visitation with the children, this benefit disappears, as we will see.)

Having an opportunity to heal emotionally. Children are capable of remarkable resilience and recovery if given the opportunity and the support. The first step toward healing is for the source of injury to stop flowing—which in this case means for them to stop having an abusive man in their daily lives, harming their mother and indirectly or directly harming them.

Having an opportunity to mend their relationships with you and with each other. Just as individuals can bounce back from their emotional hurts, so can the damage done to relationships be repaired if a long enough period of calm and safety can create the opening, without the abuser's constant interference.

As you can see, there are multiple ways that your children's lives can improve when your abusive partner is out of the home, and you will think of additional benefits that I haven't included. There is often tremendous healing and regeneration for children who are liberated from living with the abusive man.

Let's turn now to the downside, which is undoubtedly very much on your mind as well. Some of the possible costs to your children of parental separation include the following:

Missing their father. If your partner is a father or father figure to your children, they will almost certainly miss him when he is no longer living with them, even if on some level they were dying for him to go. Most children don't really want their father to leave permanently, they just want his abusiveness to stop, and it is difficult for them to understand why he can't change.

Feeling envious of "normal" families that get to all be together. Children whose parents separate compare themselves to others, and sometimes look longingly at intact families.

Economic deprivation. If breaking up with your partner means that you have to sell your home, or that you end up with no home at all, the loss to your children is substantial. Many abusive men resist paying child support or sharing any of the family's assets after a breakup. You face additional concerns if any of your children have special needs for medical procedures or equipment, educational services, or mental health services that they may lose if you suddenly have no money, or if you are forced to move to another neighborhood or town. And if you do have to move, whether for financial reasons or because you are in danger from him, the children may undergo multiple sacrifices of friends, stability, and community. Welfare has become harder to get than it used to be and in the United States is generally not provided for more than twenty-four months.

(However, in families in which the abusive man didn't share his money prior to the breakup, or wasted family resources on addictions or affairs, economic circumstances can improve rather than deteriorate post-separation, especially if the mother works or has other sources of money.)

Increased fear or danger. Depending on the abusive man's style and tactics, being away from him can be scarier for the children than living with him. If after you leave him he stalks you or the children, threatens to kill you, or assaults you, children may be terrified or injured. Many physically violent abusers continue assaulting the woman or even escalate their violence when she attempts to end the relationship, and some mothers (roughly a thousand per year in the United States) are killed by their abusive partners or ex-partners.

Being required by a judge to go on unsupervised visits with the abuser, or to live with him. A high percentage of family law judges across the United States and Canada do not understand the profile and tactics of men who abuse women and have not been informed about the impact on children of unsupervised contact. Some mothers report to me that their children have deteriorated emotionally since the parents split up, because of the abuser's mistreatment or manipulation of the children during his court-ordered time with them. Courts are gradually waking up to the misuse of visitation by abusive men, but there is a long way still to go.

How is a mother to consider this dizzying array of points? It is no wonder that some women feel paralyzed for a while, finding the thoughts of staying and leaving equally unbearable, and so try hard simply to not think about it. But you really can sort out these questions. You just need some time and, ideally, supportive and patient people around you. You may find it helpful to keep a few underlying concepts in mind as you wrestle your way through this tangle of feelings:

1. *Your situation is unique.* No boilerplate solution fits all families. You are the person who knows your children the best, and most understands their needs. You are also the expert on your abusive partner, including how he is likely to react if you attempt to leave him and how severely he may try to involve the children as weapons against you. If anyone tells you that your children are definitely better off if you stay, or that they will automatically benefit if you leave, they are wrong. No one has such a clear crystal ball. You have to follow your own intuition about what is most likely to happen, and plan accordingly.

2. *Long-term planning is important.* If you decide, for example, that your children would be at risk if you attempted to leave your partner right away, start looking six or twelve months down the road. What plans and services would you need to have in place for yourself, and for your children, in order to be able to leave safely and successfully then? Start working now on laying the groundwork to get away later. If you don't want to leave, or can't do so safely, look for ways to increase your rights in your relationship and to decrease your children's exposure to abuse, such as by involving the police or getting a protective order, asking your church to support you, or making safety plans with your children (see chapter 15).

3. *Your own well-being is an important factor.* If you are desperate to leave your abusive partner, it is unlikely to benefit your children if you stay with him. Similarly, you may not help your children if you leave a relationship that you are not at all ready to say good-bye to, or if breaking up with him also means losing your friends, relatives, or community. Children reap rewards when their mothers are feeling happy, safe, and socially connected (as opposed to isolated). So in considering what is best for your children, remember that what is best for *you* should weigh heavily in that equation, along with the other factors I've listed.

4. *An abuse-free life is possible.* Whatever your struggles may

be in the immediate future, however much you may feel that you are paddling a boat upstream against a strong and unrelenting current, keep dreaming of a life where you and your children live with kindness, patience, and nonviolence. You can get there. I would never propose that you stay permanently with a man who abuses you; if he refuses to change but you simply can't leave for now, continue building toward a time when you can.

Bear in mind also that leaving is not necessarily an all-or-nothing decision. Taking a few months' separation from your relationship can give you and your children an important time to heal and recover, can put some pressure on your partner to get himself into an abuser program and to deal with other problems he has (such as substance abuse or repeatedly losing jobs), and can help you sort out for yourself what you want in the longer term. Some abusive men will accept a separation if the woman says, "I just want to take some time apart," rather than, "We're done for good," and the break can buy you some time to think and evaluate how he reacts to being apart from you. Taking the future a step at a time can be a favor to yourself.

Allow me to share a few concluding thoughts. First, domestic violence researchers have found that children who have been exposed to physically violent abusers tend to start feeling and behaving better quite rapidly—within just a few months—once their mother is no longer with the abusive man. There is a catch here, though: These studies mostly look at children who are having little or no contact with their fathers. Staff members from programs for abused women, and abused mothers themselves, report to me that children's emotional and behavioral symptoms often begin rapidly to reappear once the children start to have visitation with Dad. Spending time with the abuser reawakens traumatic memories for the children, frightens them, and creates an opening for him to begin manipulating them or using them as weapons against the mother. But due to a tragic combination of ignorance and prejudice, many judges do not look favorably upon women who try to keep their children out of unsupervised contact with the father, even when he has a history of serious abuse toward the mother. Chapters 12 and 13 look at this dilemma and some possible solutions to it.

Second, the reports that you may have heard regarding research on the damage to children of growing up without fathers have been exaggerated and distorted. Most of these studies ignore the fact that single parents tend to have less money, and that poverty is hard on children. It is worth noting the gender bias in these discussions as well; we almost never hear reports of how emotionally harmed children supposedly are by being raised by single *fathers*. The reality is that single parenting is very challenging, but that millions of children have been raised by single mothers or single fathers and have grown into well-adjusted, high-functioning members of society. And they are far better off than children who grow up with abuse.

Third, your choices can be considerably less complicated if your partner is not the legal father (biological or adoptive) of your children, and if they are not attached to him as a father figure. In these cases, your children can more consistently be expected to benefit from getting the abusive man out of the house—unless he is of the style that will terrorize you or them.

In my experience, a majority of abused women eventually find a way either to make the abuse stop or to get away. When I say "make the abuse stop," I don't mean that you can control or manage your partner's behavior by changing your own. In fact, abusive men don't change unless they admit that they are abusive and decide to accept full responsibility for their actions. The only role an abused woman can play in her partner's change is by setting limits on what she is willing to live with, leaving him for some substantial period of time, and using police and restraining orders if that is a reasonable option for her. (All of these issues are covered in chapter 14 of *Why Does He Do That?*)

Leaving a relationship permanently often turns out to be the only realistic option for ending abuse. And it is an option, at least in the long run, even if you can't figure out how to escape him immediately. I have spoken with dozens of women over the years, many of them former partners of my clients, who have successfully gotten to freedom, and who are enjoying much healthier, happier lives as a result. Have faith that you and your children will reach a safe and kind environment, even if it takes some time to get there.

Key Points to Remember

- Getting away from your abusive partner can help your children, but the benefits are not automatic. Weigh the pros and cons of leaving, consider when and how it is best to end your relationship, and make a long-term plan for how to move life forward safely for yourself and your children.
- Your own needs and your children's needs are both important. Think hard about what would be best for them, but think about your own well-being, too.
- Seek assistance with the process of making decisions about your future, contacting in particular your area's program for abused women. At the same time, remember always to rely ultimately on your own best judgment.

Chapter Ten

Dealing with Child Protective Services

"The social worker said that I am responsible for my children's problems because I'm exposing them to my partner's violence. She called it 'failure to protect.' "

"The child protective worker said that I have to get a restraining order against him or they'll take my children away. But if I get a court order against him, he'll hurt me, for real."

"The man from the state said that they just want to help me with the domestic violence and that they won't take my children away as long as I cooperate. I'm afraid to trust him, but he seems like he really understands my situation."

"I was so upset when I found out the school called child welfare on us, and my husband went ballistic. But honestly, getting them involved ended up being the best thing that ever happened to our family, because I finally had someone on my side about his abuse."

The voices of these women illustrate both the risks and the opportunities that can arise when child protective services get involved in a family in which the mother is being abused. Child welfare workers can feel like a scary presence in a woman's life, since they have the power to remove the children from her home. Some workers are bossy and judgmental, so the woman feels like there is a new bully in her life, as if living with her abusive partner weren't bad enough. And people feel a stigma attached to state involvement in their lives, a finger pointed that seems to say, "You're a bad parent."

But there can be another side to the experience for an abused woman. Some social workers, male or female, are kind, supportive, and helpful, with some training in domestic abuse and how it affects families. The state often offers various kinds of free services to the family, such as therapy for the children and parents, educational advocacy, essential supplies for your home if you are low-income, or help finding a job. If the social workers learn about your partner's behavior toward you, they may pressure him to participate in an abuser intervention program, and help you get into a support group for abused women. Quite a number of women have reported to me that child protective involvement has ended up being a tremendous boon to their families. Here are examples of cases I've known of:

- Jamie, a mother of three, said to me, "My workers really get domestic violence, and they weren't fooled by how smooth my partner is, which I was glad of." The social workers helped her get on an emergency list for Section 8 housing, accompanied her to court to get a protective order to keep her boyfriend away from her and from the children (whom he was the father of), and arranged for her children to be in a counseling group for children of abused women.

- Anna recounted to me how the child protective workers had contacted her husband's probation officer—he had been convicted of punching her about nine months earlier—and persuaded the probation officer to bring him in front of a judge for violating his probation. Until receiving the call from the social workers, the probation officer had been misled by the husband's charm and dishonesty, and was not considering the case very serious even though she was aware of his probation violations.

- Georgina's social worker told her ex-boyfriend that he couldn't see the children unless he enrolled in an abuser program and did serious work on himself there. He finally joined, which Georgina had been attempting unsuccessfully for years to persuade him to do.

Abused mothers sometimes feel that involvement with child protective services is the next thing to a death sentence for the family. You may have heard from relatives, or received the impression from news stories, that social workers come and take children away immediately, and that parents have to fight a huge battle to get their children back again. While there are cases that go this badly, they are more the exception than the norm, and genuine assistance is offered much of the time. And in many cases, the mother can have a strong influence on the outcome by knowing how to build a successful relationship with the child protective service.

This chapter is devoted to preparing you to make the most of a challenging situation. It focuses on three areas: (1) what the social workers should be doing, (2) what mistakes they may make and why those occur, and (3) how you can best navigate the child protective system to meet your children's needs, get the support and services you are looking for, and protect yourself from being negatively labeled.

How Child Protective Systems Work

I first need to provide a brief explanation of governmental child protection, for readers who may not be familiar with these systems. In each state and province there are laws regarding child abuse and neglect, and there are government employees whose job it is to investigate allegations that a child is at risk and craft an official response. These employees are typically called "child welfare workers" or "social workers." The government agencies they work for are called by many names, such as Department of Social Services, Department of Human Services, or just plain Child Protective Services, depending on where you live.

The child protective agency has the power to demand that the parents participate in various kinds of services, such as substance abuse treatment or family therapy, to address the problems the social workers feel exist in the home. The workers also have the power to take children out of the home for a few days on an emergency basis, and to petition the court to give the state custody of the children, in which case they can place the children in foster care for weeks or months. The parents' rights in these proceedings vary from place to place. The ultimate authority regarding when and whether children can be taken out of homes, and when they are to be returned, usually rests with a juvenile court or dependency court judge, although a family court judge may also be involved if the parents split up. In order to keep children out of a home, the agency generally has to prove in court that the children are in serious danger and that the parents are refusing to cooperate with getting help for themselves and their children, and courts do not always side with the child protective service.

A woman's involvement with child protective services typically begins when someone, often a professional such as a schoolteacher or a police officer, calls the child protective agency and reports that a child appears to be suffering mistreatment. Perhaps the child told a school nurse that she had been hit by one of her parents and showed the nurse a bruise, or maybe a child told a daycare provider that he had been touched sexually by an adult in his home. A relative might have stopped by the house and found young children at home alone, or found the parent drunk and the child playing with dangerous objects. Any of these people could file a child abuse report.

Occasionally, child abuse reports are made maliciously by people who are seeking revenge against a parent. For example, abusive men sometimes call child protective services accusing the mother of abusing or neglecting her children, as a way to control her or retaliate against her.

Nowadays, callers to child protective services sometimes call to report abuse toward the *mother*, not toward the children; there is an increasing understanding in communities that exposure to domestic violence can be psychologically harmful—or physically dangerous—to children. But the response by the government agency is not always what the caller would expect; child protective workers don't always have adequate training and sensitivity regarding the dynamics of partner abuse, including the impact on a mother's relationships with her children. They therefore sometimes underestimate—or overestimate—the risk to the children, or recognize that the children are being emotionally harmed but blame the mother for "choosing to live with an abusive partner," without paying adequate attention to the complexities of her circumstances. Fortunately there is an increasing number of social workers who do understand domestic violence and strive to hold the abuser accountable, so abused women are having more positive experiences with child protective interventions than before.

More commonly, though, the child protective service is called because a child was hurt by the mother or her partner, or was left in unsafe circumstances, or the mother or her partner are abusing substances. In such cases, the workers may have no knowledge of the fact that the mother herself is being abused, unless she chooses to tell them. For a mother who is already feeling ashamed because of being accused of neglecting or abusing her child, it can be especially difficult to expose herself further by discussing her partner's frightening or demeaning behavior.

In some cases, a mother becomes involved with child protective services voluntarily, placing the call herself because she knows her situation has become too difficult for her to handle alone, or because she knows she herself is hurting her children and needs help to stop. In my experience, a woman who reaches out in this way appears to receive more compassionate and supportive responses from social workers than one who is seen as having been "caught abusing her children" or "caught exposing them to domestic violence."

Proper Child Protective Services for Abused Mothers

In my experience, child protective interventions are rarely all good or all bad. The workers are often motivated by a genuine caring for the well-being of children, and try to offer as much help as they can. How much concrete assistance they can offer depends partly on the kinds of services that exist in the area where you live, and partly on the budgetary limitations of the child protective service. Workers sometimes make mistakes from having too many cases to handle, or from not adequately grasping how hard parenting can be under circumstances of poverty, racism, or abuse. Their level of understanding of domestic violence varies tremendously, which in turn can have quite an impact on their effectiveness as helpers.

This section describes how a child protective agency should

properly handle a case, especially one in which the mother is being abused by her partner. You are unlikely to find that all of these standards are being met all the time by the workers you are dealing with, so I do not wish to raise unrealistic hopes. But the list below will give you a guide to measure by, so that you know whether your rights are being respected and your circumstances treated with awareness and sensitivity. If a review of these points persuades you that your case is being handled badly, there are some avenues to improvement that you can pursue, as we will see.

When child protective interventions are based in a real grasp of the challenges faced by abused women and their children, and in-depth knowledge regarding abusive men as parents, social workers should do the following:

Make every effort to join with you as a team. The social worker should speak to you with respect and show interest in drawing out your own knowledge and wisdom about the situation facing you and your children. Rather than starting with warnings, threats, or criticism, he or she should proceed on the assumption that you are doing the best you can, given that you have no control over what your abusive partner does. If you and your social worker can work together on ways to best keep your children safe, encouraging possibilities open up.

Give you time. Simple solutions rarely exist for an abused woman with children. As we saw in chapter 9, conditions for children don't automatically improve when a mother leaves her abusive partner, and in some circumstances they can get worse. Leaving at the wrong time, or without an adequate and realistic plan, can be more dangerous for children than staying. The social worker needs to recognize that you need time to figure out whether your partner is capable of changing, to develop a plan for leaving him safely if he won't change, to pull your own strength together (which the abusive man may have torn away), and to arrange for your children's economic and emotional survival. The child protective service should not treat you as if the situation is an immediate emergency unless it really is—in other words, unless your children are in serious danger or are being severely abused.

Receive extensive education on domestic abuse and its impact on families. Child protective personnel should be trained on the dynamics of domestic violence, the obstacles abused women face in leaving their relationships, and the impact abusive men have on mothers and children. Social workers should understand the post-separation risks to children, so that they grasp that leaving is not an immediate solution, nor necessarily the best one.

Not bully you. The last thing an abused woman needs is more pressure and coercion in her life to add to what her partner hurls at her. If a woman feels bullied from all sides, she will simply decide to trust no one—which is exactly what happens when child protective interventions are ill informed. Your social worker should therefore avoid using warnings or threats—unless, as I said, your children are in dire and immediate danger—and instead should help you make decisions that *you* believe are best for you and your children, and assist you in gathering the resources and the courage to take the necessary steps.

Assess the severity of the effects your partner has had on your children, and his current level of dangerousness. As I have discussed, each child is affected in a unique way by suffering exposure to an abusive man, and some appear to be far more psychologically harmed than others. How serious a particular child's emotional or behavioral symptoms may be depends on such factors as:

- His or her own internal sources of strength and resilience (personal qualities).
- His or her external sources of strength (friends, other important adults in his or her life, activities, skills, hobbies).

- How much the child has seen or heard the abuse, or heard about it.
- How terrifying the abuser gets.
- Whether the abuser is also hurting the child directly with verbal, physical, or sexual abuse.
- How close the child feels to you, and how free from abuse and neglect your own treatment of the child is.
- How attached the child is to the abusive man (research shows that children who feel closest to the abusive man tend to suffer the worst symptoms from exposure to his abusive behavior, probably because they have the greatest tendency to blame themselves and blame their mothers).

Rather than assuming that your child has been deeply scarred by your partner's treatment of you, the social worker can offer more effective assistance if he or she examines the particular experience of each family member. Some children survive the storm of witnessing abuse remarkably well intact, especially if their mother shields them as much as possible and gives them love and support.

Your partner's level of dangerousness to you and to your children should also be assessed. Abusive men vary tremendously in how much of a risk they pose. Various books, including *Why Does He Do That?*, describe ways to assess the likelihood that a particular abusive man will seriously injure or kill someone in the family.

Assess your efforts to protect your children. The social worker owes it to you to learn about your current and past attempts to keep your children safe from your partner's abuse, rather than assuming that you have been uncaring or neglectful. The box below shows a scattering of the dozens of strategies that abused women use to try to lessen the emotional or physical injuries to their children.

Strategies Abused Women Use to Protect Their Children

- Staving off fights with the abusive man until the children are asleep or out of the house.
- Lying to the abuser to protect the children (e.g., covering for mistakes they make that might lead him to abuse them).
- Getting the abuser mad at her to distract him from his anger at them (in other words, taking their punishments for them).
- Putting them to bed early every night to avoid his late-night eruptions.
- Leaving them with relatives or baby-sitters frequently to keep them out of the house so they aren't around him.
- Enrolling them in activities to keep them busy and away from him.
- Becoming extremely cooperative and compliant with him ("putting up with the abuse") to reduce their exposure to the extreme reactions he has when she stands up for herself.
- Punishing the children in a less severe way than he would (e.g., spanking the children quickly before he gets a chance to do it, because he hits them hard).
- Not saying anything to him when he mistreats the children (this item applies if he is the style of abuser who retaliates against her by hurting the children *more severely* whenever she tries to stick up for them).

You can probably think of other efforts you have made on your children's behalf that aren't included here. You deserve to have these courageous steps recognized and respected—to be given some credit as a mother, in other words—rather than having child protective personnel view you as uncaring or neglectful.

At the same time, you can do even better in the future, and may need to. You deserve information that can help you improve the support and assistance you provide to your children—the kinds of insights and suggestions offered in this book, for example.

If you go through a period of separation from your abusive partner and then get back together with him, be prepared for tension in your relationship with your social workers. Having the abuser back in the home can be stressful and confusing for your children, and in some cases may make them feel that you are choosing your happiness over theirs. It is common for abusive men to promise to change, but rare for them to keep their word unless they are arrested—either for domestic violence or for a restraining order violation—and required to participate in a specialized abuser intervention program. Your social workers are likely to be upset if they feel you are believing his assurances. If you are reuniting with him for other reasons, such as economic survival or because he was becoming too dangerous during your separation, you will need to explain these circumstances to your social workers and make plans with them for how you will be able to leave successfully the next time you try.

Offer you resources to protect yourself and your children. The child protective agency can help you find out how to get help from programs for abused women, counseling and childcare programs for children, welfare and food stamps, parenting classes, housing agencies, Medicaid, job training programs, faith communities, therapists, and a continuing list of community and government resources. It is unreasonable to expect a woman to be able to successfully protect her children from an abusive man, especially one who is physically violent or threatening, if no one is offering her proper assistance or if she has no economic resources.

Respect your history of efforts to seek help. By the time a child protective agency is involved with your family you may have made countless efforts to get help or advice from friends or relatives, clergy, therapists, police, judges, books, and other sources. Instead of labeling you a "victim" or "passive," the social worker should learn from you about ways you have reached out in the past and what kinds of helpful or unhelpful advice and interventions you have run into. Have you called police a number of times before, and they kept leaving without arresting your partner, or they arrested you instead? Did you talk to your clergy person, and he or she told you to "work it out for the good of the children"? Did you flee into hiding once, only to have your partner track you down and drag you home? Understanding this history might help the social worker to sympathize when, for example, you don't feel immediately ready to jump at a new help-seeking strategy that he or she wants you to try, after you have already run into a dozen roadblocks in the past.

Take into account the abusive man's impact on your parenting. Perhaps your social worker would be willing to read selected sections of this book, so that he or she could get a glimpse of some of the ways in which abusive men tend to:

- Undermine the mother's authority.
- Sow divisions in the family, which cause a lot of fighting that the mother is left to try to sort out.
- Interfere with the mother's parenting, such as not giving her money for the children's basic needs or not letting her take them to medical appointments.
- Cause depression or substance abuse in the mother so that she has difficulty looking after her children.
- Cause children to have difficult behavioral symptoms, which the mother is left to manage on a daily basis.

These insights can help the social worker feel less judgmental and critical of you as a parent, and focus on seeking constructive and creative solutions.

If you are facing serious emotional effects from the abuse, such as depression or post-traumatic stress symptoms, or have a problem with abusing substances, it is important for you to explain to the social workers any ways in which you have continued to be a good parent to your children despite these obstacles. At the same time, it is critical that you show your willingness to take steps to overcome the problem.

Place the focus on the abusive man at least as much as on you. Social workers should meet with your partner and get him involved with services, including a specialized abuser program if one is available in your area. They should work collaboratively with police and probation departments, and with other community agencies that can help hold the abusive man accountable and impose consequences for his actions. The child protective agency should consider him to be every bit as responsible for your children's well-being as you are—in fact *more so,* since his abuse is at the root of most of the problems your family is facing. However, they should not ask you to participate in couples or family counseling with him, as this approach is neither helpful nor safe in dealing with abusive men.

Understand if you can't talk about the abuse right away. Abused women don't tend to immediately trust their social workers, sometimes for good reason. The following questions may be racing through your mind:

> *"If I tell them about the abuse, will they take my children away?"*

> *"If he finds out I spoke about the abuse, will he hurt me or kill me?"*

"He has dragged me into some illegal activities in the past— am I going to end up in jail for those now if the child protective workers find out? And what will that mean for my children?"

In the face of these fears, you may feel that your only safe route is to deny that your partner is abusive and insist that everything is fine. Your social worker should not respond by immediately labeling you as being "in denial" or "protecting him," but instead should recognize that you are trying to survive in complex and potentially dangerous circumstances, and are trying to keep your children from being taken away from you, which could traumatize them further. (But remember, in most states child protective services remove children from homes in only a small minority of the cases in which they intervene.)

Treat you in a nondiscriminatory way. Whether you are poor or rich, a woman of color or a white woman, a lesbian or a straight woman, you have the right to be treated with respect and professionalism by child protective personnel, to have the facts of your case examined without bias, and to be offered the services you and your children need. Your strengths as a mother should be valued—including the strengths of the culture and community you come from—so that you are not judged solely in terms of the mistakes you have made, and not judged at all for the abuse your partner has perpetrated.

Keep mothers and children together absolutely as much as possible. Children who are suffering from exposure to domestic abuse desperately need their connection to their mother, who is their crucial source of security, stability, and positive role modeling. If they are taken away from Mom they feel punished and may become convinced that their mother must have been largely responsible for the violence, which reinforces the most destructive messages sent by the abusive man. Children of abused women should be placed in foster care only when their lives are in danger and the woman is completely unable to take steps to protect them, when she has severe substance abuse or child abuse problems that she has been unable to address even when offered supportive, high-quality services, or when they are dramatically deteriorating emotionally.

One word of caution about the points above: Some mothers can get focused on the mistakes that the child protective service is making as a way to avoid facing their own. Usually—though not always—when social workers become involved, they are there because there is good reason to be worried for the children. I am thus encouraging you to walk a somewhat difficult line. On the one hand, you have the right to have the child protective system treat you well, and look seriously at how your partner's abusiveness has affected your ability to be a good parent to your children. On the other hand, you have to be willing to accept responsibility for your own actions, at least from this point forward, and not blame everything on your partner or on the state. So do your best not to adopt an overly defensive posture, and instead be as proactive as possible, collaborating with your social worker so that you have as much say as possible over what kinds of services you and your children participate in. To the extent that you can take charge of the progress of your case, you will feel more like a survivor and less like a victim.

Common Errors in Child Protective Responses to Abused Women

Although it is my fervent hope that you will receive support, respect, and constructive intervention from your child protective agency, it is unfortunately necessary to be alert to what can go wrong, so that you prepare yourself to respond to the obstacles that may arise. Here are some of the mistakes that abused women report to me on the part of their child welfare workers:

Refusing to believe her about the abuse. Social workers still typically believe that abusive men are monsters, so when they encounter a friendly, charming, calm, manipulative abuser, they sometimes become convinced that the woman's reports about him must be false or exaggerated. In a case I am currently involved in, for example, a therapist reported to child protective services that a man was hitting his young daughter and hurting her. The mother then revealed to the investigator that he was emotionally abusive to her as well. But the social workers unfortunately developed a strong fondness for her husband, and so began closing their eyes to the ample evidence of risk to the child from him—including reports that came in from other professionals who knew the father was a child abuser.

Not understanding the dynamics of abuse. One of the most widespread and harmful errors made by child protective personnel in domestic violence cases is to assume that the children will automatically be better off if the woman leaves her abusive partner right away. The reality is that if the woman leaves at the wrong time, the result could be:

- Hunger, homelessness, or being forced by poverty to move to a dangerous neighborhood.
- Severe assault on the mother by the abuser, stalking, or murder (women are in the greatest danger from a violent abuser when they attempt to leave him).
- Loss for the children of critical special services and/or sources of emotional support and resilience (see chapter 14).
- *Increased* exposure of the children to the abusive man be-

cause he wins custody or unsupervised visitation from a family law judge.

Also, social workers who do not understand the impact abuse can have on a mother's ability to look after her children may label her an incompetent or uncaring parent when actually she is struggling with trauma and her parental authority has been undermined.

Holding mothers exclusively responsible for their children's welfare. An important historical bias creeps into much of child protective work: Mothers tend to be held to higher standards than fathers, and are considered to have the primary responsibility for taking care of their children and keeping them safe. Letting the father off the hook in this way is even more unfair in partner abuse cases, where the father's conduct should usually be the *main* focus.

In 2002, a federal judge gave a strong reprimand to the City of New York, ruling that social workers were routinely holding mothers responsible for the conduct of their abusive partners without taking into account the realities of the women's lives, and without offering proper assistance to help them toward safety. This ruling has the potential to serve as a wake-up call to all child protective systems to improve their treatment of abused mothers.

Racial, cultural, or class discrimination. Poor women and women of color can find themselves judged with unusual harshness by child protective personnel, and their children are pulled out of the home and placed in foster care at higher rates. A Hispanic woman whose case I was involved in, for example, was accused by her violent ex-partner of abusing drugs, and although he had no evidence to back up his claim, the children were taken away by the state. Teresa kept asking to be given drug tests so she could prove that the accusation was false, but the social workers ignored her requests. The children were placed *with her ex-partner,* who had beaten her up a number of times and once put a gun to her head. Teresa didn't recover custody until *he* got jailed for drug dealing.

Bullying you. Occasionally a woman finds herself confronted with a social worker who is cold and dictatorial, so that she winds up reliving her experience with the abusive man. She may be harshly criticized, told she doesn't care about her children's welfare, or bullied into getting a restraining order against her partner even though her children are not at serious risk—or she may be forced to get an order against a man who is *too* dangerous, the kind who may kill a woman for taking him to court. A woman has a hard time healing from abuse if her social worker is treating her the same way her partner does.

If you have been subjected to any of these discriminatory or re-victimizing actions, you may still be able to turn the tide. Some mothers manage to get child protective services to improve the handling of a case through building better relationships with other staff members, cooperating steadily with requirements even when they are not altogether fair, demanding hearings or appeals, or finding good legal representation. So don't give up.

What Can I Do?

The approach you take to dealing with the child protective system can have a great impact on the direction your case takes. Three basic principles underlie the advice in this chapter:

- Get along with the professionals in your case as well as you possibly can.
- Draw on available resources, getting yourself as much support and assistance as you can find.
- Research your rights, and advocate that those rights be honored.

QUESTION #11:
How can I get the child protective workers to stop viewing me as the problem?

Keep these concepts in mind as you work your way through the following suggestions for working successfully with child welfare workers:

Be cooperative. No one is eager to have child protective services involved in their lives. But avoid allowing your anger to lead into a combative stance, like a mother I was assisting recently who kept saying, "I'm going to show those people they can't get away with this!"—but they did. If you turn your relationship with the social workers into a battle to the death, the loser may be you, no matter how justified you are. Try to put your outrage to the side for the sake of your children, and enter into the most cooperative relationship with the workers that you can. Except when they ask you to take impossible steps, or clearly violate your rights, try to meet their requirements and give them the information they are looking for. You want your social workers to come to like you and develop a willingness to go to bat for you.

When things feel tense between you and your social workers, try to bear in mind their two primary concerns: (1) they feel responsible to make sure that your children are safe, and (2) they need to know that you are willing to cooperate with them in taking steps to keep the children safe. At times their demands on you may feel—or be—unfair, but try to understand their worries, and do everything you possibly can to follow through on the steps they want from you.

Deal directly with any problems you have developed. The two most common parenting problems I see in abused mothers, besides emotional distance because of trauma, are: (1) substance abuse, and (2) verbally abusing, neglecting, or hitting their children. An abused mother whose judgment or alertness is impaired by drugs or alcohol has a harder time keeping her children safe and meeting their emotional needs. If you have a problem of this kind, it is best to admit it to yourself and to your social workers, get into a recovery program, and completely give up all use of the substance (even if you believe you "have it under control"). Denying the problem can turn your social workers against you, and in the long run harms your children.

Abused women have about twice the rate of non-abused women of hitting their children, due to stress, trauma, and the undermining of the mother's authority. As with substance abuse, your denial of the problem can count against you with your social workers. You can bolster your chances of avoiding a foster placement for your children if you admit that your discipline approaches have not always been appropriate and agree to get help with your parenting and your stress. (But the social workers, for their part, also need to recognize the role your partner's abuse has played in eroding your maternal authority, and to help you reestablish your ability to gain cooperation from your children nonviolently.)

Seek specialized services. Above all, participate in a support group or in individual counseling through a program for abused women if one is available anywhere near you. A few women's programs have services that are specifically directed at mothers who are involved with child protective services or who are trying to recover custody of their children. In a handful of states, advocates for abused women are available to become directly involved in a mother's child protective case, including attending case conferences and other important meetings; ask your social worker and your abused women's program whether this resource exists in your area.

Many states have in-home family support workers available, who sometimes have considerable training in domestic violence. If it is logistically impossible for you to get to an abused women's support group, you may be able to get similar assistance and information through a family support worker.

Cultivate supporters and get them involved in your case. If you attend therapy and have a good relationship with your counselor, for example, ask him or her to write letters on your behalf, to meet with you and your social worker together, or to attend case conferences. (First, though, check the laws in your state or province to make sure that doing so doesn't compromise your right to confidentiality regarding any issues you do *not* want your therapist to disclose about your history.) Your children's schoolteachers and daycare providers, clergy, or even neighbors may be able to put in a good word for you if you have earned their respect over the years, or may be able to get more directly involved in your case. If you have personal or blood connections to influential members of your community or local government, don't hesitate to see if they can put in a word on your behalf. Reach out in every direction you can think of.

Focus on the long haul. If your child protective case is going badly, you may have to take a longer view. In some cases, expecting or demanding instant results, whether from yourself or from your social workers, can backfire. Take a deep breath and focus on what you need to accomplish over a period of months to persuade child protective personnel that you are dealing seriously with your issues and are fighting hard to do what's best for your children. As I said early on in this book, you are not responsible for your partner's dangerous behavior, but you are the one who has to find a way to protect your children from his impact, because no one else can do it. Take the fullest advantage possible of any assistance that the state is offering you.

Attempt to educate your social workers about partner abuse. As patiently and respectfully as possible, see if you can help your workers understand the dynamics of abuse and how your relationships with your children have been affected. If you have a cooperative relationship with the social workers, photocopy a few selected pages of this book for them. (But don't pile dozens of pieces of paper into their laps; smaller amounts of information are more likely to successfully get their attention.)

Educate yourself about the overlap between partner abuse and child welfare. Several books and websites are available, as are organizations that will send information to you free or cheaply. These include publications that inform you about your rights in dealing with child protective services so that you can be aware of times when you may be entitled to a court-appointed attorney, to appeal certain decisions the social workers make, or to have access to your family's official file. (See the Resources section in the back of this book, under the heading "Child Protective Service Issues," page 349.)

Get legal help if possible. If you can afford legal representation, or you qualify for a free or low-cost attorney through legal services or pro bono programs, I recommend that you strongly consider hiring a lawyer who is experienced in child protection issues. I observe repeatedly that women who have legal representation encounter more professional and responsible conduct from social workers involved in their cases, as unfair as that reality may be. Some women have said to me, "I don't want one of those court-appointed attorneys," but in reality they often handle child protective cases very well because they specialize in the relevant laws and legal strategies.

Allow me to close with just a few more words about the other side of child protective intervention: the times when women tell me that they are actually—one might even say miraculously—happy that the system got involved with their lives. The arrival at your door of an official representative from your state or province is not necessarily bad news. In the best cases, the involvement of social workers can:

- Break down the isolation that the abusive man has imposed, so you have supportive people to talk to and to give you ideas and resources.
- Make free or low-cost counseling, housing, and job-training programs available to you and your children.
- Help you understand your right to live free from abuse, including your legal rights.
- Lead your abusive partner to experience legal consequences for his violent or scary actions, through cooperation between child protective services and the police, courts, district attorney, or probation.
- Get your partner into an abuser program, substance abuse program, or other services that he needs.
- Make it possible for you to escape from your abusive partner when the time is right.

Though you may find it hard to believe, I have spoken to women who feel that they owe their very lives to the child protective workers who came out to help, and who feel that the official intervention was the turning point for their children toward healing, freedom, and recognizing that abuse is wrong. So I recommend that you not assume that the best course of action is to chase the social workers away as quickly as possible; feel the situation out cautiously, and figure out where and when you can take the leap to trust. You and your children may stand to gain tremendously.

Key Points to Remember

- Child protective workers often have not received adequate training on partner abuse to be able to understand how complicated your situation as a mother is.

- You will need to be a strong but cooperative advocate for yourself and your children, and may have to educate your own social workers about abusive men.

- For the sake of your case, and for the good of your children, be honest with yourself about issues of your own that you need to face and work on, such as substance abuse or child abuse.

- Draw on as much assistance as possible, including getting legal help if you can.

- Despite the initial shock, women sometimes find that child protective intervention ends up eventually being a blessing.

Part III

The Abusive
Man and
Your Children
Post-Separation

What Separation and Divorce Mean for Your Children

"Everything is so much calmer now that my boyfriend is out of the house. What a difference it makes."

"My son came right out and said to me, 'It's about time you and Dad split up. We couldn't take the fighting between you two anymore.' "

"They were so bitter toward their father and so eager to have him leave, but now that he's been gone a few months they're talking about him like he's the greatest guy in the world. It seems like the past has disappeared for them."

"My children come home so upset sometimes after seeing their dad, but they won't tell me what's wrong. They've gotten kind of secretive."

Mariel dreaded each fight that would break out between her parents. She would wish she could magically sail to a warm island, with no sound but the wind blowing in the trees and the birds singing. The mounting tension between Mom and Dad, the voices growing louder, Dad's rage and Mom's panic more palpable with each passing second, all felt so familiar to her that she could almost act out the scenario herself. Yet her heart raced each time, because the ending was unpredictable. Sometimes the yelling would be followed by one parent or the other storming away and slamming a door, and then an hour or two of thick tension would pass, after which life went on as if nothing had happened. Other times Dad would call Mom crude, demeaning names, or they would both yell mean things at each other, and Dad would scatter a pile of papers into the air with an enraged sweep of his arm and yell, "You're going to be sorry if you don't shut up!" Once, two or three years earlier, and then again only a few weeks ago, Dad had shoved Mom hard, leaving her trembling and choking back her rage.

Mariel was eleven years old, and she had two younger brothers, Joel, who was eight and a half, and Marty, who was five. She worried about the boys because they would get upset when their parents had loud fights, with Marty sometimes crying and shaking. She was also disturbed by how filled with hatred Joel seemed at times, such as the night a couple of months earlier when he had said to Mariel, "We're big enough now, let's plan a way to kill Dad." A couple of weeks later, he had said to her, "I mean it, Mariel, if he makes Mom cry one more time, I am going to beat his brains in with my baseball bat while he's sleeping." Marty had overheard what Joel said and started to have violent nightmares.

One night Mariel woke up to hear her parents fighting in their bedroom. "I'm sick of this, Kaleigh," her father was yelling. "It's been weeks! I don't want to hear any more of your fucking excuses about how your head aches or you're too tired. I know you've got something going with that guy you work with. I'm not an idiot, you know! That's why you don't want it with me anymore! You're all kissy and lovey-dovey with the children, but you don't give a shit about me, do you? Well, I'm out of here, you fucking bitch. By the time I get back here tomorrow, I'd better not find you here, or you'll be sorry. You can go sleep under a bridge for all I care." Mariel could then hear drawers opening and slamming, and the sound of glass smashing, followed by her father's car screeching out of the driveway. She quickly went to comfort her brothers, and she found Marty pale and trembling. Her mother did not come out of her room. Mariel stayed with Joel and Marty and eventually fell asleep in Marty's bed with him, drifting off into a night of haunted dreams that left her drained and pale.

The children were awoken by their mother at the usual time, and the preparations for school followed the normal routine, but Mom was off in another world. Her lip seemed to quiver slightly when she spoke. As she was saying good-bye to the children, she told them, "Don't get on the bus after school. I'm going to pick you up."

That afternoon, Mom arrived at the school with a car full of packed suitcases. The children were startled. "We're going to stay at Aunt Sheila's for a few days," she explained. "We need to take a little trip because she needs me to help her with some things." But it was obvious to the children that they were fleeing because of the previous night's fight. They sat in stunned silence during much of the two-hour drive.

During the days that they stayed at their aunt's house, the children heard Mom crying several times. One day she left them in Sheila's care for several hours, saying that she had some errands to run. (But in fact she was going to court to obtain an order removing their father from the home because of his threats.)

A few days later—once Kaleigh received confirmation from the police that Felix had been served the protective order—they drove back home and resumed their daily routine. Only Dad wasn't there anymore. Mom explained to them, "We need some time apart to work things out so that we won't fight so much." They wanted to know how long Dad would be away, but she had to tell them that she didn't really know. "A few weeks, maybe, or a couple of months," she said evasively. Marty cried for his father at bedtime every evening for the next several days.

Mariel and Joel both felt a flood of relief, bordering on elation. "I can't believe that fucker is finally out of here!" Joel said to his sister. "I hope we never see him again. I hate him." Mariel responded with sharp disapproval. "Don't talk about Dad like that. You don't hate him, you love him." Joel shot back at her, "Love him? You're crazy! All he ever does is yell at people and put them down. It's much better without him. Don't be stupid."

For a few days, the house was peaceful. They spoke to each other in soft voices, they snuggled close on the couch to read stories, they watched movies without interruptions. They felt happy.

But happiness began to have its price. Mariel worried about how her father was doing, and she felt guilty for being so happy about his absence. Joel started to feel that his resentments toward Dad had driven him away (though this belief might seem illogical to an adult). And Marty sometimes wanted everything back the way it was, simply because that was the life he was familiar with.

For several weeks, Felix made no effort to see the children, or even to contact them by telephone. He felt too bitter and upset, and would tell friends and relatives, "They all ganged up against me. She has brainwashed the children to think everything is my fault."

Joel made a point of saying to Mariel, and to his mother, "Who cares if he calls? He should go to hell." But in reality he felt abandoned by his father, and worried that maybe Dad hated him for taking his mother's side. Marty cried less often for Dad than at first, but began instead to talk incessantly about him, turning him into an almost mythical figure: "Daddy is a pilot now, he flies all over the world"; "Daddy is going to come for us one day and take us to meet the president"; "Daddy had to do some really important secret work, and they're going to pay him tons of money."

With Felix out of the house, Mariel's relationship with her mother became better in some ways and more difficult in others. Mom was noticeably more patient and less grouchy. She would even smile and laugh sometimes, and the attention she paid the children was more focused than any they could remember in many years. But Mariel was put off by her sense that Mom was starting to act less like a troubled friend who needed Mariel's support and assistance, and more like—well, more like a *mother*. She was imposing more discipline, and she was keeping her private thoughts more to herself, confiding in other people instead of in Mariel. Mariel wasn't sure she liked this change. She didn't want her mother to have a kind of authority that Mariel wasn't used to, and she felt somewhat pushed away emotionally. Yet at the same time her mother seemed more present and loving. The changes left Mariel feeling confused.

After two or three months had gone by, the relaxed and cooperative atmosphere in the home began to deteriorate. The children's complicated and often contradictory emotions about their parents' separation began to erupt in various ways. Back when their father was still living at home, the children had for years stuffed away their bitterness, sadness, and fear about the abuse of Mom that they heard and saw, and the times when Dad targeted them directly with his unkindness. This backlog of distress was now tightly interwoven with their upset and guilt about the recent changes. And now that Dad wasn't in the home anymore, and with Mom visibly stronger and happier, the children felt safe to let loose demons they had been keeping tightly caged. Mariel, who for years had been hypermature, like a second mother in the house, started regressing into whining and demanding. She wanted help choosing her clothes in the morning, complained that she didn't understand any of her homework, and became unable to fall asleep without her mother. Marty couldn't settle down at night, convinced that a monster was going to come to the house to kill them all. The slightest disappointment or frustration would send him into sobs or tantrums.

The direction that Joel was taking was perhaps the most worrisome. Since roughly three years earlier, he had shown a tendency to pick up certain aspects of his father's conduct, particularly the swearing and yelling. But he had rarely exhibited that behavior when Dad was around, since he was afraid of being punished. With Dad now out of the picture, though, Joel felt emboldened, and he not only became more frequently mouthy and defiant, he also developed an array of new ways of being disrespectful to his mother, most of which looked hauntingly similar to Felix's style. He would, for example, mimic his mother's voice to insult her when she was angry, call her "stupid idiot," and scold her like a small child when he didn't feel catered to—such as times when she sent him to school with lunches that weren't his favorite.

In a peak of frustration one day, Kaleigh yelled at her son, "You're turning out just like your father!" Joel shot back, "Fuck you!" Kaleigh was so shocked by her son's vulgarity that she slapped him across the face. Joel was deeply hurt by his mother's words, and by being hit, but he was determined not to let his emotional wound show, and instead became even more superior and demeaning.

Kaleigh felt overwhelmed by her children's unexpected emotional and behavioral backsliding. Her own recovery could have been a full-time job, but she had to support her children economically and care for them on top of everything that was stirring inside her. Her inner turmoil was following a trajectory similar to her children's; her initial elation and sense of freedom from getting away from Felix was giving way to rage, sleeplessness, and anxiety about the future. *Both Mom and children were, in short, ex-*

periencing how distance from trauma can create a space to begin feeling its true impact, a natural stage in the healing process.

No one had provided Kaleigh with a map of the terrain she was crossing, and she made numerous errors as she worked her way through, such as the time she slapped Joel. She could be grouchy and short-tempered with the children, and sometimes blamed them for not being more appreciative of how hard she had been fighting to get the three of them into better circumstances. There were days when she felt that she couldn't listen to the three of them cry at bedtime anymore, or squabble with each other all afternoon, and would yell at them to snap out of it. At times she drifted off into her fear and bitterness about her years with Felix, and about having to be the healer of the psychological harm to the children that he had left in his wake.

But she didn't give up. She would apologize to her children when she needed to, and work hard to do better the next day. She told Joel she had been wrong to slap him, and that he was *not* just like his father. At the same time, she kept setting limits with her children, requiring them to behave respectfully toward her and guiding them to overcome the negative attitudes they had absorbed from Felix. She began rebuilding a social life for herself so that she had people to talk with about the hard but satisfying life of a single mother building a life of freedom. And her tenacity bore fruit; by the time they had been out from under Felix's heavy hand for five or six months, they were starting to get back to calm and closeness. Healing was unfolding as it should.

About nine months after the separation, Felix suddenly reappeared, demanding to have the children on weekends and a couple of evenings during the week. Kaleigh resisted, since the children were now doing so well, and Felix took the matter to court. Kaleigh explained to the judge that the children were recovering well from their exposure to his abusive behavior but still needed more time of peace and quiet, and that Felix had vanished for almost a year, so she didn't see why it was so urgent to him now to have so much time with the children. She also asked that his visits with the children be supervised. Felix responded that Kaleigh's allegations of abuse were completely trumped up as a way to keep him away from the children because she was upset that Felix had a new girlfriend. He said that she had actually been the one with the abuse problem, and claimed that Kaleigh had hit him several times and used to hit the children. He said that the reason he had stayed away for nine months was because she had completely turned the children against him and he had "given up hope," but that now he wanted to try again to prove to his children that he was not the monster she was telling them he was. He told the judge he would be happy to pay child support. "I of course want to contribute to my children financially, I'm their father." The judge was impressed with Felix's commitment to be an involved father, and made no issue of the fact that Felix hadn't sent any support during his absence.

Felix was granted unsupervised visitation on Tuesday and Thursday afternoons, with overnights on alternate weekends. The judge said, "I don't know whether to believe these abuse charges, but anyhow that has nothing to do with the children. The children need to have close relationships with both of you. I'm not going to deny Felix the opportunity to be back in their lives."

The children were happy that Felix had returned to them. For the first few months he put a great deal of energy into making the visits fun, and was much more patient with the children than he had been when the family was together. Joel went from despising his father to declaring that his father was a great person. "He's really changed, Mom, he's completely different from how he was before." Felix explained this transformation to his children by telling them that he had just needed to get away from the stress of the terrible relationship he and Kaleigh had shared. Felix's new partner, June, was kind to the children, and was very impressed by what a great father Felix was. June was disgusted that Kaleigh would try to restrict the children's contact with him, and that she would call during visits to check up on how they were doing.

All three of the children regressed emotionally and behaviorally as contact with their father resumed. Joel returned to imitating his father's disparaging and bullying behavior toward his mother, and Mariel drifted back into bottling up her feelings and looking after her younger brothers. Marty resumed having trouble falling asleep at night and biting his nails during the day. Kaleigh complained to the court about these effects, but the court social worker told her that the children were just struggling with the transitions in their lives, and that they felt caught in the middle between the two warring parents. She said that they were probably reacting largely to Kaleigh's hostility toward Felix rather than to feelings of their own, since they obviously loved their father and were eager to see him.

As the months went by, the children began to come home with distressing reports about certain aspects of their visits. They would report that Felix had made an insulting comment to his new partner, June, or Mariel would express upset that her father had punished Marty too harshly and that he would call Joel a "spaz" when they played whiffle ball. One night Marty cried at bedtime, telling his mother that when they were on visits, Felix and June would make "mean jokes" about Kaleigh, and that Mariel and Joel would laugh about the jokes, "but they make me feel sad."

When Kaleigh would ask the children to explain more about any of these events, they would clam up. They felt loyal to their father, and they also worried that if they revealed the worst aspects of his behavior they would lose him again. They were swayed further by his steady stream of spending on them, buying them boom boxes, dirt bikes, and other expensive enticements, and taking them on costly outings to restaurants and amusement parks.

After several months of growing closer to her father, Mariel began to pull away again, and after a year or so told her mother that she wished she didn't have to go on visits with him at all "because he says mean things to the boys or to June, and sometimes he makes fun of me, like about being so skinny." Yet Mariel would never skip a visit, and Kaleigh became increasingly convinced that she was afraid to leave her younger brothers alone with their father.

Kaleigh did not want to speak badly about the children's father to them, but she also could tell they needed help in making sense out of their conflicted feelings, the strong affection they held for him that collided with his periodic selfish or mean actions. Watching Mariel become burdened once again, seeing Joel taking up the role of mini-abuser that he had overcome, wincing as Marty descended back into insecurity, Kaleigh felt anguished. Would her beloved children be able to get through this next phase, which seemed as hard as any they had faced? Was she going to lose her closeness with them, as they drifted off into secret-keeping about their visits?

Kaleigh found herself in a quandary about how to guide her children through these treacherous waters. It was clear that, at least for now, the court was not going to permit her to restrict her children's exposure to Felix's abusiveness and manipulation, and to the reawakening of traumatic memories that his current behavior caused them. Kaleigh wished urgently to protect her children, and began searching in every direction she could think of for an avenue that was open to her.

The ups and downs that Kaleigh and her children ride through are typical of the experience of families who break away from an abusive man. Each family has its particular dynamics, of course, and not everyone meets with as many obstacles as Kaleigh does— though she handles them admirably. Your own challenges will be shaped by the ages and gender of your children, the level of divisiveness or solidarity that exists between them, the level of cruelty or irresponsibility toward children that your ex-partner is capable of, and the quality of response you get from courts, child protective services, or police. These are all issues we will examine in the chapters ahead.

Although Kaleigh's story largely speaks for itself, there is a handful of concepts I want to select out for special emphasis:

Your children feel caught in the middle. Unless they feel no bonds of affection for your ex-partner—as is sometimes true if the abusive man is simply horrible, or if he is not the children's father—children feel trapped in the tension and undergo some loyalty conflicts. I am not saying that you share equal responsibility for your children's stress, which is primarily caused by your ex-partner's abusiveness; but the reality is that you are the one left to assist them with it, and you will be more successful if you can be sensitive to the vulnerability and confusion they feel.

Children's hidden emotional injuries from witnessing abuse can rise to the surface post-separation. The abuser's absence from the home can make children feel safe for the first time in years. Many children respond by falling apart, which can be confusing for mothers. Rage, fear, and sadness that they have felt unable to show over a long period of time can now come rushing to the surface. In addition, they may have habits of disrespecting your authority, and without their father around to keep them in line, they may explode in difficult behavior. In some cases, boys in the home begin to abuse the mother, as if they were filling their father's vacant shoes. You can help your children work through this phase successfully and reach easier times, especially if a family court doesn't exercise poor judgment, as it did in Kaleigh's case.

Separation and divorce can be especially difficult for children who have been exposed to an abusive man. Children who have grown up around abuse sometimes feel less initial sadness about the parental separation than other children, because of the relief they experience, but after a while they start to struggle with grief that is at least as deep as that of other children of divorce. Even if family life was unhappy much of the time, the breakup means that children lose their dream that things might one day take a turn for the better. And those feelings of loss can be intensified by the guilt, isolation, and rage they carry about the abuse they witnessed. Your children will need you to understand the complexity of what they have to sort out internally, and will be looking to you for support and reassurance. They can and will heal with time if you hang in there with them through this process.

Information about children's reactions to separation and divorce can help you to help them. You will find some recommended readings under the heading "Divorce and Separation Issues" in the Resources section (see page 345). Bear in mind, though, that most of the published writings on divorce do not adequately take into account the effects of years of living with an abusive man. You may read books or pamphlets that tell you, for example, that you should "lay your differences and resentments aside, get along with your ex-partner, and cooperate for the good of your children." This can be an impossible—and unhealthy—assignment for an abused woman; an abusive man can make it impossible to "get along" or "cooperate" post-separation unless you *abandon* what is good for your children and cater to everything he wants, which no one should advise you to do. So don't follow advice that conflicts with your internal sense of what is realistic and what will genuinely be good for your children.

Some abusive men let go. I have been involved in quite a number of cases where abused women report to me, several years after separation, that their ex-partners have been reasonably responsible fathers, have not used the children as weapons or tried to turn them against their mothers, and have not provoked major conflicts, preferring instead to move into the future. Your intuition (along with his past behavior) can be a useful guide for you in assessing whether your partner is going to allow your relationship to end in peace or is going try to keep bullying you through your children.

But take steps to prepare yourself either way, just in case. Occasionally women get nasty surprises, when an abusive ex-partner who seemed fairly trustworthy regarding the children suddenly comes forward seeking custody or engaging in other destructive parenting behaviors. This sometimes happens, for example, when an abuser gets into a new relationship and wants his new partner to raise the children, or wants to impress her with what a great dad he is. Put all agreements about your separation or divorce in writing, including the terms of child support and child visitation, and try to retain sole legal custody for yourself. If possible, get an attorney to review all papers you sign, and to accompany you to court for any hearings that may take place.

We will continue to draw from Kaleigh's experience as we explore some of the obstacles to keeping your children emotionally well post-separation, and many strategies for meeting those challenges. The future holds great hope and promise, if you can keep moving forward courageously but cautiously.

Key Points to Remember

- Children can undergo a powerful set of mixed feelings when their mother leaves her abusive partner, particularly if the abuser is their father.
- Your own feelings about your ex-partner can be a source of useful insight into the kinds of anger, sadness, denial, and ambivalence that your children are likely to go through.
- Don't give up on yourself or on your children. Healing takes time, but it does happen.

Chapter Twelve

Abusive Men as Post-Separation Parents

"They come home from visits with their father an emotional mess. I spend days putting them back together, and just when they are finally feeling good again, it's time for the next visit."

"When we were together, he would hardly ever give our children the time of day. But now that we've split up, he's suddenly turned into SuperDad."

"He cries about how much he loves his children, but he quit his job so he wouldn't have to pay child support."

"There has never been a worse day in my life than the one when I opened the papers saying that he was asking the court for custody of our children."

A woman whose life is being constrained or made painful by a controlling or abusive man needs images of freedom to sustain her spirit. She needs to picture birds flying, or porpoises leaping through the air and diving back down into the sea, or rivers running and jumping, or whatever scenes sustain her spirit. She has to hold onto a vision of a life without coercion, to know that freedom is possible.

For some women, ending the relationship is all it takes. Some abusive men more or less accept the breakup and move on with life. If you are leaving your partner, I hope he turns out to be among those who are willing to say good-bye. But there are abusive men who are determined to find a way to keep their claws dug in. They try to cause their ex-partners financial harm, or they stalk and threaten, or they try to abuse and control her through the children. For a woman facing this style of abuser, the path to freedom can be longer and more arduous. Successfully protecting your children during this phase requires some new understandings and fresh strategies. This chapter will help to prepare you for some of the post-separation difficulties an abusive man can cause children, and will lay out approaches you can use to minimize his impact, so that you and your children can keep moving toward that freedom you have been envisioning.

Undermining of Your Parenting After Separation

In chapter 7, we examined the ways in which abusive men may erode a mother's parental authority. We also saw that some abusers do much more deliberate undermining than others. If your partner frequently interfered with your parenting while you were living together, it is important to prepare for the probability that these tactics will continue post-separation, though in somewhat different forms.

One particularly common behavior that I find among my clients is using visitation to undercut the mother's efforts to establish discipline at home. If your ex-partner knows that you try to restrict the children's intake of sugar, for example, he will make a point of pouring sweets into them while they are with him. One woman recounted to me how each Saturday morning when her ex-husband came to pick up their son, he would pull out a huge chocolate egg as the boy climbed into his car, unwrapping it with flair and handing it over to the smiling boy in the backseat. He made a point of carrying this out dramatically in front of the mother each visit.

Similarly, he may allow the children to watch any movie they choose at his place, regardless of the inappropriate sex or violence it may contain. (And inappropriate movies can be especially disturbing, yet also addictively appealing, to children who have witnessed abuse or violence at home.) Meals may be pure junk food. Bedtime may not exist; part of being the "fun" parent is to allow the children to stay up until they collapse.

A mother finds, predictably, that her children's behavior is hard to manage when they return home from a libertine weekend of this kind. The normal kinds of restrictions that she imposes suddenly feel extraordinarily chafing to them, and they don't want to hear about homework, bedtimes, eating vegetables, and watching their language. They may come right out and say, "Why can't you loosen up, Mom, and be more like Dad? He knows how to have a good time." This kind of "Disney Dad" behavior is especially unfortunate for children who have witnessed abuse, who need to feel close to their mother and respectful of her authority.

Some other common post-separation undermining tactics that you may run into include:

- Feeding tensions in your home by giving the children a lot of positive attention and reinforcement when they speak negatively about you to him.
- Criticizing your parenting to them.
- Explicitly encouraging them to be defiant or disrespectful to you when they get home.

In a recent case of mine, for example, a five-year-old girl kicked her mother, something she had never done before, and did so again several times over the next three days. Her mother pressed her to explain where this behavior was coming from, and the girl finally said that during her weekend away with her father, he had told her that she should kick her mother.

The Children as Weapons Post-Separation

For the abuser who is determined to perpetuate his control over you, or who seeks revenge, the children can look like the perfect vehicle to cause you pain or intimidate you. The box below shows the most common tactics that I see abused women struggling with from their ex-partners:

Post-Separation Use of the Children as Weapons

- Persuading the children that you are to blame for the separation.
- Having the children transmit messages to you.
- Pumping them for information about your current living situation, your finances, or your new dating partners.
- Returning them dirty, unfed, or emotionally distraught from visits.
- Frequently buying them presents or taking them on expensive outings, to buy their affection and loyalty.
- Turning the children against you through verbal conditioning and manipulation.

- Undermining your parenting by making his home a place with no rules, structure, or safety precautions.
- Having special toys or pets at his house that they cannot take home, so they have to go to his house to enjoy them.
- Making the children feel sorry for him about the separation, such as telling them he cries when they aren't there, so they will feel obligated to spend more time with him.
- Taking them for visits and returning them late, or not returning them at all for days or weeks.
- Not calling them or spending time with them at all, especially when he is angry at you about something.
- Not paying child support, underpaying, or paying late.
- Causing you and the children to become homeless by not contributing financially, by getting you evicted, or by forcing the sale of your home.
- Threatening various kinds of harm to you if you allow the children to get to know your new partner.
- Destroying their relationships with therapists (by scaring them out of talking to the therapist, by threatening the therapist, or through manipulation).
- Dragging you into court repeatedly regarding visitation or financial matters.
- Seeking custody of the children through the court, or threatening to do so.
- Kidnapping the children, or threatening to do so.
- Physically or sexually abusing the children during visitation, especially when he's angry at you.
- Filing unwarranted child abuse reports.
- Promising to see the children and then canceling at the last minute, in an effort to control your schedule and free time.

If your ex-partner is using these kinds of tactics, you no doubt have days of feeling like you still haven't gotten away from him. Some abused women have said to me, "He's just never going to let me be." Healing is of course more difficult—but not impossible—if the abuse has never really ended.

Three repeating themes run through the post-separation maneuvering of abusive fathers, and are worth exploring as you prepare to defend your family against these incursions:

#1: Getting Children to Blame You for the Separation

The abusive man does not believe that he's abusive. So when his children break into tears in front of him and say, "Daddy, we miss you, how come you aren't living at home anymore?" he does not admit his problem to himself, much less to the children. Instead, he says:

"I moved out because Mommy doesn't love me anymore."

"Mommy is very angry at me right now, and I need to stay away until she calms down."

"Mommy called the police and said I hit her, even though I didn't."

"Mommy told the judge that she gets scared when I yell at her, so the judge said I couldn't go home. Of course, she didn't tell the judge about how she screamed at me."

Children miss their fathers even if they have witnessed a great deal of his abuse. They want a break from him so that they can catch their breath, but then they wish he would return, magically transformed into a loving partner to Mom and a kind, available father to them. So the same children who six months ago may have been saying, "Please, Mommy, we can't take listening to this yelling anymore!" may do an abrupt about-face and confront their mother reproachfully: "Dad cries because he misses us so much, and he feels so bad about how he acted. Why can't you give him another chance?"

Some of my divorced clients know how to pile on guilt. Nate, who was physically violent to his wife, rented an especially dingy apartment when they split up, though he could have afforded something better. He tossed a mattress on the floor, left the walls bare and the rooms empty, and allowed the children to be shocked by his living conditions. He cried about how much he missed them, and told them that he felt like an outsider to the family now. He dressed sloppily and stopped shaving. Predictably, the children began begging their mother to let Dad come back home. Another man kept telling his three-year-old daughter that his kitten missed her and cried for her after she went back home from her weekend visits. Ironically, he would also kick the cat occasionally while she was there. The combined effect of these behaviors was that the girl began telling her mother that she needed to spend more time at Dad's.

Children's worries or sadness about their father's absence can weigh a mother down. You may already feel some guilt about his loneliness—no matter how many times you remind yourself that it isn't your responsibility. You may be struggling with your own sadness about the loss of the family life you had dreamed of having someday. And some days you undoubtedly miss your ex-partner yourself, in his better aspects. Depending on his style, you may also be scared that he is going to do something destructive because he is so angry or desperate about your breakup. Try to remember that the abuser is trying to manipulate you into going back to him, or is trying to settle old scores. Stay as strong as you can, and work on helping your children understand what is happening.

#2: Using Children to Control and Upset You

Some abusive men just seem to be fixed on hurting their ex-partners through the children any way they can. A father who is deeply abusive in this way may drag you repeatedly into court, call you constantly to criticize you as a mother, or pry information out of the children about your current activities. If he hears you are planning to go on a trip during one of his weekends with the children, he may call at the last minute claiming that he is too sick to have them over, in order to ruin your plans. He may turn minor complaints about you by the children into major ones, or report you to child protective services.

In some cases, the man doesn't seem to care how much pain he causes the children, as long as he can upset the mother. I've had a number of women complain to me that their ex-partner leaves the baby in a soiled diaper for hours during visitation, knowing full well that a bad rash will result. I had one client who reduced his children to tears by telling them that their mother was putting the family house on the market and getting ready to move them all to another town, which she wasn't even considering.

As he uses these tactics he is likely to claim that he actually has the children's best interests at heart. If, for example, he files legal actions against you for custody or visitation, he will adopt a posture of deep concern regarding the atmosphere in your home; he or his attorney will write in the court papers that you have a stream of boyfriends coming through the house, or that you have trouble waking up in the morning, or that you are leaving the children unattended. Similarly, if he puts you down constantly as a mother, he will insist that he is just trying to "stick up for the children"— except, of course, that he won't be willing to examine any of *his* behaviors that are hurting them.

#3: Establishing His Ownership of the Children

A client of mine named Paul came to group increasingly agitated over a series of weeks. He reported that his ex-wife, Nina, "has a man living at the house." I pointed out that they had been apart for over a year, he was on probation for assaulting her, and she now had a restraining order against him. Paul grudgingly agreed that she did have the right to start a new relationship, "but she shouldn't be bringing him around my children!" I explained to him that when a divorced parent has young children, there is no way he or she can have a serious relationship without the children having exposure to the new partner and developing some level of attachment to that person. And in our times, couples typically move in together once their relationship starts to look long-term. I hoped that Paul would find a way to accept this reality.

But unfortunately he didn't. He abruptly stopped showing up for group, and when I contacted his probation officer, I found out that he had been caught peeking in the windows of Nina's home, and had been jailed for violating the restraining order and the terms of his probation.

Paul's actions illustrate the tendency among some abusive men to see their children as personal possessions, and to feel that ownership threatened by divorce or separation. This conflict can be intensified by the fact that some children decide to distance themselves from the abuser post-separation, as they start to discover how much better they feel with less contact. His response can be to try even more fanatically to control them. He typically will blame the mother for the fact that his children are pulling away from him or are disclosing how abusive he has been; many abusers say that the mother is guilty of "parental alienation" to shift attention away from their own conduct. Underlying this accusation is often his own projected desire to turn the children against their mother so they will be exclusively his.

The Real Perpetrators of Alienation: Abusive Men

Among the most cruel attacks that an abusive man can carry out is a campaign to alienate children from their mother. The children who are turned against their mothers sometimes appear on the surface to feel triumphant, because they get in good with Dad—what is known as "identifying with the aggressor"—and escape Mom's limits and discipline.

But beneath this thin facade are boys and girls who feel frightened, confused, lonely, and self-hating. The loss of their mother means the loss of their one hope for a non-abusive role model, and for a source of love and affection that doesn't come with a set of exploitative strings attached. With proper support and intervention—especially if professionals or the legal system get involved and offer assistance—children who have been alienated from their mothers by an abuser can find their way back to her.

QUESTION #12:
Why does he want to turn our children against me?

As women in such a situation fight to preserve their relationship with their children, they try to understand what would drive the abuser toward such an abominable goal. The motivations that come to light when I work with abusive men of this style are the following:

He wants power, control, and vengeance. If he wins the children to his side and turns them against you, he feels like he's gotten you back for standing up to him over the years.

He believes his own distortions about you, and about himself.
Your ex-partner's entitlement and self-centeredness cause him to
perceive *you* as being the one who is volatile, unreasonable, and unkind. He also may start to believe some of his own lies, from repeating them so many times.

He sees children as owned objects, as I discussed above.

He wants your life to fail. The abusive man wants to be able to
say to himself, to you, and to other people, "See, my life is going
well and hers is falling apart. What's more, the children feel close
to me and not to her. I always said that she was the one who was
messed up, and now you can see how right I was."

He has contempt for women in general. Some of my clients stand
out for their extreme attitude of superiority toward women. A
man with this attitude sees the mother as having a disease—
femaleness—that she will spread to his children unless he can
quarantine her. He tends to be particularly worried about infection
spreading to his sons.

He blames you for the effects he has had on you. When an abusive man sees the depression, mistrust, or emotional explosiveness
that he has caused in his partner, he thinks the problem is in her.
So rather than recognizing that both the mother and her children
need distance from him so they can heal, he believes that the cure
is for them to have *an even heavier dose* of his influence over their
conduct, thoughts, and values.

If you are struggling with the kinds of behaviors and attitudes
in your ex-partner that I describe in this chapter, you may be finding that it is an uphill climb to persuade people around you to
take seriously the harm that he's causing your children. Perhaps
you are receiving responses such as:

"He's the children's father, and they need him, too."

"Children always struggle when their parents divorce."

"Your own feelings are probably coloring your view of what is going on for your children. They obviously really love their dad."

Though such comments can have aspects of truth to them, they do nothing to address the realities of how the children are being ground up emotionally by the abuser's ongoing tactics of power and control. In order to find validation and support for your concerns, you may need to seek out an advocate for abused women who specializes in post-separation issues, or find websites for abused women who are in custody or visitation conflicts (see Resources, page 345).

How Bad Will My Ex-Partner Become Post-Separation?

Abusive men vary greatly in the extent to which they draw children in as pawns of abuse after relationships split up. Some of my clients are fairly responsible fathers post-separation, while others are at the opposite end of the spectrum, harming children through mistreatment and determined to drive mothers and children apart. But most fall somewhere in the middle. They cause some hardship and stress for their children, but without reaching extremes. They provide an unhealthy role model, but don't seem determined to teach their sons to abuse women. And they don't destroy mother-child relationships, so the mother is able to use her ongoing influence with the children to counter his example and, above all, she doesn't lose her precious loving bonds with her children.

If you are leaning toward leaving your relationship or have already done so, there are indicators you can examine to help predict the severity of the problems that lie ahead in attempting to co-parent with your ex-partner. Among the most important pre-dictors is his history of behavior as a parent *before* the breakup. Some questions you can ask yourself include:

Has he hit the children or been scary to them?

Does he disrespect their boundaries?

Has he tried to turn them against me or keep them apart from me?

Does he undermine my authority?

Is he sometimes cruel to them?

Does he take his anger toward me out on them?

Does he profoundly neglect their needs or feelings?

Does he manipulate them, such as showering them with gifts or positive attention when he is angry at me?

If these behaviors were already a problem while you were to-gether, they are unlikely to vanish post-separation—unless he him-self vanishes from fathering, as some abusive men do. More commonly, behaviors like the ones above get worse after a breakup because he loses his other avenues to control you. On the other hand, if he has mostly stayed away from hurting or manipulating the children in the past, and generally respects their need to feel close to you, then he may permit you and your children a reason-ably peaceful future.

However, there are several additional questions to consider. I encounter cases where the father has not involved the children in his abuse pattern while the family was together, yet begins to do so when the relationship ends. Here are some of the factors that can help you evaluate his likelihood to cause future problems, even if he hasn't done so in the past:

Is he focused on the idea that his children belong to him?

Has he been threatening or scary to you about the fact that your relationship is ending, or shown other signs of refusing to accept the breakup?

Has he ever made threats that involve the children, such as saying that he will seek custody if you leave him, threatening to leave you with no child support, threatening to kill the entire family, including himself, or anything similar?

Has he tended to abuse you verbally or physically in front of the children, or to use them as weapons against you?

Is he dictatorially controlling, or severely and relentlessly demanding?

Does he abuse drugs or alcohol, or have other important addictions?

Does he have extreme reactions to the possibility that you may have a new partner whom the children will come to know?

Has he turned his relatives, or your own relatives, against you?

Does he have serious psychological problems, such as severe depression, narcissism, anti-social personality, or major mental illness?

"Yes" answers to these questions are indicators of an abusive man whose tendency to use the children as weapons may worsen post-separation. If you find that many concerns are arising for you, it's important to apply the suggestions from this chapter and the next one carefully, in order to help prevent problems before they grow.

Could His Parenting Improve?

In my experience, it is rare for an abusive man's parenting—meaning not only his direct care of the children, but also his ability to respect your relationship with them and to meet his broad range of parental responsibilities—to improve post-separation. The only exceptions I've seen are men who get professional help through a specialized abuser program and simultaneously deal with any additional problems such as substance addiction. Women report to me that parenting classes for the man don't seem to help in themselves; abusive men tend to twist parts of what they learn in such courses to their own purposes and ignore the rest.

One cause of confusion is that non-abusive men sometimes do make significant improvements in their fathering post-separation. Having to care for their children independently jogs some fathers out of patterns of passivity or self-involvement, so that children sometimes grow closer to their fathers after their parents divorce. But I do not encounter these kinds of spontaneous improvements in abusers. Some of my clients do indeed turn more attentive to their children for a period, lavishing attention and gifts upon them, but these superficial changes turn out to be part of a campaign to win custody or damage children's relationships with their mothers, rather than signs of learning to better understand and prioritize their children's needs and feelings.

My clients who do make true changes in their roles as fathers are those who also confront seriously their abusiveness toward the mother, and change their way of treating her even though the relationship is over. Change comes from the hard work of overcoming denial, developing empathy for his partner and children, and taking responsibility for the effects of his actions. It doesn't come from magically waking up one day with a new outlook.

The Role of the New Wife
or Girlfriend

"He spent so little time with our children for a year and a half after we split up. They felt so hurt by his lack of interest. But then he got a new girlfriend that he's serious about, and suddenly he started coming around constantly, demanding more time with them, sending them presents, calling them up, and they are enraptured by him."

"His new wife is so nasty to me. She treats me like dirt. To tell you the truth, I'd rather deal with him than with her, bad as he is."

"He's saying he needs more time with the children, and he's even filed for custody now. But when the children are over there, his girlfriend is the one who looks after them, not him. They come back from visits saying, 'Carrie got us lunch. Carrie took us to such-and-such a place. Carrie washed our hair. Carrie this, Carrie that,' and they barely mention their father's name."

"She's written terrible things about me in the court papers, complete lies. I don't know what is going on with her."

"To be honest, I'm glad his new wife is there. I don't like having my children be alone with him, and I feel like she might help make sure they're okay. She seems pretty nice. If she only knew what's coming for her down the road, though—he puts on such a good show when a relationship is new."

"He finally got involved with somebody new, and now he pretty much leaves us alone. The children feel hurt, but I'm kind of relieved. He would hassle me a lot and play a lot of mind

games with them, but now suddenly he just wants to be off with the new girlfriend, so he makes excuses to shorten his visits with them or doesn't show up at all."

As you can see from these common reports I receive from abused women, your ex-partner's new relationship can affect his parenting in a range of ways, depending on his personal style and the personality of his new partner. If, for example, he gets involved with a woman who loves children, he is likely to want to show off to her what a terrific dad he is. In order to excuse the fact that he had been largely ignoring his children until he got involved with her, he may tell her that you have been keeping them away from him out of vindictiveness, which can tug on her heartstrings. If, on the other hand, she does not get along well with children—even if she's a mother herself—then she may join him in being verbally rough on your children, and she and your ex-partner may make insulting comments about you in front of them.

In *Why Does He Do That?*, I discuss various issues about the new partners of abusive men. I will briefly recap three central points here. First, assume that he is shaping her perceptions of you, including getting her to feel sorry for him about how abusive *you* supposedly were. Her hostility toward you may be largely the product of indoctrination, so that she may not really be as bad as she seems. Second, he is probably blaming his explosiveness toward her on you. His new partner may see glimpses of his aggressive side, but he will excuse those behaviors by saying that he is reacting to how hurt he feels by injustices that you did to him, such as "falsely" accusing him of abusing you. Third, he enlists his new partner as an ally. She sees how nice he is to her—because their relationship is still fairly new—so she trusts his word about your relationship and your character. In this way he can manipulate her into speaking badly about you to other people.

A client of mine named Riley provided an illuminating example of how an abusive father can draw his new partner into his behavior pattern. Riley's children were at his house for the weekend, and he asked his girlfriend to handle the exchange of the children on Sunday afternoon so he could run an errand. He told her that his ex-wife, Charlene, was due to pick them up at six, knowing full well (though he told me he "forgot") that the actual pick-up time was five. When Charlene showed up to bring them home, Riley's girlfriend was angry and accused her of trying to cut into Riley's weekend visit. A few days later, Charlene heard that the girlfriend was telling mutual friends, "That bitch shows up an hour early and starts demanding that I let her take the children home right then. She's always doing stuff like that, she's crazy."

The solution to this kind of splitting is not easy, but I have seen women overcome it. Do your best not to hate his new partner, reminding yourself that his invisible hand is working in the background; if you come to despise her, you are playing into his design. Keep being as pleasant and reasonable with her as you can stand, to help her see through his propaganda about how volatile you are. Put agreements in writing as much as possible, striving to word your handwritten notes or e-mails in a cordial tone. When possible, speak with the new partner face-to-face or put notes into her hand so she hears your side directly, rather than giving him a chance to distort what you said. And if you are on good terms with anyone who is friendly with her, send peace messages out and try to build bridges. Your children, and you yourself, stand to benefit if his divisive efforts fail.

If your children are reporting to you that their father's new partner is unkind to them, or if they are upset by derogatory comments that she makes about you, keeping peace will of course be more difficult. In this case, you will need to strategize with your children for ways they can protect themselves, whether by complaining to their father—if that will do any good—or having you attempt to intervene.

Financial interests sometimes cloud the judgment of the abusive man's new wife or girlfriend. As their lives become more intertwined, she may begin to resent the way in which his child support payments or legal fees are limiting the money available to her, especially since he quite likely characterizes you as being unreasonable about money. Again, if you can get any accurate information into her hands about your financial picture, do so, and keep trying to build a relationship with her. Within a couple of years, she will probably be seeing what he's like. I have been involved in cases where the abusive man's new partner became an ally to his ex, as they started to recognize their common struggles.

What Can I Do?

To a great extent, what your children need from you post-separation remains the same as it was while you and your partner were together: love, affection, validation for their feelings, and assistance thinking for themselves through the confusing or upsetting behavior their father exposes them to. But new challenges also call for some new solutions. Here are some of the concepts that I have seen abused mothers have successes with during this stage in their children's recovery.

QUESTION #13:
Should I encourage my children to be close to their father?

Don't push your children and their father toward each other. Your ex-partner's relationship with your children is his responsibility. You may feel tempted, or even obligated, to press them to spend more time together, especially if you see your children getting hurt by their father's lack of interest. I talk to women who bend over backward to make visiting easy for the father, who call him to set up visits if he doesn't take the initiative or pressure children to see their father when they don't want to. Down the road, though, these same women express regret about the steps they took, as the father's manipulativeness, selfishness, or intimidation begins to take a toll on the children's well-being. When a man who has abused you wants to fade away, or when your children want to take a break from him, *let it be.* If an abusive man has to be pushed into having a relationship with his children, that demonstrates how selfish he is and how little he values them as people—characteristics in him that are almost guaranteed to create serious problems in his parenting down the road. And if children are reluctant to visit with him, that indicates how badly hurt they have been by his abuse of you, or of them.

Researchers have found that the closer children feel to the abusive man, the more deeply hurt they are by his mistreatment of their mother. Children who are more tightly bonded to their father are more likely to blame their mother or themselves for his cruel behavior, and are more vulnerable to his efforts to turn them against their mother. At the same time, studies have found that the closer children feel to their abused mothers, the *better* they do. So make your own relationship with your children your priority, and let their relationship with their father take its own course.

Limit contact between the children and their father if you find it necessary, and if you legally can. If your ex-partner is not the children's biological or adoptive father, you are under no obligation to permit visitation. Even if he is the father, you may find that he does not know how to use the family court to force contact. If he does take you to court, there is still the chance that the court will back you up on limiting his time with them—though the family court system does not generally tend to understand the emotional damage that abusive men can cause children, as I examine in the upcoming chapter.

Avoid having your children go on overnight visitation unless you are confident that he will treat them well and will not try to turn them against you. If your children are distressed by visiting with him, or are being emotionally harmed by his abusive tactics, try to arrange for his visits to be supervised by a professional (see chapter 13).

Seek professional assistance for your children. Look first for a specialized program for children who have been exposed to domestic abuse. For example, some abused women's programs offer specialized individual or group counseling for children, which is the ideal resource if it's available. If this service is not available in your area, try to locate a child therapist who has training and experience in domestic abuse. By getting your children involved in professional services you not only give them some potentially valuable assistance, you also help to avoid a situation where "it's your word against his" about how your children are responding to their relationship with him. Choose a therapist who understands the parenting tactics used by abusive men and the effects of exposure to domestic abuse in children.

Keep working on your relationship with your children. Make it a priority to be close to your children and maintain healthy, open communication with them. Read *How to Talk So Kids Will Listen and Listen So Kids Will Talk* (see the Resources section, page 348). Be affectionate and loving with your children, but firm about limits at the same time. Admit when you are wrong and apologize to them. Struggle your way through difficult conflicts with them, avoiding breakdowns in communication as much as possible. Consider using professional counseling to help you work through your greatest difficulties with each other, and if your children already see a therapist, ask to be included in some of the sessions to work on improving your communication. Abusive men have a harder time pulling mothers and children apart when relationships are strong.

You might also review the suggestions I make in the "What Can I Do?" sections of chapters 7 and 8, many of which remain relevant in the post-separation context. Draw upon as many community supports for your parenting as possible, such as parent education classes, play groups, and support groups.

Teach your children skills in critical thinking. Because the legal system often does not permit women to protect their children from abusive men the way it should, you need to equip them to protect themselves as well as possible. One indispensable step in this direction is to help them learn to think independently and analytically, so they will recognize control and manipulation that they encounter from their father—or on any other front in their lives. This important subject is examined in chapter 15.

Seek male role models for your children. Both boys and girls need to see examples of kind, respectful, noncoercive adult men. Boys need to see that their father is not the only example of how to be a man, and girls need to know that they aren't obligated to tolerate their father's style of behavior in other men they love. Encourage healthy male relatives or friends to take an interest in your children and spend time with them, sign your boys up to get a "Big Brother" (though there may be a waiting list), or inquire at schools about mentoring programs in your town.

Don't speak badly to the children about their father, but do validate their concerns. This can be a balancing act, but an important one. Avoid involving the children in your bad feelings toward your ex-partner, as your criticisms of him will just tend to make them stressed from feeling caught in the middle, and defensive of him. But do take seriously the concerns they raise about his behavior, and be honest with them when you think his conduct sounds inappropriate or hurtful. Be careful not to minimize their complaints; they may be trying to alert you to serious issues. At the same time, try not to overfeed their grievances with your own emotional energy in a way that could blow minor problems out of proportion. In short, focus on your children's feelings about their father, not your own. Make room for them to share with you their positive and affectionate feelings about him, which will in turn help them to feel that they can open up with you about his more destructive aspects.

Prepare for a legal battle even if you don't think one is coming. Better safe than sorry. Some abusive men insist that they aren't interested in litigating, and then run furtively down to court and start filing motions. As soon as you know that you and your abusive partner are headed for a breakup, start keeping a diary about important events; save letters, e-mails, and handwritten notes from him; keep copies of your correspondence to him; and make similar efforts to build a documentary record of his behavior. Seek legal representation if you can afford it, or apply for a legal aid attorney if you qualify under their income guidelines. (See chapter 13 for detailed suggestions on handling custody and visitation litigation.)

Use resources on divorce where appropriate. There are many helpful books and other resources to use with children to help them process their feelings about the end of their parents' relationship (see Resources, page 345). Many materials for children of divorce emphasize to them that they have the right to love both parents, a message that can help children resist their father's efforts to alienate them from you. However, look carefully at books or videos before using them, as some contain messages that are not appropriate for children who have been exposed to abuse. They may, for example, not allow space for children's valid feelings of fear toward their father, or for their bitterness about his verbal or physical brutality toward their mother. Divorce specialists sometimes mistakenly believe that children's resentment toward their abusive fathers is strictly a "loyalty" issue, greatly underestimating the painful impact on children of seeing abuse or intimidation happen to someone they love and depend on.

Help your children to heal emotionally from the verbal or physical abuse they have witnessed. Give them room to talk about how hard the family tensions and the abuse have been for them. Validate the reality of their experiences. Permit them to express and release painful emotions through crying and tantrums, and let them know that it is okay to feel and show anger. In chapter 14, you will find extensive suggestions for how you can facilitate emotional recovery in your children.

Key Points to Remember

- Leaving your abusive partner does not guarantee that life will get easier for your children; they are likely to continue to need assistance from you with their feelings and experiences regarding their father.
- Some abusive men continue to use the children as weapons of abuse post-separation, and your ex-partner may even become worse in this regard than he was when you were together.
- By leaving your abusive partner you can help create an opportunity for your children to recover. However, you may have to fight for them to actually get the chance to do that healing, in the face of your ex-partner's efforts to sabotage their progress.
- Preparing for difficulties before they arise can help prevent some of the post-separation distress that abusive men tend to cause. You and your children can get through this next phase if you stay by each other and keep working on your relationships.
- Continue to build your resources and support system.

Chapter Thirteen

Making Your Way in the Family Court System

"Several people advised me that I absolutely had to have a lawyer. But I feel like my lawyer has hurt my case a lot more than helped it."

"The court in my county requires divorcing parents to go into mediation together, so I have to sit in the same room with him, and he scares the daylights out of me."

"My husband is telling the judge all kinds of lies to make me look like the bad one, and she's believing him instead of me."

"The people at the court are finally starting to catch on to what he's all about, but it has taken so long for them to get it."

I now undertake to illuminate some of the most difficult and critical issues that an abused mother can face. My hope is to leave you empowered to guide your children through a minefield laid down by their father, so that your life and theirs can move forward toward peace and healing. But in order to map the route to safety, I have to speak bluntly about some disturbing realities that exist in family courts today. Abused women who come into the legal arena in disputes over custody and visitation are sometimes shocked by the unsympathetic atmosphere they encounter there, and by the court's inexplicable eagerness to back up the abuser. It is essential for you to prepare yourself ahead of time for the challenges that family court litigation can present, to help avoid outcomes that could be destructive to you and your children.

I begin with the stories of two court cases in which I've been involved. In the first, it took years for the children to recover from the effects of their father's violence because the court refused to protect them. In the second case, the court did ultimately protect the child, but not before monumental judicial errors had been made, and the mother—like so many other abused women—had to show heroic perseverance and resourcefulness to get her child safe.

In this book I use the term "family court" to refer to any judge who has jurisdiction over custody, visitation, child support, or division of assets issues. In some states no separate family court exists, so the same judge who hears these kinds of cases also handles a wide range of other legal issues. In a few states, your case may be split up among multiple courts, with child support addressed in one arena, divorce in another, and custody and visitation in yet another.

Rhonda

Rhonda began divorce proceedings when her children were preteens, after years of being beaten by her husband, Fritz, a highly respected anesthesiologist. The court did not take Rhonda seriously about the history of violence, largely due to Fritz's public reputation and smooth image, and not only granted him extensive unsupervised visitation but actually gave him temporary custody of their older daughter, Michelle. Fritz then remarried, and a couple of years later it came to Rhonda's attention—because a friend clipped a newspaper article—that Fritz had been arrested for beating his *new* wife, and Michelle had been in his home when it happened. Michelle had not told her mother about the incident, and perhaps had been ordered to keep it secret.

Rhonda then heard about my work and called me to discuss her case. I happened to have a connection in a police department who was able to leak me a copy of the police report for the incident—which police had refused to give to Rhonda—and I gave it to her. Here is some of what the sergeant wrote (with identifying information changed):

> I arrived at 18 Downing Ave. and spoke with the victim, Fritz Carlson's wife. She related that Mr. Carlson "lost his temper," grabbed her forcefully by the throat with his hands and then bit her in the face with his teeth. He then threw her down the outside, front, masonry stairs of the house. I observed a laceration involving her lip which she stated had been caused by the bite. I further observed redness around her throat, and she complained of neck pain and pain in her right elbow. Ms. Carlson told us that she was pregnant and was reluctant to obtain a restraining order or go forward with criminal charges as she was concerned that these would have an adverse effect on Mr. Carlson's standing as a physician.

The report revealed that Michelle had actually been *the subject of the conflict* that had led to Fritz's violence:

> Ms. Carlson indicated that she and her husband Fritz were in a downstairs area arguing about the defendant's fourteen-year-old daughter Michelle over her newly acquired suspension from

school. The defendant demanded that the plaintiff give him the application papers to the private school. The plaintiff refused because she wanted to speak with the defendant regarding the problems they've had to face having Michelle reside at 18 Downing Ave. (Michelle has been living there for about two months.) The plaintiff indicated she is unable to handle or control Michelle in any way.

Now, this case would seem open-and-shut to most people; the father is violently assaulting his new wife, just as he did to his ex, the daughter was present during the assault, and the stepmother is revealing that Michelle is completely out of control at their home. Clearly, the girl needs to go home to her mother, where she should have been all along.

But unfortunately, this is not what occurred. Rhonda took the police report to the family court, *and the judge refused to read it,* saying it was irrelevant unless Fritz was criminally convicted of the new act of violence. (And there never was a criminal prosecution, because Ms. Carlson refused to cooperate, just as she had told the arresting officers she would do.) The judge instead made permanent her order that Fritz was to have sole legal and physical custody of Michelle.

Michelle's behavioral problems continued to escalate after this incident, including an arrest for a severe assault on another student, but the court still refused to return custody to Rhonda. In fact, during the time I was attempting to help Rhonda with her case, the court took the astounding action of giving Fritz permission to send Michelle away to a residential program for troubled teenagers *because he couldn't manage her,* rather than return her to her mother's care.

When Michelle was seventeen years old, she took matters into her own hands and moved back to living with her mother and her younger brother, too old now for anyone to stop her and sick of dealing with her father's selfishness and intimidation. Rhonda called to tell me the happy news that Michelle was back home, but she also said, "She is so hurt, as is my son. Things are difficult here. It's going to take a long time to repair the damage that Fritz and the judge did."

Paula

Paula split up with her husband after six years together. His abusive style had consisted primarily of scary threats, raised fists, severe selfishness, and relentless put-downs and psychological cruelty, although once he had also thrown Paula up against the refrigerator. Their daughter Rowana was only fifteen months old when Kenseth moved out. Paula held hopes that Kenseth would be a good father, and pushed him to spend time with Rowana. He showed little interest for several months, but suddenly perked up as a father when he got involved in a new relationship, and he began to take their daughter on alternate weekends.

Over the following year and a half, as Rowana went from just under two years old to well over three, she returned from visits with her father exhibiting increasingly strange behaviors and reporting upsetting events, such as being left alone in her father's apartment. Then she began to behave in sexual ways, such as kissing her mother with her tongue, and finally disclosed that her father was touching her inappropriately.

Paula went to family court requesting that visits be suspended and that a professional evaluation be conducted to look into her daughter's disclosures. The judge, however, took the stunning action of forbidding the mother to take the child to any kind of evaluation, *forbidding the mother even to continue taking her daughter to the therapist that Rowana had already begun seeing,* and allowing the father to have extra time with the child, under the threat that he would give custody to Kenseth if Paula didn't cooperate. Her daughter continued to slide rapidly downhill psychologically.

The tide was turned by a stroke of good fortune: Paula managed to persuade the state's child protective service to release a letter saying that the girl should be evaluated by a sexual abuse team at a hospital. Armed with this letter, Paula went back into court, ended up before a different judge, and the evaluation was ordered to go forward. Months later, the hospital team released a report concluding that the risk to the child was high and that the father's visits with the child needed to be supervised for at least a few years. (However, the court never did require the father to undergo any treatment.) According to Paula, Rowana recovered rapidly once she stopped spending time alone with her father.

Unfortunately, there is nothing terribly unusual about the experiences of these mothers; the poor response to protective mothers by family courts has been documented in the book *The Hostage Child* (Indiana University Press), the award-winning video "Small Justice" (see Resources, page 346), and a human rights report called "Battered Mothers Speak Out" (see page 346), in addition to various newspaper exposés. Organizations have sprung up attempting to protect the rights of abused mothers and children. (Look under Resources for more information.)

In this atmosphere, it is important that you inform yourself about the court process and about approaches that have worked for other protective mothers, in order to create the best chance that your children's rights, and yours, will be honored. This chapter explains basics about how custody and visitation litigation works, what can go wrong, and how you can keep your case headed in the best direction possible. I will draw from the recurring themes that I have observed in those family court cases that go well for the mother, or where they go badly for some period of time but she manages to get the court to improve its response.

Misconceptions About
the Family Courts

An abused woman can be vulnerable in family court if she comes in with unfounded expectations. Perhaps the most widespread myth is the belief that mothers are favored by courts in custody disputes, which stopped being true decades ago. It is true that for roughly the first half of the 1900s the "Tender Years Doctrine" was influential, and mothers had some advantage in gaining custody of young children. (Prior to about 1900, mothers had *no* rights regarding custody at all.) But in the 1970s the tide was turning back, for various reasons, and by the 1980s fathers were winning at least joint custody in a majority of the custody battles they undertook, and winning sole custody more often than mothers, a situation that remains today. And the fathers who are taking advantage of this imbalance are largely abusive ones; researchers have found that abusers are twice as likely as non-abusive men to seek custody.

Why do abusive men turn up disproportionately in custody disputes? First, abusive men don't do well at separating their own needs from those of their children, so they don't consider how injurious it could be for the children to be taken away from the primary care of their mother, where they feel secure. Second, the abusive man is focused on power and control, and may ignore the harm he causes the children in his desperate race to settle old scores. And his lack of respect for the mother's humanity, a core aspect of the abusive mentality, can permit him to believe that she is the one who will harm the children, not him. Occasionally, the abusive man's main reason for seeking custody seems to be a desire to avoid having to pay child support.

Another common but mistaken belief is that a court would of course not grant custody to an abuser, especially a physical batterer. But the sad reality is that many judges say, "You aren't together anymore, so his aggression toward you is no longer an issue. Does he beat the children? If not, there is no reason to curtail his relationship with them." This is the case despite the fact that almost every state has laws that say that domestic violence *is* relevant to custody and visitation disputes. Even where the father has been physically abusive to the children, the mother may not have proof, or the judge may say, "Well, that only happened a few times, and he knows not to do that anymore." Other judges conclude that the parents mutually abused each other, because the abusive man claims to be the victim.

Even—or perhaps especially—a mother whose children are being sexually abused by their father cannot assume that the court will allow her to protect them. In recent years, evidence is emerging that mothers who raise sexual abuse allegations in custody disputes run a serious risk of losing custody of their children to the abuser, a scandal that has been brought into the public eye by the documentary "Small Justice" and articles by journalist Kristen Lombardi. If you have concerns that your ex-partner is violating your children's boundaries, be sure to read "When You Have Concerns About Child Sexual Abuse," page 248, for guidance on how to keep your children's disclosures from backfiring against them.

How Family Courts Handle Domestic Abuse Allegations

QUESTION #14:
Why doesn't the family court get what he's doing to our children?

The typical judge, custody evaluator, or divorce mediator, even if he or she has impressive degrees and licenses, has had very little training on domestic abuse, and none at all on abusive men as parents. Instead, court personnel tend to operate on the basis of myth and outdated beliefs, sometimes combined with prejudices against women. Specifically, court personnel and court-appointed evaluators tend to be unaware of the following:

- The well-established profile of abusive men, and the fact that these characteristics can have profound implications for their children (as I discussed in chapter 2).
- The widespread tendency among abusive men to undermine the mother's authority and damage her relationship with her children.
- The extremely low rate of change in abusive men except among those who participate for an extended period of time in a specialized group for abusers in combination with criminal prosecution.
- The fact that abusive men have far higher rates of physically or sexually abusing children than other men do.
- The fact that being a target of chronic abuse can leave a woman with many emotional difficulties—and sometimes physical ones as well—from which she may need time to heal.
- The tendency of abusive men to abruptly start paying focused attention to their children when they decide to seek custody, and the powerful emotional impact this positive attention can have on children who have been traumatized by the man's abusiveness, and who simultaneously are starved for his approval.
- The fact that abusive men usually present themselves as likable, calm, reasonable people in court, do not seem in any obvious way abusive, and often play the role of hurt, misunderstood victim.

- The fact that abusive men are unhealthy role models, and that their children grow up with high rates of involvement in domestic violence themselves, and in other kinds of aggressive or anti-social behavior. (For some reason even a man who is physically violent to his partner is not considered a bad role model by most family courts, whereas a drug dealer would be, even though abusers do at least as much damage in society, including causing a similar number of deaths annually.)
- The tendency of many abusive men to sabotage children's recovery, such as by ruining their relationships with therapists.
- The fact that, for the reasons above, unsupervised or unwanted contact with their woman-abusing fathers impedes children's recovery.

This lack of information about abuse can be compounded by an active prejudice against women who raise abuse allegations. I train family court personnel all over the United States, and at each workshop there are a few judges and evaluators who make comments such as, "I think most abuse allegations come from women trying to get a leg up in the divorce," and "Women are just bitter about the breakup so they try to cut the father off from the children." These statements use infrequent occurrences as an excuse to ignore most well-documented abuse.

Courts are highly reluctant to curtail fathers' access to their children. As a number of court employees have said to me over the years, "There are so many fathers out there who abandon their children, and here I have a dad who *wants* to be involved; you're telling me I should discourage him?" As a result they tend to hold fathers to much lower standards than mothers. Supervised visitation is not often imposed, and usually gets lifted within a few months as long as the father behaves well under supervision, as most abusive men do.

The abusive man can often discern the court's lack of will to hold him to proper parenting standards, with the sad result that he feels emboldened. I cannot count the number of times women have said to me, "He finally crossed a line where I thought the court would realize how out of hand he is, but they just went ahead and let him get away with it again. It seems like there's nothing he can't slide by on."

QUESTION #15:
How can I get the family court to listen to me?

Thus in order to persuade the court to take seriously the implications of your ex-partner's abusiveness, you are forced to work doubly hard to get the court unstuck from its well-worn path. Specifically, you need to:

• Come up with as many objective sources of evidence as possible of your ex-partner's abusiveness, such as police reports, medical records, letters from schoolteachers and other professionals, letters from people who witnessed important events, and other documents that can help you avoid being in a situation where court personnel say, "Well, it's just your word against his."

• Bend over backward to present yourself as friendly and non-vindictive in hopes of overcoming the anti-female stereotypes that often reign in courthouses (even among female judges and evaluators). Hide your anger, no matter how justified it is, because court employees are harshly discrediting toward mothers who show bitterness or raise their voices, though these tones are generally accepted from fathers.

● Be as concrete and specific as you can about why your partner's behavioral history causes you to be concerned *for your children,*
because court personnel will often fail to make the appropriate
connections, and will insist that you are really just thinking about
yourself.

Dealing with a Custody Evaluator

Custody evaluators can be either employees of the court or private
practitioners appointed by the court. They tend to be either lawyers
or mental health practitioners, though some have other backgrounds. It is rare, unfortunately, for courts to appoint evaluators
whose primary professional experience is in domestic violence. In
some states the custody evaluator is referred to as a "guardian ad
litem," though this title does not make much practical difference
in most cases. (In many cases, no evaluator exists at all, because neither the court nor the parents have resources to pay for one.)

The majority of custody evaluators proceed on the misguided
assumption that the truth or falsehood of abuse allegations, and
the level of risk to children from an abusive man, can be determined by interviewing the parties and seeing who sounds truth-
ful. Evaluators who are mental health professionals add the
dimension of "clinical evaluation," which is equally unsound in
sorting out domestic abuse concerns. If the clinical assessment indicates that the father has no major mental health problems, for
example, the evaluator may declare that the abuse allegations must
be false because the father doesn't fit the "profile" of an abuser—
even though the reality is that no mental health profile of an
abuser exists. Extensive research and clinical evidence demonstrates that some very destructive abusers of women and children
perform normally in clinical evaluations and psychological tests,
but courts continue to ignore these findings.

The evaluator's eye then turns to the abused woman. Because

she is carrying the effects of many years of abuse, clinical assessment may suggest that *she* is actually the one with greater problems. Tests may indicate that she has symptoms of paranoia, depression, histrionics (meaning that she exaggerates for dramatic effect), or mistrust of others—all symptoms that are present to at least some degree in most women who have been traumatized by abuse, especially when the woman now has the additional stress of fearing that the court will forbid her to protect her children. But these predictable symptoms of abuse are used by many evaluators *as evidence that her allegations of abuse are false,* and that the main risk to the children is actually the mother's mental health.

In recent years, both custody evaluators and abusive men themselves have developed increasingly distorted reasoning for blaming abused mothers for their children's reactions. Mothers who take appropriate protective steps—such as reporting to the court what their children have told them about incidents during visitation—can get labeled as guilty of "parental alienation." Children's detailed and explicit disclosures of sexual abuse are sometimes dismissed with a quick wave of the hand by an evaluator or judge, who declares, "The child is just trying to please the mother by joining her in her campaign against the father."

I do encounter cases in which the custody evaluator has caught on to the abuser's mentality and tactics, and has taken seriously the risk to the children of being drawn in by him as pawns, but this outcome appears to be more the exception than the rule. So I recommend that you cautiously follow the steps below when dealing with a custody evaluation:

Don't request or voluntarily accept the appointment of a custody evaluator unless you know who the evaluator will be, and know how that person has dealt with other abuse cases. Abused mothers often feel, understandably, that as soon as a trained professional looks carefully at the facts and sees the effects on the children, he or she will of course stop letting the abuser get away with what he's been doing, and will allow the mother to protect her children. But the reality is often otherwise. More often than not, custody evaluators are committed to the belief that children must have extensive involvement with both parents, and often refuse to look carefully at evidence of abuse.

Proceed with caution even if you are told, "This individual is known to be trained in domestic violence"; some custody evaluators present themselves publicly as sensitive to domestic violence issues, while actually handling their cases irresponsibly. Be sure to talk to people who have dealt with the person's evaluations directly before accepting their appointment.

If you have a lawyer, bring him or her to all meetings that you have with the evaluator. Some evaluators try to dissuade women from having legal representation at interviews—perhaps saying, "I just want us to have a relaxed, friendly conversation, and as soon as attorneys are present, everything gets much more adversarial"—and some lawyers are reluctant to attend, saying to the client, "Evaluators don't like having attorneys present, and you don't want to get the person irritated." But the reason evaluators don't like having the attorney present is that they know they will have to be much more careful and professional about what they do, and will not be able to intimidate or manipulate the parent the way some evaluators do. Any evaluator who is professional and objective won't mind having the lawyer in the room; and if the evaluator doesn't meet that description, then that's all the more reason why you'd better have your attorney there.

Try to avoid inflammatory language. Many custody evaluators, whether male or female, are quick to label mothers as hysterical, too angry and bitter, incapable of separating their own feelings from their children's, and out to cut the father off from the children. In this context, it is important for you to describe your concerns in calm, reasonable language. Express your willingness to support your children's relationship with their father, but ask that steps be taken first to get him into proper services, including a high-quality abuser education program and any additional help he needs for substance abuse, mental health, or parent training. Explain that you want your children to have some time to catch their breath and some assistance with healing. Say that you believe your ex-partner will be a better father if he is held to some realistic measures of change and knows that he will be made accountable. Always talk of "our children" rather than "my children," and speak of your concerns in terms of what each child needs, not what *you* want, even though the two tend to be the same.

Put a bad evaluator on the stand as quickly as possible. If you receive an irresponsible or biased report from your evaluator, move quickly to put the person on the witness stand and discredit his or her qualifications on domestic abuse and the handling of your particular case. I find that the longer a bad report is allowed to sit unchallenged, the more damage it does; most judges proceed on the assumption that the evaluator is incapable of making any really serious mistakes unless they are shown otherwise. Powerful cross-examination is sometimes the only antidote.

Don't give up. An unfavorable or biased report does not mean that the battle is over. Judges are sometimes willing to throw out some or all of an evaluator's recommendations, especially if strong testimony is presented at a hearing or trial. In some cases, the abusive man agrees outside of court to terms that are better for the children than what the evaluator recommended, in order to avoid the expense and hassle of a trial and the possibility that the judge will see through him. Below, I address long-term strategizing further.

When You Have Concerns About Child Sexual Abuse

Although men who abuse women are more likely than non-abusive men to violate children's boundaries (see chapter 5), only a small percentage of the women I have spoken with over the years have received disclosures of outright incest from their children, or have seen behaviors in the child that caused the mother to worry about violations of this severity. However, when such concerns arise, the mother's life gets turned upside down; few events can cause as much pain, rage, and desperation for a mother as discovering that her child appears to be an incest victim. If you find yourself in this position, I recommend above all that you acquire a copy of John Myers's humane and wise book *A Mother's Nightmare—Incest* (see Resources, page 347), which will prepare you for the best chance of successfully protecting your child.

The next piece of advice I offer is one of the most difficult: Try with all your might, from whenever your concerns first arise, to respond to your child in a calm and matter-of-fact way, hiding your own upset and fear as much as you possibly can. A measured response is important for several reasons, including:

• Your child may be responding to an innocent, appropriate interaction that was misinterpreted by him or her, or that you are misinterpreting. It is normal for children of various ages to exhibit certain degrees of sexualized behavior, such as masturbation, which are not cause for concern in themselves, and it is not uncommon for them to make ambiguous or confusing statements about their physical contact with people. If you react very strongly prematurely, you could cause your child to become distressed about an event that was not actually upsetting to the child originally.

• If your child was indeed inappropriately touched or exposed, the experience is likely to have been frightening and confusing for him or her, and you do not want your own reaction to upset the child more.

• Overly strong reactions from a parent can cause a child to be afraid to say anything further about what is happening or even to retract the disclosure, out of fear that the perpetrator will get in serious trouble, that you can't handle the full truth, or that the child himself or herself will be deemed to have done something wrong. Children typically feel that they are complicitous in some way in the violations that have taken place; in addition, they sometimes are threatened by the perpetrator that disastrous consequences will result for the child, their siblings, the perpetrator, or the mother if the child discloses. If you are concerned that your child may be experiencing sexual abuse, it is critical for you to react in a way that keeps lines of communication open between you and your daughter or son, so that over time you can get as accurate a picture as possible of what is taking place.

If your concerns about sexual abuse are serious—for example, if your child has made an explicit disclosure—or if the issues are more subtle but persist over time, try to involve a professional, such as a therapist who has experience with child sexual abuse. Unless your situation is dire, however—for example, your child is disclosing penetration—don't pressure your child to repeat his or her disclosure to the professional, because:

- Children have a hard time talking to professionals about sexual abuse, and feeling under pressure to do so can quickly lead them to clam up and say even less.
- If the child does talk to the therapist under pressure from you, the accuracy of the disclosure may be called into doubt in court, *even if the child simply repeats to the therapist exactly the same details he or she told to you.* For example, if the therapist asks your child, "Did your mommy tell you to tell me these things?" and he or she answers, "Yes," the court begins to assume that the child's statements were false, even though all you actually had said to your child was, "You need to tell the evaluator what you told me." In addition, a child who comes to see the therapist's office as a place "where we

go to talk about the bad stuff that happened," or "where we go to talk about how Daddy hurt me," may soon start refusing to go, especially during periods when the father is buying him or her gifts or using other tactics to silence the child about the abuse. The child needs to view the therapist's office as a place where he or she goes to have some fun, to develop a special relationship with a new adult, and to talk about feelings, so that the exploration of possible boundary violations or of negative feelings about visits with Dad are just one aspect of a multifaceted therapeutic experience.

Now comes another delicate matter: It is important to encourage the therapist to contact the father and build a relationship with him. You may feel reluctant to do this, since your experience may be that he is always able to charm everyone he talks to, so you fear that he will soon have the therapist on his side. But if the therapist has a relationship with you and not with your ex-partner, his or her letters or testimony may be discredited in court as biased in your favor. If you feel that you can't trust your child's therapist not to be hoodwinked by your ex-partner, the solution is not to keep them apart, but to find a therapist with better training on abuse.

If the therapist agrees to write letters or affidavits to the court on your behalf, ask him or her to stick to describing clinical observations and carefully drawn clinical conclusions. The therapist should avoid sounding overly invested in the case, and should not tell the judge what to do. For example, a letter from a professional can appropriately say, "I have observed that the child is upset after visitation with the father," or "The child has made clear statements about boundary violations by the father that do not sound rehearsed or coerced," but should not make statements such as, "The child has clearly been sexually abused," or "Visitation with father should be immediately suspended." Statements that overtly advocate for one side, or that seem to draw overly strong conclusions, can give the professional's observations less credibility and impact in court.

Depending on where you live, a number of resources may exist in your area to support you though the turmoil that sexual abuse concerns bring. Call your local program for abused women, hospitals, and mental health clinics to look for such services as support groups for non-offending parents of incest victims, therapy groups for the child, workbooks and picture books to help you in working directly with your child on processing what has occurred, and more. (Look also in the Resources section, under "Child Sexual Abuse," page 347)

It is important for any abused woman facing custody and visitation litigation to find good legal representation if possible, and that issue becomes even sharper where sexual abuse arises. Below I talk more about how to find and choose a good attorney—and how to represent yourself if necessary.

Should I Go into Hiding with My Child?

While I cannot answer this question for you, given the number of factors that are involved in the decision, I can draw your attention to a few crucial issues. Mothers who have gone underground describe their lives as extremely difficult, with the fear of being found ever present. All contact with people you used to know has to be avoided, which is sad and isolating. If you are found, which happens in the great majority of cases, you risk jail, and your child is likely to end up in the full-time custody of the perpetrator. In such an event, your child loses almost all contact with the one person who can keep her or him sane and hopeful: you.

So before deciding to go on the run, make sure you have exhausted all other possible strategies to help your child survive emotionally. Children have a remarkable capacity for healing, as I discuss in the coming chapter. I am not denying the urgency of your child's plight. But the way out for him or her may come into view over the next couple of years where none currently seems possible, whereas once you go into hiding, there is no turning back. If you hang in there, you may finally get before a different judge, or child protective services might finally wake up and decide to take steps to protect your child, or a protest group might form around you that succeeds in publicly pressuring the court enough that the judge is forced to examine the evidence. Sometimes battling for your child over the long haul is the approach that holds the best prospects for your child's mental health and ultimate enjoyment of life. This is a determination that only you can make.

Should I Involve Child Protective Services?

Child protective services can be reluctant to get involved "in one of those messy divorce cases." Some departments take the stand that behavior by a non-custodial parent is outside their purview, because the mother can protect the child by getting the family court to curtail the visits. This stand ignores the fact that most family courts do not have investigative staff, certainly not of the kind that child protective services have, and are not generally trained well on child abuse and neglect issues. Furthermore, when a child protective service fails to take action on a case, the family court generally interprets that failure to mean that *no protective intervention is necessary,* and that the mother must have made a false allegation, even if that isn't what the child protective service meant to indicate. And therein lies the main risk in making a child abuse report; if the social workers decide not to get involved, you may be in a worse position than before you reported.

So begin by asking advice anonymously from your local pro-

gram for abused women, to see what type of response they consider likely from your child protective service based on their experience. (If you give your name, they might feel obligated to
make a report even if you don't want them to.) Consult also with
your lawyer if you have one. If you decide it's best to involve child
protective services, see if a professional such as a schoolteacher,
an advocate at the abused women's program, or your child's therapist can file on your behalf, since the state may investigate more
carefully if the report isn't viewed as being "a weapon in a custody
conflict."

If you find out that allegations against non-custodial parents are
not handled well in your area, gather up as much evidence as you
can and ask for a hearing at the family court. Whenever possible
avoid going into court with only your own word as evidence. Try
to bring witnesses, or at least letters from them, to provide independent accounts of what your child is saying or doing that raises
red flags, and get support from a professional if you can.

Negotiating with an Abuser

Because court hearings and trials can involve tremendous expense,
anxiety, and time away from being with your children—a bitter
irony indeed—you will probably be involved at one or more points
in efforts to negotiate an agreement with your ex-partner regarding custody, visitation, and finances. It is quite common for courts
to *require* parents to participate in mediation, even if the man has
abused the woman physically, so you may end up negotiating with
him even if you don't wish to. If you can reach an accord that you
can live with, by all means do so. Some abusive men do consent
to move into the future rather than get stuck in the past, having
their own reasons for wanting to avoid costly and stressful court

battles. And your ex-partner may even turn out to be one of those abusive men who follow their post-separation agreements reasonably well and don't mistreat or manipulate the children. If the agreement breaks down months or years from now, whether because your children are sliding downhill emotionally or because their father stops honoring his commitments, you can litigate the case later. However, be aware that proving abuse, and persuading the court to consider it relevant, gets more difficult the further back into the past it goes.

Negotiating with an abusive man can be perilous. You may feel intimidated by him in the mediation process itself; I just recently spoke with a woman who described how her ex-partner yelled and swore at her right in front of the mediator, who neither did anything to stop him nor mentioned his conduct in her report. You may also feel pressured to agree to a plan that you aren't comfortable with for fear that the judge will end up ordering something even worse if you don't reach an agreement. There is no easy answer to these challenges. In a few courts, mediators are available who have been trained on domestic abuse, and some may even follow special protocols, as they should, when dealing with an alleged abuser. You should have the right not to be involved in face-to-face negotiations with a man who has abused you, but state laws and court policies don't always respect that right.

A large proportion of abusive men do not feel obligated to honor agreements they make, because of their high level of entitlement and their extensive collection of excuses and justifications. An abuser who may seem calm and reasonable, ready to bargain in good faith and leave the past behind, may erupt into his old ways weeks or months later as the reality of the breakup starts to sink in. Therefore, it is best to include provisions in any agreement that address how future breaches by either party will be dealt with. If you are not represented, pay a lawyer to review any documents before you sign them, helping you structure the agreement in an enforceable way and watching for loopholes that need to be closed.

What Can I Do?

Although I have included advice throughout the sections above, several points remain that can help you increase your chances of getting a fair and safe response from the court, making your children's healing the priority that it should be:

Either find an attorney who can really fight for you, or represent yourself. People may advise you to enter a divorce or separation action with a lawyer at all costs, suggesting that it will be disastrous for you to be unrepresented. But the hundred or more accounts I have received from abused mothers in custody litigation show that the picture is not so simple. An ill-prepared, uncommitted, or dishonest lawyer can cause your case, and therefore your future, more harm than good, and can leave you penniless in the process, as is powerfully described in Karen Winner's book *Divorced from Justice* (see Resources, page 346). I have been involved in several cases in which, for example, the lawyer assured the mother that he or she was filing certain court papers but actually failed to do so, and once the deadline had passed it was no longer possible to take the actions the woman needed to initiate, such as to appeal a judge's ruling.

Finding the right lawyer to represent you in a custody or visitation conflict can be a challenge. Contact a nearby program for abused women to see if there are lawyers in your area whom they recommend. The fact that a lawyer is smart and high-powered does not necessarily mean that he or she can help your case; your attorney needs to be versed in the specific statutes and case law (previous rulings by higher courts) relevant to domestic violence and child abuse. Equally important, he or she needs to understand the tactics that abusers use in litigation, the types of psychological harm that unsupervised visitation can cause children who have witnessed abuse, and strategies for successfully pursuing cases in the long haul.

Your lawyer needs to be neither overly passive nor too aggressive; he or she has to have a good sense of when is the time to fight hard and when it's necessary to compromise and show flexibility. Some issues have to be let go of, even if they are upsetting ones, in order to increase your chances of victory on the most critical points related to your children's well-being. You and your lawyer need to present yourselves to the court as reasonable and willing to work things out for the good of your children, but at the same time not be pushovers. Show the judge that you respect him or her, but at the same time don't be afraid to point out legal errors. Some judges will handle your case more conscientiously if they sense that you are prepared to appeal decisions that are irresponsible or that ignore the law. In short, you need a lawyer who is clear-thinking and shrewd, knows the relevant laws, and is sympathetic to the plight of abused mothers and their children.

If you cannot find or afford an attorney you feel confident in, or if you are finding that much of your energy is going into fighting with your own lawyer, consider representing yourself. Although the first choice is certainly to have a good lawyer, going *pro se* or *pro per* (terms for being your own lawyer) is the next best option, while having an ineffective or uncaring lawyer comes in a distant last. If you are going to represent yourself successfully, though, you will have to be prepared to do the following:

- Spend time at a law library (sometimes available within courthouses) researching relevant laws and court cases.
- Find other women who have been through custody and visitation litigation who can guide and advise you.
- Try to find a lawyer whom you can pay on an hourly basis

to help you with basic procedural issues, such as how to file motions, how to give appropriate service, and how to request necessary hearings.

- Obtain the free book *Managing Your Divorce: A Guide for Battered Women* (see Resources, page 345).
- Use Internet resources for custodially challenged mothers.
- Be prepared for the fact that your ex-partner and/or his attorney will attempt to intimidate you, by such tactics as lying to you about the law or threatening to go to court to request even more frightening judgments than they have already asked for. For example, I was recently involved in a case in which the abuser, who was a lawyer himself and was *pro se,* informed his ex-girlfriend that he had appealed the judge's trial ruling on custody and division of assets—which was true—and proceeded to tell her that he did not have to give her the many thousands of dollars he had been ordered to pay her because "the judge's ruling is automatically put on hold when you file an appeal"—which is not true in their state.

Effective representation of yourself demands of you that you be courageous, willing to do extensive research and able to find good emotional support from friends or relatives for the stresses you are undergoing. On the positive side, you will save thousands of dollars that you can put to better purposes—such as hiring an expert witness for your trial.

Be careful whose advice you follow. Women repeatedly tell me of mistakes they have made in their court cases because someone who sounded knowledgeable, and who genuinely wanted to help, gave them bad advice. Consult broadly, move cautiously, and listen carefully to your own intuition.

Consider compromising on economic issues. The financial concessions that abused mothers are sometimes forced to make in order to keep custody of their children can be terribly unfair. Nonetheless, you may decide at times that it's best to let him get away with it. I recently spoke with a woman who went into court seeking an increase in child support, and her ex-husband retaliated furiously by filing for custody of the children, and ten months later he won. She had no idea of the risks involved in seeking the additional economic support that her children deserved. If you can trade alimony, assets, or part of your child support for sole legal and physical custody, and maybe even get him to agree to take only limited or supervised visitation, it might be worth it. However, be aware that there is no ironclad way to stop him from later seeking custody or increased visitation.

A general principal to follow when you have children with an abusive man is that if he is leaving you alone, and not harming your children, avoid doing anything that might rouse him into action against you.

Hold onto custody if you can, even if you are having serious difficulties. Sometimes a woman comes to feel so exhausted or beaten down that she is tempted to give custody to the abuser voluntarily, so she can stop fighting with him for a while and collect herself. But it is extraordinarily difficult to recover custody once you have given it up, even if the history of abuse toward you provides an understandable reason for doing so. So try to muster up another reserve of strength, and carry on, keeping your children in your care as much as possible.

Work hard to get along with people involved in your case. Depending on how your luck goes, you may sometimes have to deal with court employees, judges, custody evaluators, or mediators who are arrogant, disrespectful, irresponsible, or simply not terribly smart. You may be horrified when you see them getting sucked in by the same man who was so cruel to you—and perhaps to your children as well—and fawning over him as if he were the Father of the Year; some days you may feel an overwhelming urge to scream. But in the family court system, mothers tend to be judged by stricter standards than fathers, and a stark bias turns up in professional responses to women's anger. When a man expresses anger, or even somewhat explosive rage, court personnel may say, "What do you expect the guy to do? He feels like he's gotten such a raw deal, and he sees the court system as stacked against him." But faced with a furious woman, they tend to react with strong disapproval, and may begin to discredit her reports because she is "too angry" or "aggressive." So as unjust as it is, try to absorb the subtle insults and injustices from these professionals who have so much—too much—power over your destiny and that of your children, and wait until you can vent your fury alone or with loyal friends. Stand up for yourself as calmly and reasonably as you can, and stay focused on living to fight another day.

Face up to your own issues and deal forthrightly with them. You are unlikely to succeed in custody and visitation litigation if you are running away from your own problems with alcohol or drugs, emotional instability, or abusing or neglecting your children. Try to be honest with yourself and move quickly to seek help where you need it, such as substance abuse treatment or parent training courses. I do not mean that you should be carelessly honest with court personnel, as they may use your openness against you later, but do confront your issues rather than avoid them. In the long run your chances of keeping custody of your children and protecting them from abuse will grow if you yourself are growing.

Draw on a wide range of resources. In the back of this book is an extensive list of books, videos, toll-free numbers, and other resources for abused women who are involved in civil litigation. Reach out for help in every direction you can think of, and even more so if you are *pro se* or have a lawyer who is not carrying the ball well. Custody litigation can take a powerful toll on a woman's emotional health, especially when she is already carrying the effects of abuse, so reach out for professional help if you need it, making sure to work with a therapist who understands post-trauma symptoms and appropriate healing approaches.

Testify. I have been involved in several cases that were going badly until a trial or hearing finally occurred where the woman got a chance to testify, and that turned in a significantly better direction once the judge heard her tell her own story in detail. No strategy in family court is foolproof, but making your voice heard in a context where you get to speak for an hour, or for many hours, instead of for five minutes, can strengthen the position of the abused woman and weaken the ability of the abuser to put on a false front.

Focus on the long term. Many abusive men, though not all, eventually unravel in litigation, hitting a limit on how long they can convince everyone, including their own children, that they have no abuse problem. In some cases you may not be able to defeat an abusive man in court right now, but if you are able to create structures that give him some responsibility and accountability, he will sink himself over time. Keep working on yourself and on your relationships with your children, and focus on helping them heal and grow emotionally—which is the subject of the upcoming chapter.

Involve yourself in the growing movement demanding rights for protective parents. If your court case has gone badly, you can help yourself heal from this double experience of abuse—first by your partner and then by the court system—by getting involved in organizations that are fighting for the rights of mothers to protect their children from abuse. Your own struggle need not be in vain, because you can help to ensure that other women and children are not put through the hardships that you have endured. (See the organizations listed in Resources, page 345.)

Key Points to Remember

- Your chances of succeeding in protecting your children in family court increase if you go in with realistic preparation for the challenges you will face there.

- Family courts generally do not take domestic abuse seriously as a key factor in custody and visitation disputes, so you may have to fight hard to have your concerns properly heard and investigated.

- Find time to educate yourself and develop your abilities as your own advocate, even if you have a lawyer, and draw on a wide range of resources.

- You and your attorney can increase your effectiveness in court by reading *The Batterer as Parent* (see Resources, page 343) and drawing from the argument and the research summarized there.

Part IV

Children
Moving
Forward

Chapter Fourteen

Helping Your Children Heal

"For several years, my children kind of idealized him and drifted further and further away from me. But one by one they have seen through him, and I feel close again to all three of them now."

"My son has wild tantrums after he comes home from visits at his father's house, almost like he's possessed. I'm not sure what I should do when that happens."

"My children have gradually forgotten the hurtful things that happened, and I don't want to remind them, but I can still see the effects they carry. So how do I help them work through those wounds?"

"I don't know how to describe it—both of my daughters kind of crumbled before my eyes. It was the worst experience of my life. But, amazingly, they have both bounced back, and I can't believe how well they are doing now. They had some incredible inner strength I guess."

We now turn our attention to sources of hope and renewal, paths that you and your children can take out of the dark shadow cast by abusive men and toward healing and renewal. Survivors of abuse, whether children or adults, show an inspiring, at times awesome, capacity for recovery and rejuvenation. By offering some guidance, a great deal of patience, and above all an abundance of love, you can help your children escape the oppression of life with an abusive man, and enable them to overcome the emotional wounds of witnessing his frightening and demeaning behavior. You and your children are partners in healing, moving together toward freedom, mutual respect, security, and kindness.

Where Does Healing Come From?

I am haunted by some of the heartrending accounts from abused women that I have listened to over the years, stories of sweet, loving boys who have turned bitter and aggressive, spirited girls who have become withdrawn or self-destructive, children who have grown to dislike themselves or look down on their mothers. But these lives are not over. There are other stories that I hear from mothers, inspiring examples of hope and renewal, of the breaking down of divisions, of natural allies finding their way back to one another, of hearts growing whole again:

• Ursula told me of her three-year-old daughter Inez who had said to her, "I hate my life," and who had pulled away from all contact with other children, sitting by herself even when her best friends were playing together nearby. Yet within just a few weeks after the court finally agreed that visits between Inez and her father needed to be supervised—following nine months of efforts by Ursula to get the judge to take seriously her daughter's deterioration—Inez began to enthusiastically join groups of active children, joking and laughing again as though she had been reborn.

• Katie's teenage daughter Holly had faded away from her mother emotionally, becoming increasingly superior and critical and ultimately opting to go live at her father's home. But a little over a year later, when Holly's father was hospitalized for a week so that she had to go back home, she spilled out to Katie how intimidating her father behaved toward her, and the role her fear of him had played in her decision to move. "He wanted me to come live with him," she said through her tears, "and he was making my life miserable for refusing, so I didn't know what to do." This courageous leap toward truth-telling showed that Holly had never really given up—and demonstrated how critical it was that Katie had kept reaching out to her no matter how difficult it became to sustain the effort.

• Tracy described how all three of her children, a daughter and two younger sons, had grown fearful, hypervigilant, and aggressive with each other in the years leading up to their parents' divorce, during which their father, Peter, was physically violent to Tracy and constantly verbally abusive to the children. The relationship between Peter and their oldest daughter had descended to constant screaming back and forth as the girl had taken on the role of trying to protect her younger brothers from Dad's put-downs and explosiveness. But after Tracy and Peter broke up, Tracy managed to help her children back to calm and happiness, partly thanks to the support and assistance of her new partner, who became a loving stepfather to her children and showed them a different model of how to be a man.

The research on children's resilience provides additional reasons not to lose heart. It demonstrates clearly that children *can* recover, not just from exposure to abuse, but from all kinds of traumatic experiences, and that their chances increase further when they have the opportunity to live in safe, healthy environments and are given access to healing experiences.

My professional work and the published research on children's recovery both point to the same overarching point:

The single most important avenue for your children's recovery is their relationship with you.

QUESTION #16:
How can I help my children heal from their pain?

Many an abused woman has said to me, "I don't know how to help my children, except to give them a loving home and encourage them to believe in themselves"—as if that were a small thing. But in reality the kindness and affection you bring to your children, the example you set for them of sharing and listening rather than bullying and selfishness, and the safe haven you give them in a home without violence or intimidation—if you are able to get to such a home—these are the most precious gifts you can give to your children. Being a good parent is one of the most demanding jobs a person can undertake, even without the challenges of helping children with their abuse-related wounds. Don't ever underestimate the important, intelligent, and exhausting work you are doing by being a mother, striving to bring a healthy next generation into the world despite all the shrapnel that your abusive partner has strewn across the landscape.

Children heal through relationship. Their connection to you teaches them the power of love, which is ultimately so much more satisfying and life-giving than the power to abuse or dominate. Your love brings them a sense of their own goodness in a deeper way than words of praise could ever do. Your encouragement and faith in them leads them to self-confidence—not overnight, but in time. Your assistance in working out their fights with each other gives them the knowledge that bullying is not the answer, that people can listen to each other's needs and feelings and work out solutions that are good for everyone. Your insistence that they treat you with respect models self-respect for them. And at the same time, your willingness to listen and respond to their grievances provides a model of flexibility and of accepting responsibility for one's actions. You are probably already contributing far more to your children's recovery and healthy development than you ever give yourself credit for.

Always be on the lookout for ways to enter into their world. Play sports with them even if you feel you aren't competent at them. Ask them about their projects or fantasy games and take part in them. Even if your time is fairly limited, every effort you make will communicate to your children that you really want to know who they are, and that they can share their lives and thoughts with you.

Remembering that you are your children's bedrock, you can move into constructing a healing environment for them. Children can best build a healthy outlook on life and recover their happiness in an atmosphere where as many of the following elements as possible are present:

Key Elements of Children's Healing

- A close relationship with their mother (regardless of the child's age or sex).
- Safety.
- Good relationships with siblings.
- Connection to other loved ones, to peers, to self, and to creation.

- Opportunities to talk about events and express feelings.
- Opportunities to release distressing feelings.
- Good information about abuse.

I have already explored the importance of their relationship to you, so I will continue by examining each item in the box above.

Safety. Children have trouble healing from past events if they continue to be exposed to new acts of abuse. Seek strategies to make the abuse in your home stop, whether by using police, getting friends and relatives to pressure your partner to deal with his problem, leaving him for a period of time, or leaving for good if you safely can.

If you yourself are contributing to your children's lack of safety because you hit or threaten them, or you rage in scary ways at them, or you drink too much, or you get involved with new dating partners who aren't good choices, make it a top priority to get assistance for yourself. Consider such resources as programs for abused women, Alcoholics Anonymous, and parental stress hotlines (see Resources). Be honest with yourself about your problems, and remember that it is okay to need help.

If for any number of reasons you can neither make the abuser stop nor get away safely—for now—by all means keep helping your children in as many other ways as you can, using the suggestions in this chapter and throughout this book. You *can* make a difference to your children even within your current circumstances. But keep the dream of safety and freedom alive.

A final word on safety: If you are reading this book as a woman who is no longer with her abusive partner, your children need you to do everything in your power to ensure that your next relationship does not expose them to more verbal or physical abuse. Any re-creation of their earlier experiences could represent a big setback for their recovery. Familiarize yourself with the warning signs of abusive men (which you can find in chapter 5 of *Why Does He Do That?*), and take your time about getting involved with a new man, even if—or perhaps *especially* if—you are feeling desperate for companionship or financial assistance. Women who are still recovering from the emotional devastation that abuse brings are not always in the clearest state of mind to make good choices about a new partner. Take time for your own healing and make sure you start any new relationship with your eyes wide open.

Good sibling relationships. If you have more than one child, be aware of what a deep well of support and strength siblings can be for each other, even at a young age. Insist that they be kind and respectful to each other, model for them ways to be loving and supportive, and help them work out their conflicts. At the same time, don't try to require them always to feel close to each other, and do make it acceptable in your home for children to express anger to each other as long they don't use violence or put-downs. They will remain closer in the long term if you give them some room to have bad feelings toward each other, and help them talk their disputes out; given the kinds of tensions between siblings that exposure to abuse causes, ignoring their mutual resentments won't help.

Connection. Abuse causes a rupture in children's experience. The world begins to feel like a hostile place, secrecy blocks communication and truth-telling, distortions of perception and reality creep in. The child starts to feel separate from others, disconnected from nature and from creation, and distant from himself or herself. You can help heal these ruptures in several ways:

Connection to others: Support your children's loving connections to emotionally healthy relatives, family friends, and other loved ones. Keep photographs visible around your home of their favorite people, and have your children call or write letters. Have them remember people who are central to their lives in their evening prayers, or make up stories to tell them in which they and their loved ones are characters. Facilitate opportunities for them to play with other children, ideally with age mates of both sexes. Show them in your words and actions that you value their love for other children and adults, and work to keep those connections strong.

As I discussed earlier, this goal can be a challenging one for mothers whose partners isolate them by forbidding them to go out, denying them money for gas or entertainment, or retaliating against them for seeing friends or relatives. But don't give up.

Connection to self: Value your child's interests, hobbies, and fantasies, seeing him or her as a unique individual. Stay away from painting a child with a broad brush with statements such as "Ellen only likes to play with girlie toys," or "Vincent is the artistic one in the family." If you make room for all the different facets of each child's character—and children are far too complex to reduce to simple terms such as "brainy" or "athletic"—your children will have an easier time knowing themselves well.

Treat your children with respect and encourage them to treat *themselves* with respect by standing up for themselves, caring for themselves well, and speaking positively of themselves. At the same time, don't deny your children's frustrations or weaknesses. When a child says, for example, "I'm no good at drawing," avoid sweeping those feelings away by saying, "Oh sure you are, you're a wonderful drawer." Instead ask, "Are you feeling bad about how you draw? Would you like some help with it?" This response helps children feel connected to all aspects of who they are and of what they feel, rather than believing that they have to hide or deny aspects that they don't like or are struggling with.

Encourage children to participate in vigorous physical activities, such as dancing, running, or playing sports. Sustained exercise releases stress, strengthens children's self-confidence, and causes chemical reactions in the body that can elevate mood. Physical activity also connects children to their own bodies, further grounding them in a strong sense of self.

Connection to creation: Seek ways to bring spiritual connection to your children through participation in a faith community, through outings in nature if possible, and through introducing them to books, music, and art that bring them experiences of beauty, universality, and humane values. Be careful, though, about raising them in a religion that primarily teaches rigid or unquestioning adherence to a dogma or set of rules, as these messages can reinforce the authoritarian values that their abusive father has modeled for them. Try to make sure instead that their religious training focuses on introducing them to the joy of living a rich life, to the importance of deeply held values and treating human beings and the world well, and to the love of a community. Help your child find sources of hope and strength in your faith. If you are atheist or agnostic, you can still seek ways to bring your children a sense of connection to the wider world, to nature, and to beauty, thereby helping them to heal the ruptures that abuse causes.

Opportunities to talk about events and express feelings. I have covered this topic in earlier chapters, but I will add a few more points here. First, children cannot resolve complicated feelings in one or two conversations. You will find that they need to discuss certain topics or events over and over again, and some days you may feel impatient and be tempted to say, "But we've already covered this so many times!" They may ask you repeatedly, for example, whether their father hates them (because of extreme behaviors they witnessed), or whether you hate them (because he told them you do). If your partner has moved out, your children may ask you every night for months whether "a monster" is going to come in the home and get them; what they are really expressing are their fears that Dad will return, which are mixed often with confusing feelings of missing him and wishing that he *would* return, so that sorting out all those conflicting emotions takes time. Go over these points with your children as often as they feel the need to, offering them reassurance and validation each time.

Second, allow your children to express deeply bad feelings. If a child tells you that she wishes she could kill her father, or that he hates his sister, resist the temptation to cut the child off with, "Oh no you don't, don't say that, you love your father (or your sister)!" Instead say, "You must feel very angry to say that. Tell me what has made you so angry." Your children's deep bitterness is real and can't be chased away—but it *can* be healed, if they are taught that those rageful feelings are okay to express and process. When children hold in their resentful and bitter feelings, they start to think that those feelings *are part of who they are,* and so they come to believe that they themselves are bad. If they can get them out, on the other hand, they are able to move back toward love.

Last, talking is not the only way children express feelings, and for some it isn't even the primary way. You can ask your child to draw you a picture that shows you her feelings about an event or a person, to act out his feelings or memories with puppets or doll house figures, or to make up an emotionally expressive song while strumming a toy guitar. Any of these approaches is as valuable as talking for breaking the silence and loneliness that surrounds abuse.

Opportunities to release feelings. Releasing feelings is not the same as expressing them; both are critical to healing, and neither can substitute for the other. Children release painful emotions through:

- Throwing tantrums, having "fits."
- Crying, especially loud sobbing with lots of tears.
- Raging, stomping their feet, and making other angry movements.
- Screaming or trembling from fear.
- Laughing, especially hysterical or extended laughter.

Tantrums

> **QUESTION #17:**
> **What should I do when one of my children completely "loses it" emotionally?**

Mothers tend to get upset by their children's tantrums, which may come once or twice a day for a few days following a scary, confusing, or guilt-inducing event. When parents split up, I commonly hear of children who have tantrums after returning from visitations with their abusive fathers, even if he has not hurt them in any overt way during the weekend. Tantrums are widely misunderstood as a form of bad behavior, and parenting guides sometimes recommend that you ignore them, stating, "If the child does not receive any attention for the tantrum, the behavior will gradually stop being repeated." But for children who have had traumatic experiences, tantrums can be an important cathartic release. You can assist your child through a tantrum by doing the following:

- Offer your loving attention, and name for your child what he or she appears to be feeling (e.g., "You sound angry, you look scared," etc.).
- Keep your child away from objects or hazards that could cause harm.
- Do not permit your child to break things, throw things, or hit anyone. (The only exception to this should be cases where you give the child explicit permission, as in, "Here's something you can heave," or "You can hit this pillow, but not me or yourself.") Put something within reach that the

child can pound or kick without causing harm or getting
hurt, such as a couch cushion or a mattress.

* Allow the tantrum to go on, with your caring attention,
until it ends by itself. (The tantrum may end by the child
switching into crying, or may include crying throughout.)

For most parents, the above suggestions represent a startlingly
new approach to children's tantrums, requiring the abandonment
of previous habits of either ignoring the child or criticizing him
or her for the tantrum and demanding that the "behavior" stop.
If you treat a tantrum as a healing event, in which your role is to
be a loving witness to the child's distress and to keep him or her
from getting hurt or doing any kind of damage, you are likely to
observe a surprising outcome: Your son or daughter comes out of
the tantrum feeling relieved and refreshed, ready to cooperate with
you, and in buoyant spirits. Tantrums are a natural emotional healing process in children.

Odd as it may seem, most children can learn to follow your
rules about how they can throw their tantrums, once they discover that you are not going to stifle them. I have observed countless times, for example, how a child who is told, "You can't punch
me but you can hit this cushion," will turn immediately to pound-
ing the soft, safe object. (Note, though, that an adolescent who is
having a tantrum can be impossible to manage or channel, so you
may need to reach more quickly for professional assistance.)

If you can hold your child during part or all of a tantrum, he
or she may feel more secure. Tantrums are sometimes indications
of a child who is quite frightened and feels that some aspect of life
is spinning out of control. Express your love in the midst of the
tantrum, and try to let the child see that you are not afraid of his
or her feelings; in the long term, this will help the child feel less
afraid also. Come down physically to your child's level during a

tantrum, perhaps sitting on the floor so you don't tower over him or her, and so your support feels close.

Many tantrums begin when the child does not get something that he or she is demanding, and in most cases it is best to lovingly refuse to accede to the demand. By holding the line on your original decision, you send the message to your child that tantrums are for releasing emotions, not for creating a scene to get your way. Offer the child constructive solutions or alternatives; if he or she angrily refuses your suggestions and continues the tantrum, that is probably a sign that the tantrum needs more time.

Tantrums can be quite wearing and upsetting for the parent, especially when they go on for a long time. Remind yourself that you are not a bad parent—despite the voice of your partner or ex-partner, who may insist that the tantrums occur because you don't handle the child well. In reality, tantrums can be a sign that the child feels safe with you, just the way adults who don't like their jobs tend to hold it together at work, but then fall apart once they are safely home. One mother said she says a sort of mantra to herself during her daughter's tantrums, "Don't get mad, don't give in."

When some time has passed after the tantrum, perhaps the next day, sit alone with your child and speak in a loving way about what happened. Ask the child if he or she is now able to explain what was underlying the tantrum, and gently restate limits regarding behavior. Some mothers report that this approach has succeeded in making it possible for children to express feelings that they were having a hard time putting into words or were afraid to reveal.

Crying

Crying is commonly misinterpreted as an *expression* of grief or fear, when actually it is a form of *release and healing* for those feelings. As with tantrums, children who have suffered trauma or serious losses may cry hard and long as much as one to two times per day, or even more. Frequent crying is nothing to worry about in itself—unless you can't figure out what is upsetting the child—and can actually be a sign of healing and recovery.

If you permit your children to cry deeply and for a long time, they will actually come to cry *less* over time; a child who starts crying a dozen times in the same day is trying repeatedly to have that one cathartic, sobbing "fit" that will relieve his or her sadness. As you stop your child from crying each time, you are actually setting yourself up for a hard day, as he or she will keep finding small excuses to try again. Once the child cries out the feelings that are causing the distress, the rest of the day will tend to move toward better spirits and more cooperativeness. (Sometimes food and sleep can help, too, of course.)

Children get the most relief from a kind of crying that is deep and long, with lots of sobbing and tears. Don't be surprised or concerned if your child cries for fifteen minutes or even half an hour a day. (Though you may notice if you watch the clock that what feels like a half hour of crying usually turns out to be only about ten minutes.) Children who are held and loved through their upset will cry longer and harder and will show more noticeable benefits from the release, switching at the end of the crying into high spirits and energy, sometimes quite abruptly.

Parents are sometimes confused by the fact that children so often cry *after a source of distress has passed.* You may observe, for example, that your child gets frightened by a strange dog but doesn't burst into tears until the dog has run away. You may feel tempted to say, "Don't cry, honey, everything's okay, the dog didn't hurt you and now it's gone." But the child is crying precisely *because* the dog has left and it is now safe to release the fear of attack that he or she went through.

This dynamic—that is, the fact that most healing takes place after an upsetting experience has ended—is one important reason why your children are having their tantrums and their deep cries with you, not with their father. Children will, for example, smile and laugh their way through a weekend visitation with an abusive man during which they feel quite unsafe, and then fall to pieces within minutes of arriving back at home to the security of being with Mom. Understanding that this response is normal puts you in a better position to be there for your children when they need you.

Boys need to cry just as much as girls do, and it will make them stronger, not weaker. One of the best ways to make sure that your son doesn't "turn out like his father" is to make sure that he has safe opportunities with you to have long, deep cries without fear of shame or ridicule.

Research shows, by the way, that crying is important to the mental and physical health of adults as well, and that a large majority of both men and women feel significantly better after having a good cry. So seek opportunities for deep emotional releases for yourself as well.

Raging

Your children have plenty of reason to be angry. They are enraged at their father for being mean to you; at having to live in a scary and unpredictable atmosphere; at you for not finding a way to make the abuse stop (and you need to try to accept this anger while also not blaming yourself); at themselves for not being superheroes who bring everyone in the family to safety. Anger can be an especially hard emotion for your children to express and release in constructive ways; from observing your partner's conduct, they come to feel that anger is a *bad feeling* because it appears to them to cause abuse. So they will need reassurance from you that anger is a natural and acceptable emotion, and that it does not cause verbal or physical violence—anger is just an *excuse* that violent people use to justify their actions.

Anger can have additional complications for your children. First, their fear of your partner may have led them to repress their angry feelings for years. On some level they are aware of how much rage they have built up, and so may be afraid that if they let any of it out they will burst into flames from the accumulated force of it all. If you have a child who has learned to stuff anger away or turn it all against himself or herself (such as by self-injuring behavior), you may need to say explicitly sometimes, "It's okay for you to feel how angry you are, it won't hurt you and you'll get through it with my help."

Second, the abuser's model may condition them to believe that bullying people or acting aggressively toward objects is the way to release anger. If one of your children shows this behavior pattern, you may have to repeatedly set limits on aggressive behavior, explaining each time that anger and destructiveness are two different things, and offering the child channels for positive release of anger.

Children release much of their anger through crying. However, they also need some direct release of anger through furious talking or yelling, along with angry motions such as waving their arms in the air and stomping their feet. Make sure not to imitate these behaviors or do anything to make the child ashamed of being enraged, and insist that siblings show respect for each other's angry releases. If a child is calling you names or speaking disrespectfully to you while storming angrily, say, "You can be angry with me and yell and stomp, but if you call me those things I am going to walk away. If you can be angry with me without saying disrespectful things, I can stay here and help you through it." Most children will gradually adopt constructive anger discharge if they are guided into that option, since they would rather have your company as they go through their rage than be left alone with it. They will periodically test these limits, naturally, and you will sometimes have to leave or impose a consequence.

In some cases, a mother finds that a child is simply not willing to release anger safely, so she is forced to try to prohibit her child from raging, seeking professional assistance if possible. If your child's anger is too frightening for you, or doesn't stay within the bounds you have imposed, don't push yourself to handle it alone.

Deep Releases of Fear

Children who have been exposed to scary behavior by the abusive man can have recurring difficulties with nightmares or "night terrors," where the child is awake or half-awake and badly frightened, sometimes imagining that there are monsters in the room or that he or she is in a different location. One mother told me, for example, of an evening when her three-year-old daughter had just returned from a weekend visit with her abusive ex-husband. The girl woke up to use the toilet in the middle of the night and panicked while in the bathroom, shaking her head around and opening her eyes wide. Her mother tried to calm her by saying, "Everything is okay now, you're back home with Mommy," and the girl answered her loudly, "No, I'm not, I'm at Dad's house, I'm at Dad's house!", continuing to whimper until her mother held her tightly.

When your children begin to express or release deep fear, they need for you to appear completely solid. If your son or daughter is "freaking out," look at him or her with an expression that conveys love and concern but not fear, and make it clear through your tone that you have the situation completely under control—even if you are not entirely convinced that you really do. Give reassurance in a soft voice, saying, for example, "You've just been through a really scary experience (or dream), but everything is okay now and you will feel better soon." When children scream or tremble, move in close, holding them unless they are thrashing around, but don't attempt to stop the release; screaming, trembling, whimpering, and thrashing can be important healing mechanisms for feelings of terror, and will help the child recover more quickly.

One mother told me that she says to her daughter, "If you tell me all about your nightmare, that will give it to me, and then I can take care of it for you." Other parents report success with relieving children's fears through playing games that help them gain a sense of mastery, such as defeating a monster or locking a giant in a cage.

Laughter

Laughter is a physiological process through which children and adults can relieve fear and anxiety, as multiple studies have shown. People sometimes find themselves emitting peals of laughter at times that don't seem appropriate—at funerals, for example—and then may berate themselves, "How can I be so uncaring? A few minutes ago I was so upset, so why am I suddenly laughing now? That's terrible!" But it isn't terrible; in times of high stress, laughter naturally alternates with periods of crying or just plain feeling sad or scared. The tensions that are released through laughter bring strength and hope. If you know ways to get your children involved with humor during difficult times, and especially if you can periodically get the family into uncontrollable laughing fits, you will see that relaxation follows and tension dissipates.

A few words of caution. Avoid humor that makes fun of anyone in the family (except in extremely good-natured ways), as the person who is the target of the laughter is likely to feel quite hurt, even if he or she superficially laughs along in order to appear tough. Equally important, don't try to push a child into laughter who isn't ready for it. For example, children who are crying should never be joked with, as they will feel that you don't take their sadness or hurt seriously and are making fun of them for letting their pain show; the result will be that next time they may decide to hold their sadness in instead of exposing themselves, an outcome you urgently need to avoid. As I explained earlier, crying is necessary to healing, so if you jostle a child out of tears with humor you may short-circuit his or her recovery.

All of the forms of emotional release that I've described here have their most potent healing impact when they go to a deep level and continue for an extended period of time. They also commonly run together, so that it is entirely normal for a child who is laughing wildly to suddenly burst into deep sobbing, or vice versa. You may notice that yawns are mixed in as well, even when the child is not at all tired; yawning plays its own role in the release of emotional stress.

Should I Worry About My Child's Releases?

Anytime your child's emotional condition is causing you serious concern, or you feel it is too much for you to take on alone, consult a professional. However, there are a few points to be aware of that could ease your mind. First, a child who is releasing emotions deeply is generally one who is doing fairly well. Children (and adults) who are depressed, for example, actually tend to cry less often, or to cry frequently but in a way that is superficial, intermittent, and unsatisfying; depression actually makes it difficult for people to have deep, sobbing, cathartic cries.

Watching a child in a deep tantrum or night terror is scary for adults. Children who have experienced trauma can appear possessed when they enter into deep releases, perhaps yelling things out that sound extreme or bizarre and becoming hysterical. However, these processes are normal ones. The more worrisome signs to watch for are:

- Is the child incapable of any self-control during rages or tantrums, so that harm is being done to self, to others, or to important objects?
- Does the child continue to exhibit extreme thinking or to

make bizarre or illogical comments even after the emotional release has stopped? (For example, a child may insist during a deep cry or tantrum that he or she is somewhere or someone else, but if this belief continues after the child is calm again, professional help should be sought.)

- Does the child seem more depressed, withdrawn, or self-destructive after the release ends, rather than appearing unburdened, energetic, or happy?

Although studies indicate that most people benefit from deep emotional discharge, not everyone does, and a few individuals even find that their emotional condition gets worse through releasing their feelings rather than better. If your child's release mechanisms don't seem to bring him or her any healing or relief, trust your instincts and seek professional help.

Of course, if your children are reporting new injurious events, as opposed to processing long-standing feelings, your assistance to them will have to include seeking ways to protect them from ongoing harm.

Good information about abuse. Children need to know that they are not at fault for what happened to their mother; feelings of guilt can be a great preoccupation for those who witness abuse. Children need to know that their mother is also not to blame, and that the perpetrator is entirely responsible for his own actions. They also need to be offered, at an age-appropriate level of detail, insight into the dynamics of abuse, including typical excuses and tactics of manipulation used by abusers, and the fact that the goal of abusive behavior is power and control.

A closing thought about the basic elements of healing: *Ask your children what they feel they need.* Parents, and other adults, often forget that children and teenagers have knowledge and insights into their own feelings and recovery, and can sometimes give us crucial guidance on how to best help them, if we remember to ask.

Seeking Professional Assistance

The first place to begin looking for professional help for your children is your nearest program for abused women. Programs typically have a children's advocate on staff, and counseling groups for children are sometimes available. In some cases, groups for mothers and for children are scheduled at the same time, so you can attend together and compare notes after the meetings. An advocate recently told me of a case in which children were in the custody of their abusive father, but slipped out each Wednesday night to a domestic violence support group for children, telling Dad that they were going to the library. Their mother reports that their participation in this group was the key to their emotional survival, and eventual recovery, in the face of their exposure to their father. Research interviews with children of abused women have found that they are especially eager to have the opportunity to meet and speak with other boys and girls who have lived with frightening or violent fathers.

If you live in an area where therapists are available who work with children, and you have insurance or personal resources to pay for their services, therapy is another option. If you feel that your child's emotional or behavioral struggles have become too much for you to handle alone, getting a therapist involved with your child is a way for *you* to get more support, as the professional can share insights with you about your child's needs and hurts, and can offer strategies for you to use in managing destructive or self-destructive behaviors.

The success of your child's therapy will depend partly on the quality of rapport that you have with the therapist. Ask your program for abused women for any referrals they can offer, and interview a number of therapists before making a choice, seeking one who talks to you with equality and respect. You and the therapist need to be a team working together on your child's behalf. Avoid therapists who talk down to you, who make snap judgments about your child's circumstances, or who do not listen carefully to your knowledge and expertise about your own child. A wise professional remembers that the parent is the person who knows her child best.

Ask any therapists you interview to describe their background on trauma and on domestic abuse, and ask them to explain where they think abuse comes from. Listen carefully for language that blames women for the behavior of abusive men, that assumes that abused women are "codependent" or "enablers," or that criticizes you for the effects your partner's behavior has had on your children. Inquire as to whether you will be included in some of the sessions; when children have been exposed to a man who abuses their mother, it is advisable for the therapist to devote a substantial portion of the sessions to working with the mother and child *together,* so as to strengthen the relationship and improve communication, helping to heal the wedges that abusers drive between mothers and children.

The therapist's office should be an environment that appeals to children, with plenty of toys available in a colorful and comfortable space. The therapist needs to have the ability to play with the child, as children do not generally wish to spend extended periods of time with a counselor "talking about serious stuff." For children to benefit from the therapeutic process, they need to develop a fondness for the therapist and a real connection, which generally has to be developed through participating together in a variety of activities, such as artwork, games, and eating snacks. They need reassurance, especially as they get older, that their confidentiality will be respected, and that the therapist won't tell their parents what they discuss except in emergencies.

You can find more information about working with child therapists in chapter 13, under the heading "When You Have Concerns About Child Sexual Abuse," page 248. Many of the suggestions offered there apply to all kinds of domestic abuse cases whether or not boundary concerns are present.

Does My Child Need Medication?

We live in a period of lively controversy over the frequency with which children are being placed on psychiatric medications for emotional or behavioral problems. There are particular concerns being expressed in professional journals about the risk of misdiagnosis of children who are in distress from abuse they have witnessed, and who may be treated as having attention deficit, hyperactivity, or oppositional/defiant disorders. Unless your child's behavior is so destructive that home life or school life has become unmanageable, the child is endangering you or your other children, or he or she is suicidal or self-destructive, try various strategies for helping your child to heal before resorting to medication. This chapter and other sections of this book offer a range of approaches to fostering your children's recovery. In addition, many therapists are willing to work with you on strategies for helping your child function in a healthier way, usually involving a combination of techniques that the therapist uses in counseling sessions with your child and others that you apply at home.

If you reach the decision, in consultation with a professional, that medication is the best option for your child, continue working on other healing approaches simultaneously, so that over time the medication can be reduced or phased out. The mothers who speak most positively to me about their children's experiences with medication are those who have used it on a temporary basis to get the child and the family through times of acute crisis; medication can play an important positive role in some cases but is not a substitute for healing and safety for children. (Nor is it a substitute for children's need to learn that they are responsible for their actions; this is noticeable in the case of adolescent boys, for example, who may have learned excuses that they have heard their abusive fathers use, such as, "I can't control myself when I get violent urges.")

What if I Can't Find Good Professional Help?

If you are unable to locate services for children who have witnessed abuse, through a program for abused women, and do not have luck finding a helpful therapist either, think of yourself as filling the role of therapist to your child. Many psychologists agree with this approach, especially for young children. By taking the steps laid out in this book, you are largely filling the role of what a therapist would do.

When Children Don't Remember What Happened

One of the more common questions I hear from mothers is what to do when the effects of witnessing abuse—or of being abused directly—are still evident in the child, but he or she no longer recalls the incidents. It is generally best not to remind children about distressing events they have forgotten unless they come to you asking to know, or if you have to tell them for their own safety. (For example, I have had cases in which the abuser resurfaced after disappearing for a number of years and was awarded visitation by a court, in which case the children had to be reminded, for their own protection, that their father had a violent history and that they needed to be ready to flee or call for help if he became explosive.)

But children do not necessarily need concrete memories in

order to process their feelings. They commonly project their fears or sadnesses onto other situations, real or imagined, and then work out their distresses in a symbolic way. I hear repeatedly from mothers about children who develop exaggerated fears of monsters after seeing their father's violence, or who have dreams of being abducted by strangers after overhearing their father threatening to sue for custody, or who develop peculiar preoccupations or compulsions. These "symptoms" can actually play a positive role, as they provide a channel for the child's distress to be worked out without him or her having to speak directly about, or even remember, horrifying or heartbreaking acts of violence or cruelty. Your child is unconsciously using these phobias and obsessions as a way to work through deep emotional injuries.

You can create symbolic experiences for your child by making up stories or using children's books that capture aspects of the child's distress. A child who, for example, was once blocked by the abuser from getting to you when he or she was terrified may love to hear stories over and over again about a child who gets lost in the woods but eventually gets back safely. A child who was verbally abused by his or her father can read and respond to a book about animals who are teasing and ganging up on one little animal, and who later in the story realize that what they are doing is wrong. When you are making up stories yourself, have the main character express feelings that your child has not been able to, thereby acting as a voice for him or her and helping with the naming and identifying of emotions. Stories work best when they illustrate an underlying emotion that the child has struggled with, but when the events in the story are not so similar to what actually happened as to directly trigger memories of distressing events.

Using stories and symbolic play may also help protect the mother who is involved in custody and visitation litigation. One of the tragedies of family court battles with abusive men is that children can lose important healing opportunities; for example, mothers who help their children talk through their feelings about abuse that they witnessed can be accused of attempting to "alienate" their children from the father. The mother can thereby be forced by the court to leave her child emotionally isolated, and to avoid facilitating the child's recovery. A mother can escape this dilemma to some extent by helping her children attach their feelings to fictional characters or events, indirectly letting them know that she understands their feelings and that they have a safe place with her to work through those injuries.

A final word on healing: A great collection of wise, practical, and supportive information is available in Cynthia Monahon's book *Children and Trauma: A Parent's Guide to Helping Children Heal* (see Resources, page 343). Even if you aren't sure that your children's distress rises to the level that would be termed "trauma," you will find important guidance in the pages of Dr. Monahon's book.

Key Points to Remember

- Emotional damage is rarely, if ever, permanent. The potential for recovery is always present.
- Children—and adults—have powerful inherent healing capabilities if they are just given the opportunity and support to use them.
- You can facilitate your children's healing in powerful ways, especially if you are simultaneously getting good support for your own recovery.
- Healing takes time, and involves many ups and downs and setbacks along the way. Keep your faith.

Chapter Fifteen

Empowering Your Children

"My daughter just swallows everything he says, but my son sees right through him. I wish she could recognize the abuse the way her brother does."

"My eleven-year-old is never home. It's almost like she doesn't live here. I don't know why she's always off somewhere else."

"My teenage son is getting pretty big, and one day he told my husband that if he ever lays a hand on me again, he'll 'beat the crap' out of him. My husband hasn't dared touch me again, although he still verbally abuses me."

"I'm so proud of my children. They have been through so much, but I'll tell you, they don't let anyone push them around."

Your child's emotional wounds, deep though they may be, are only a small part of who he or she is. Alongside each sadness, every fear, all the clouds of pain and confusion, there is also intelligence, toughness, quick thinking in a crisis, imagination, creativity. Helping children heal is not only about repairing damage, the way a body rebuilds after an accident or an infection, but also about recognizing the resilience in your child, the impetus toward emotional health and love of life, and helping the child maintain and strengthen those currents.

I hear from women who feel that they spend their days cleaning up messes—mostly emotional ones—that their abusive partners have made, helping their children put themselves back together each time their father shakes up their world with insults or intimidation, directed at them or at Mom. Mothers sometimes say they wish they could armor their children so their partner couldn't hurt them. Even though you can't truly prevent all hurt to your children in this way, there is a great deal that you can do to make them less vulnerable and help build them into strong, self-directed people. In the pages ahead you will learn ways to guide your children past helplessness and toward thinking for themselves, but without making them harden as people. These steps can, in turn, speed the healing processes I describe in chapter 14; empowerment supports emotional healing, and emotional healing in turn supports empowerment, so attention to both processes makes for vibrant, animated recovery.

Teaching Critical Thinking

Picture the following scene: Your children are watching television together while you perform various tasks about the house. As you pass by them at one point, a beer commercial catches your attention. In the ad (this is a real one), several men are complaining about their friend Gary because he treats his wife so well; he speaks to her kindly, brings her flowers, meets his responsibilities. One of the men declares, "Gary is ruining it for the rest of us," and they all wholeheartedly concur; because of Gary's respectful behavior, *their* wives are starting to demand better from them. So what do the men decide to do? The best course of action, they agree, is to *beat Gary up*! We don't know exactly what happens next, but at the end of the commercial Gary has decided to be "one of the boys," and they are all standing around in happy camaraderie, drinking a certain brand of beer and laughing together.

As the commercial draws to a close, you wonder what to say to your children. Do you express your outrage to them about what they just watched? Do you say nothing, hoping that the commercial didn't really register on their brains? Do you ask them whether *they* notice anything offensive about the scene that was just dramatized?

The answer is that children need to be taught to think critically about the messages they take in from their social surroundings. The process of healing is a battle not just to save the heart and the soul, but also the mind. The cruelty and degradation, the bullying and arrogance that children witness works its way not only into their feelings, but also into their ways of thinking. So children need to unravel the ways in which the abusive man has invaded their minds, developing a strength of insight that will help them analyze and reject abusive values.

QUESTION #18:
How can I keep my children from being manipulated by him?

Attempting to directly teach children to think critically about their father is a project that often fails, however. They feel defensive when you speak negatively about him, and they can come to think, "Well, both parents badmouth each other, so they're equally bad." At the same time, you do want to equip your children to see through their father's manipulations, and to recognize abusive or domineering behavior as wrong. So how do you resolve this dilemma? One answer is:

Teach your children to think critically and analytically on all fronts in their lives.

If you help them develop the ability to look below surface appearances, to ponder what is motivating people's actions, to not believe everything that adults tell them, and to distinguish fairness and respect from injustice, they will become able to recognize your partner's abusiveness without a word from you. And they are more likely to voice their complaints about him out loud to you if they don't feel they have to defend against *your* bad feelings toward him.

Media Literacy

In our times, the easiest way to teach children to think critically—because the opportunities are so plentiful—is to make your children "media literate," helping them recognize the values and attitudes that are being promoted, intentionally or not, by TV, movies, video games, rock videos, rock lyrics, and advertising. Media literacy has an additional benefit for your children, in that many messages they receive from society reinforce the destructive model the abusive man has set for them. As I explored in *Why Does He Do That?*, our media are full of depictions that indicate to children that violence and domination define what it means to be a real man (look at professional wrestling, for example); that a woman who says no to sex actually wants the man to keep pressuring her (a recurring theme in rock videos); that women are to blame for men's abuse of them (consider the lyrics to Eminem's "Kim," for example); and countless other similar messages. These unhealthy role models are especially insidious for those boys and girls who are already struggling with the question of who is responsible for the aggression that occurs in their homes; the last thing they need is to see that their heroes consider violent or abusive behavior normal, justifiable, or even funny.

Advertising

Training your children to analyze the tricks of the advertising trade is a prime place to begin, because advertising is essentially a form of manipulation; the sellers want you to buy their product or service to make money, but they want you to feel that their desire is to enrich your life. (Just as many abusive men try to create the impression that what they want for themselves is actually what is best for the family.) Television commercials, for example, communicate to your children that they will win love if they use certain hair-care products, that they will feel more freedom in life if they drive powerful cars, that if they eat the featured foods they will feel happy and fulfilled.

You can point out these manipulations to children directly, but you may be able to engage their interest better by having them treat the ad like a puzzle. "What do you think this commercial wants you to believe? . . . Why do you suppose that nearly naked woman is there, when she has nothing to do with the product they are selling? . . . What is this ad trying to make you worry about? . . ." If you ask these types of questions, rather than provide the answers, you draw your children into making the effort to think for themselves about what they are absorbing—and teaching them to think for themselves is exactly what you are after.

The beer commercial that I described provides a good example of a "teachable moment." The ad implies that men should value bonding with other men more highly than their relationships with women, that men who treat women with respect are traitors, and that drinking beer together and disrespecting women is the way to make yourself belong. Because of the unhealthy example set by their father, your children have an especially strong need to be steered away from these kinds of messages. When you see a commercial that provides this kind of opportunity to discuss important issues with your children, seize the moment.

Look Carefully at What Your Children
Are Seeing and Hearing

If you are not already disturbed by the content of the music videos and rock lyrics that enter your children's daily cultural experience, you may be once you take a closer look. Spend some time reading the printed lyrics that come with your children's CDs, and sit with them while they watch music videos or movies. Ask yourself not only, "How would these images affect children in general?" but also, "What are *my* children in particular learning from what they're seeing, given the abuse they have already witnessed?" After a movie ends, for example, engage them in a critical discussion of the story and draw their attention to any disrespect toward females, glorification of violence, racism, or other offensive portrayals that you noticed.

Should I Bar Offensive Materials
from the Home?

I have to answer this question yes and no. It isn't possible to shield your children from all cultural training that supports abuse or demeans women. If you try to shut offensive images and lyrics completely out of your home, your children may just go over to the homes of friends where there are no restrictions. To some extent, therefore, it makes sense to allow the culture to come in your door, but to sit with your children listening and watching together, and sharing with them your insights and objections. At the same time, you do need to draw a line somewhere; permitting lyrics that express open hatred for women into your home, or pornography that degrades females, or movies that are full of violence, implies that you consider them acceptable. So you do your children a favor by setting standards so that certain CDs, movies, or music videos are simply not permitted, and so that their TV watching is infrequent and carefully screened. (Even harmless-appearing shows such as situation comedies can turn out to be full of messages that support abuse.) Children who have been exposed to an abusive man need adults around them to take strong stands to counter his influence, particularly when it comes to images of violence and degradation.

You can find excellent guidelines for parents on how to help your children handle media influences in *The Other Parent* (see Resources, "Media Literacy," page 354).

Using Everyday Situations

"Teachable moments" arise every day. You might be at a playground with your children and observe another parent verbally abusing his or her child, or handling the child too roughly. After witnessing such an event, you can take your son or daughter aside and say, "I didn't like the way that parent was acting. Did you notice that? Did that upset you? What do you think that parent should have done instead?" By reflecting on a public incident in this way you help your child internalize important self-protective insights, including:

"I don't have to accept unquestioningly what adults do. Adults make mistakes, too, including mistakes in how they treat children."

"Children have rights, even when they're misbehaving."

Watch also for less obvious behaviors that you can point out to your children, such as manipulation, *especially when you see an adult (or a child) exhibiting tactics or attitudes that you know your partner manifests.* You might point out, for example, situations where a person's body language is sending a strong message that his or her words are contradicting. In this way you arm children with a language and concepts for analyzing the things their father does, without speaking badly about him at all. And just as advertising has less power over us as soon as we recognize its techniques, the abusive man has more difficulty twisting his children's perceptions if they are conscious of his maneuvers.

An excellent tool for engaging children in a discussion of manipulation is the Russell Hoban book *A Bargain for Frances* (see Resources, page 344), which you can read with children as young as four years old and as old as ten or perhaps older. The main character, the little badger Frances, is manipulated by a greedy friend of hers named Thelma into giving up her china tea set, which she loves, replacing it with a plastic set that she doesn't want. When Frances becomes aware of what Thelma did, she uses a trick of her own to get her china set back; she then persuades her friend that they should keep that kind of underhandedness out of their relationship. The book provides many opportunities to discuss issues of trust, vulnerability, and kindness, as well as to identify specific manipulative tactics so that children learn to recognize them. (See other books to read with children under Resources.)

Skepticism Need Not Mean Cynicism

There is one risk that comes with teaching critical thinking: that children will come to mistrust everyone, always suspecting that people are concealing their true motives, or that what appears to be generosity is a mask for selfishness. To avoid causing your children to harden in this way, be sure to point out what is good in their social environment as often as what is bad. Draw their attention to acts of giving and kindness wherever you observe them, and model for them a belief in the inherent goodness of human beings. Teach them to see destructive or selfish behaviors as products not of evil, but rather of *problems* that people have. Show them by the example of how you live your life that there are people who are worthy of trust and role models who are worth following. Encourage them in general to look upon others with a generous and forgiving spirit.

Such a mindset will not only help keep your children hopeful and positive about life, but will actually make them more willing to face up to their father's abusiveness; it is easier for them to digest the fact that he treats you or them badly if they don't feel that he therefore is a fundamentally bad person. They also will be less likely to be drawn into his negativity if they have learned love and appreciation.

Your positive outlook on life—which may be difficult for you to muster at times, given what you have been through with your children's father—will help your children be more open to your critical insights. I have seen children who start to roll their eyes each time their parents point out sexism or violence on television, saying, "Oh, there goes Mom (or Dad) again, always finding something wrong with everything." If your children begin to react this way to you, it may be a sign that you are being too frequently negative with them and they need more balance, focusing on what is good about their world and about human nature.

Children's Coping and Positive Resistance

An adult man recently approached me after I gave a lecture on the effects on children of exposure to domestic violence, and proceeded to share the following poignant account from his childhood:

"I grew up in a home where my father would get plastered drunk and beat my Mom with his fists. Sometimes she'd have black eyes, or blood pouring out of her nose. I hated my dad and he knew it, so he put me down constantly. He'd make fun of me in front of other people, everything I did was wrong. Some nights you could just tell he was going to go off, usually at my mom, because he'd be raging and drinking, and I would just clear out, walking for a half hour or so to get to my best friend's house, where I was always welcome, and I'd spend the night there. My friend and his parents were the only people I told about the violence. They were so good to me. I got through those years by just dreaming about the day when I'd be able to get out and not have to be around all that, and by making a pact with myself that I would be nothing like my father. I also promised myself to succeed in life, to prove all his predictions wrong about what a mess-up I was destined to be. And you know what? I did it. I'm the financial director of a foundation now, with the kind of responsibility and authority that my dad always said I'd never be able to handle. And I'm married to a great woman, a lawyer who handles workplace discrimination cases for women. . . . My mom's still with him, and he still hits her sometimes. It's hard for me to think about it. . . . One of my brothers I'm pretty close to, but the other I can't really communicate with at all, because he turned out just like my dad."

This young man's story was as inspiring as it was painful. It illustrated how careful we should be not to see children as passive, helpless victims of the abuse they have witnessed. Side by side with children's distresses are their courageous efforts to find ways to be safe, to watch out for one another, to find people who will love them, to hold onto the belief that they don't deserve to be mistreated and neither does their mother.

The box below contains just a few of the dozens of strategies that children use to resist abuse that they are immersed in growing up:

Children's Coping and Resistance Strategies

- Avoiding being at home.
- Finding other families to spend time with, developing attachments to other adults.
- Becoming protective toward Mom.
- Becoming protective toward siblings.
- Developing an active fantasy life.
- Holding on internally to beliefs that they can't say aloud (such as that the abuse is wrong and that they will not grow up to behave as the abuser does).
- Finding friends they can tell.
- Keeping the secret so that Dad won't retaliate.
- Pretending to side with Dad.
- Lying to the abuser, or to outsiders, to protect Mom, their siblings, or themselves.
- Pouring themselves into hobbies, sports, reading, music or dance lessons, or other satisfying, soothing, and creative activities.
- Treating people well, inside or outside the family.
- Taking good care of themselves.
- Fleeing the home when they sense danger.
- Learning to enjoy spending time alone, developing a special relationship with themselves.
- Staying close to Mom or to each other when they sense danger.
- Directly challenging the abuser verbally or physically, sometimes in ways that put them at considerable risk.
- Calling the police.

- Disclosing the abuse to school personnel, neighbors, or other adults.
- Defying the abuser in small ways that he doesn't know about.
- Loving Mom, loving their siblings.
- Believing in themselves, standing up for themselves (including with you).

Pay attention to your children's strengths, including both their subtle and their overt ways of fighting back against abuse. Children chafe against pity, just as adults do, and want to be seen as courageous survivors, playing a role in their own healing, and not as damaged or helpless victims, tossed about like bottles in the waves of a storm. They want your appreciation of the steps toward wellness that they have already taken, and your encouragement to grow stronger. Think of your children as needing two opposites from you: They need you to see how resilient they are and how much they have to be proud of, and also to provide them a safe place where they can periodically fall apart, where they can stop battling so bravely for a while and let out all their sadness, exhaustion, or bitterness. It is not easy to learn to play this dual role, but I have worked with many mothers who have succeeded in doing so. The more you understand your children's emotional and physical survival strategies, the better you can support them.

Remember also that your children's frustrations, their tantrums and sadnesses, their periods of defiance, do not all come from the abuse they have witnessed, or that they have been the direct targets of. They are also going through the normal trials of childhood, and the emotional highs and lows that are part of human life. Bearing this in mind will help you avoid painting your children as victims in your mind.

One word of caution: It is best not to share insights into your children's resilience with your partner, even during periods when he is being nice. Unfortunately, many abusers make mental note of the strengths of their family members, and then use that knowledge later to more effectively sabotage their independence or resistance. It is natural that you would want your partner to recognize how resourceful your children are, instead of seeing them as helpless or stupid, but think carefully about arming him with information that could backfire against the children later, when he is back in an abusive period.

Safety Planning with Children

Now we move onto another delicate balancing act, but one that, again, I am confident you can take on successfully:

As much as possible, keep your children from being burdened with adult responsibility, while simultaneously equipping them with strategies for keeping themselves—and you—safe.

QUESTION #19:
Should I talk with my children about how dangerous my partner gets sometimes?

If your partner periodically turns scary or violent, your children are almost surely aware of it. Avoiding the subject will not lessen their fear; in fact, children feel safer if they can talk to their mothers about how frightened they get, and discuss actions they might take next time their father erupts. They are afraid not only for themselves, but also for you, and they need to be able to express that concern and feel that you hear them. They also want to know how they might be able to protect you.

Find a time to sit with your children, individually or as a group, to talk about safety strategies. Begin by emphasizing the following points:

- Adults are responsible for their own safety. Children can help if they want to, but it isn't their job.
- Safety plans won't always work, and if someone gets hurt, it isn't the child's fault.
- If children make a mistake and do the safety plan wrong, they *still* aren't at fault for what happens; the abusive man is always responsible for his own actions.
- They can't manage their father or make him change.
- They don't have to make a safety plan with you if they don't want to.

Then begin the discussion by asking your children what *they* think might help, or what they would like to plan to do next time they feel scared of Dad. Elicit as many ideas from them as possible. They are more likely to be able to effectively practice actions that they come up with themselves, and in the process you will learn about safety strategies that they are already using. Then add ideas of your own, and see if you can agree on a plan. Here are some of the strategies I have learned about from families over the years, which you might try to include in your safety plan:

Safety Strategies for Children

- Run out of the home when the incident starts.
- Lock themselves in a bedroom.

- Lock themselves in a room that has a telephone, and call for help.
- Arrange a code word with friends or relatives, so they can use the phone to call for help without the abuser knowing what they are doing.
- Dial 911 (or the local emergency number if it is different).
- Run to the home of neighbors who know about the abuse, and call the police from there (if the police are supportive).
- Siblings agree to meet together in a prearranged spot.
- Make an excuse to get Mom out of the home (such as going outdoors and faking an injury, so that she has to come out to help).
- Keep a cellular phone hidden somewhere indoors, or in a garage or shed, without the abuser's knowledge, where the children know where to find it if they need to call for help.
- Plan phrases they can say to themselves or to each other to help them stay calm and get through the scary incident (such as, "We're going to be okay").
- Leave home as soon as they see that Dad has been drinking, or observe other behaviors that they know are warning signs of a scary incident.
- Hide weapons or other dangerous objects in the home so Dad won't be able to find them.
- Plan with children regarding what adults they can safely call for help if you aren't home, if you are sick, or if you are being intimidated by their father at that moment and can't help them.
- Physically or verbally intervene to protect Mom (which can be very dangerous in some cases, so children should discuss the risks of this choice).

In some cases women discover that their children have already made agreements with each other involving these elements or similar ones, but hadn't mentioned their plans to Mom because of feeling that the abuse was an issue they were not supposed to mention, or out of fear of making her feel embarrassed or ashamed.

Some people feel that making safety plans with children who are exposed to abuse is inappropriate, because it burdens them unduly with adult responsibility, reinforcing a dynamic that is already part of their experience. But in practice safety planning seems to lessen this burden rather than increase it; children already feel a profound desire, and a great need, to protect their mothers, as comes across powerfully in the interviews with children described in *Childhood Experiences of Domestic Violence* (see Resources, page 343). The only way to truly relieve that burden is to end or escape the abuse. In the meantime, most children are better off with some empowerment than without it.

Safety planning cannot relieve children's distress to any profound extent, however, nor can it protect them from direct abuse. So the long-term goal of getting the children into safe circumstances needs to continue to be pursued.

If you have not made a safety plan for yourself, I encourage you to do so before making one with your children. You can look in chapter 9 of *Why Does He Do That?* for an introduction to creating your own plan, which you should work on in conjunction with an advocate at an abused women's program if at all possible. If you don't have time or transportation to get to the program, work with an advocate by telephone.

Safety Planning for Unsupervised Visitation

As I discuss in chapter 13, it is regrettably common for family courts to require women to send their children on unsupervised visits with their abusive fathers. Safety planning for unsupervised visitation can follow the points above, but include the following additional considerations:

- Have them think through the setup at their father's home, perhaps even drawing a diagram with you, to consider where they could get behind a locked door, get access to a telephone, or both.
- Make sure they know your telephone number by heart, including area code.
- Send them on visits with a photograph of you that they can look at for reassurance, a stuffed animal they can hold, or other objects that can help them get through times of feeling afraid, insecure, or lonely.
- Let them know that they should make their own safety their top priority, even if it means they need to go along with their father in speaking badly about you or take other steps to placate him and keep him happy.
- Prepare them for how best to deal with his efforts to pump them for information about you (which a large proportion of abusers do in unsupervised visitation). Let them know they can tell him what he is asking for if they feel that their safety depends on doing so, but that it is important when they get back home for them to tell you what they told him. (For example, if he has found out from them where you work, or the fact that you are dating someone, it is important for you to be able to plan for his possible reactions.)
- As above, discuss how the children might respond if they see signs that Dad has been drinking or see other danger signals, including what to do if he attempts to drive in the car with them while he is intoxicated.

> • If you are concerned about possible abduction by the abuser, rehearse with your children their full name, the town and state you live in, and how to call 911. Discuss strategies for passing written messages to other adults to indicate that they are being abducted, or to leave messages in public restrooms (especially women's rooms, where the abuser is unlikely to go).

As with safety planning when the abuser still lives at home, try to discuss the children's anxieties openly with them while simultaneously trying not to alarm them or intensify their fears. Remind them that when safety plans don't work, they are in no way to blame. You may want to actually rehearse certain aspects of the plan, such as how they might approach another adult for help if their father is acting frightening and you aren't there.

If you are involved in a court battle with your ex-partner over custody or visitation, the fact that you talked to your children about safety planning could be used against you, as the abuser may claim that you have been placing fear into the children that wasn't there previously. Because of this risk, you might want to try to arrange with a professional, such as a therapist or an advocate for abused women, to do the safety planning with your children without your involvement. If these resources are not available to you, you might want to safety plan with children only in cases where you are confident that they will not mention the plan to the abuser.

(As I discuss in chapter 5, secret-keeping needs to be avoided as much as possible with children who are exposed to an abusive man; if you ask them not to tell their father about the safety plan, be sure to emphasize to them that in general it is inappropriate for adults to ask children to keep secrets, and that the only exception is in cases where certain secrets are necessary to keep them safe *and* where the child is voluntarily agreeing to keep the secret.)

One would certainly hope that unsupervised visits would be stopped by the court if children continued over time to feel unsafe, but in practice children's ongoing anxieties are often blamed on the mother, so long-term coping strategies can be necessary. These might include finding ways to secretly call Mom on the phone to talk, writing in journals to help keep their own sanity, tuning out their fears or loneliness by watching a lot of movies at Dad's house (although heavy video exposure can create problems of its own), and other approaches to psychological survival that you and your child might brainstorm together.

Some Closing Thoughts

Underlying these avenues to building children's empowerment is a fundamental goal: to seek to expand and strengthen children's *voice,* by which I mean their ability to:

- Make themselves heard.
- Articulate feelings and opinions.
- Develop a sense of agency—that is, having the power to shape the direction of their life events.
- Feel deeply the values of *democracy* and *equality,* so they come to feel that they have rights that no one should take away, and that among those is the right to have a *say* over the decisions that affect their lives.

The best way to increase your children's voice is to listen carefully to their feelings and opinions and take them into account as you make parental decisions, so that children come to feel that what they express makes a difference. This feeling will in turn

help them to stand up for themselves with their father and to recognize the ways in which he refuses to hear them and be sensitive
to their needs.

In addition, you can:

• Help them speak for themselves in conflicts with others,
rather than speaking for them. When your child comes home complaining about something a schoolteacher has done, for example,
ask for a meeting with the child and the teacher together, and then
assist your child in raising the issue, rather than relaying the griev-
ance yourself. Whenever possible have children use your support
and encouragement as a springboard to stand up for themselves,
and don't take the conflict over for them unless they simply can't
handle it.

• Help them write letters to your town newspaper or to elected
representatives about issues that they express concern about to
you, such as needing more supplies at their schools or wanting a
better playground facility in their neighborhood.

• Praise them for sticking up for their friends or siblings when
they observe mistreatment happening around them.

It is wise to caution your children from time to time not to
practice their assertiveness with their abusive father, unless they are
sure the potential consequences are worth it to them.

Silence can also be a powerful statement. After you have done
everything in your power to open the door for children to talk to
you about their experiences, respect the choice they may make *not*
to talk. Refusing to open up about their feelings can be a statement that their inner world belongs to them alone and is not public property, and that they are entitled to a place where they feel
safe and have complete control, even if it is only a place inside
themselves. A little later in life, when the time is right, they can

decide to let others see into those dark inner places so that healing can occur.

Finally, help keep the spirits of your children alive through the mental images you conjure for them. Describe for them a world where kindness and tenderness are the order of the day. Make up stories for them—using them as characters—in which they act powerfully to overcome challenges or heroically protect others. Keep them dreaming of what could be, and what can be, for their own lives and for their world. Keep your own healing moving forward, which will help your children feel hopeful about their own. Hope and vision keep a spirit kindled, and that flame in turn sustains life and renewal.

Key Points to Remember

- Children who are taught to think critically and analytically will, of their own accord, use those skills to defend themselves against manipulation by the abuser.
- Children are not passive victims of the abuse they witness; they strive for survival and rejuvenation.
- You can empower your children to increase their ability to protect themselves, both physically and psychologically.
- The long-range goal is to raise children who have a voice on their own behalf, and on behalf of those they love.

Chapter Sixteen

Stopping the Cycle of Abuse

"My brother has kind of taken my children under his wing, to make up for the ways they've been hurt by their father. I've been so grateful for his role in their lives, so that they can know that there are good men."

"I feel degraded each time I walk past a store that has pornographic magazines on display everywhere. And it's even worse that they have them right out where children can see them— I don't want my boys growing up to think females are pieces of meat."

"My children's therapist has been such a godsend to them, and to me."

"I was asked to come down and tell my story at the state legislature, and I did it. I was so nervous, but I wanted to do something to keep other women from going through what I went through—being forced by a judge to send my children off on visits where they were being abused by their father."

Although this book has been addressed to abused mothers, many readers will no doubt be people who are in the role of helping, rather than of living these circumstances directly. In this last chapter, I wish to include both mothers and their allies, examining ways that we all can be involved in relieving the anxiety and hurt of children who witness abuse.

The scourge of domestic violence has forced its way into public consciousness over the past two decades, largely due to the tireless efforts of the battered women's movement. Celebrity actors, athletes, and politicians have been arrested for assaulting their wives or girlfriends, followed by the predictable denials that characterize abusive men. Television public service ads show us up close the drama and fear in homes ripped apart by violence, and implore us to stop turning a deaf ear to the shouts coming from neighbors' homes. In one commercial that millions of people have seen, a young boy sits trembling at the top of the stairs listening to his parents fighting below, wincing each time he hears his mother struck.

Researchers tell us that boys who grow up in homes where their mother is battered are more likely than other boys to grow up to abuse their own wives and girlfriends. Daughters of abused women have a harder time than other women do escaping mistreatment once it starts.

At the same time, many men who abuse women—roughly half, in fact—did not learn their values and behaviors from their fathers or stepfathers, but instead absorbed abusive attitudes from peers, from other male relatives, from television, or from pornography. So when we speak of stopping the "cycle of abuse," we need to broaden our thinking beyond just transmission from father to child, but also from the *culture* of each generation to the culture of the next. If we want to stop abuse, we have to transform social attitudes.

Compassion for abused women is building across the continent, but we are still a society with deep habits of blaming victims. When people suffer misfortune, we jump to analyzing what they should have done differently: She should have fought back, she shouldn't have fought back; she was in an area where it wasn't wise to be walking; she didn't plan ahead; she didn't try hard enough or think fast enough.

These judgments can tragically limit the support and compassion that an abused woman receives from her community. She may hear, for example:

"Why did you choose a man like that for a partner?"

"What do you expect a man to do when he catches you cheating on him?"

"You're just as abusive as he is, and you provoke him."

"If you don't leave him, it's your own fault." (Or, ironically, she may hear the opposite: *"Yes, it's terrible the way he threatened you, but the poor man was so torn up over the fact that you were leaving him."*)

But almost no one—except maybe for the abusers themselves—is prepared to blame children for the hurts they suffer. When I speak to audiences about the emotional injuries to children who witness abuse, the room fills with empathy and caring, hands shoot up with questions about what community members can do to help, eyes well up with tears. I am thrilled that so many people are eager to find out what they can do, and there are countless suggestions I can offer for constructive action. But the most important point of all is this:

If we want to help children who are exposed to domestic abuse, we have to offer our wholehearted support to their mothers.

We have to give up victim blaming and start understanding the complex realities that abused mothers face. As I explain in chapter 9, leaving the abusive man is *not* a magic answer that immediately brings safety and healing for mothers and children, and we have to be willing to work closely with abused mothers toward viable long-term solutions.

In addition to oversimplifying her options, blaming the mother has the effect of reinforcing the abusive man's own messages to her. He tells her day in and day out:

> *"It's your own fault things are so bad here."*
>
> *"You're messing up these children."*
>
> *"Why don't you just get off your ass and take care of things?"*
>
> *"Why can't you do one simple thing right?"*

We cannot help her children by joining our voices in chorus with his. As I explain in *Why Does He Do That?*, to assist an abused woman effectively we have to treat her in a way that is *opposite* to the abusive man's style. Since he pressures her constantly, we have to be patient. Since he talks down to her, we have to approach her as equals. Since he believes his ideas are superior to hers, we have to draw from *her* intelligence, rather than assuming we know better than she does how to improve her circumstances. And since he makes her feel like she's a bad mother, we have to approach her as a *good* mother, one who is trying hard to figure out how to make life better for her children, and who doesn't need a lecture from us. What she needs instead is:

- Our caring.
- Our assistance in thinking *for herself* through the various options or strategies that she can consider.
- Our financial assistance.
- Our help with getting the legal system to respond appropriately to her situation, through proper prosecution of

the abuser for any laws he has broken and through re-
stricting his access to the children.

The pages ahead are devoted to proposing concrete steps you
can take within your community, and beyond, to bring safety and
healing to children who have been wounded by the actions of an
abusive man, and to break the societal cycle that keeps producing
more abusers, and therefore more abused mothers and traumatized children. But all efforts should begin with reaching out to
mothers with awareness and compassion, and striving to build
supportive relationships that can empower them to successfully
protect their own children.

Expand Your Knowledge Base

In order to advocate effectively for children in your community,
you need to be able to articulate your concerns and suggestions to
people who are in positions to make changes happen, such as of-
ficials in town government, school committee members, the police department, court personnel (including judges), and mental
health professionals. As you reach out through phone calls and letters, you are likely to encounter a mixed response, with caring and
interest being expressed by some people, and impatience or misconceptions revealed by others. For dealing with the latter group,
you will want to have facts and arguments ready at your fingertips,
so you can meet ignorance with information and meet defensiveness with realistic proposals for community change.

The best starting point for educating yourself about how communities can help children who have witnessed abuse is to read
Childhood Experience of Domestic Violence, by Caroline McGee (see
Resources, page 343). McGee's wise, readable book provides an
unprecedented depth of insight into children's feelings, struggles,

and triumphs. The interviews mostly involve cases in which the man has been physically violent to the mother, but much of what McGee learned is equally applicable to homes where the abuser does not commit frequent assaults but is cruel or intimidating in other ways.

Next, expand your knowledge about domestic abuse in general through reading such books as *When Love Goes Wrong,* by Ann Jones and Susan Schechter, Patricia Evans's *The Verbally Abusive Relationship,* and my book *Why Does He Do That?* (see Resources, pages 338–39). These books will prepare you to respond articulately to victim blaming, point out concrete ways that your community can hold abusers accountable, and help you describe the harm that can be caused by partner abuse even when it doesn't include outright blows.

Finally, to prepare yourself to advocate for reforming how family courts handle domestic violence and child abuse cases, see the powerful documentary "Small Justice," by Garland Waller, and read the human rights report "Battered Mothers Speak Out," released by the Battered Mothers Testimony Project (see Resources, page 346). All these resources are listed in the back of this book.

Educate Your Community

You can raise awareness about the plight of abused women and their children by, for example, writing articles or letters to the editor of your local newspaper. If you belong to a club or a group, or if you participate on a committee at your church or temple, offer to lead a discussion about the issue and propose some actions the group could take, such as holding a community forum. Meet with your state senator or representative to ask him or her to pursue funding for counseling and advocacy programs for children of abused women.

Schools are among the institutions best positioned to identify and assist children of abused women. Call or write your town's school committee to ask what steps the school system is taking to train teachers about the effects on children of exposure to domestic abuse. Request also that the schools develop written protocols for how teachers and administrators should respond when they see warning signs in a child's behavior, or when a student explicitly reveals that he or she is witnessing physical or verbal violence. As we saw with Nick Abbott in chapter 6, a school that doesn't recognize the roots of a child's trauma-related behavior may respond harshly, exacerbating the problem; on the other hand, school personnel who are well informed can ask children sensitively worded questions about their experiences at home and can reach out constructively (and privately) to the abused mother, finding ways to support and assist her and her children.

Community Collaborations

Any community member can initiate a community task force or "roundtable" on children's exposure to domestic violence, with successful models already in motion in some locations. The effectiveness of these task forces, which typically meet monthly, lies in bringing as many different players as possible to the table to discuss improved services for children and their mothers. To start such a group, try to get at least one representative to attend from each of the following groups or institutions:

- Currently or formerly abused mothers.
- The school system, such as a teacher, nurse, or school counselor.
- The police department.
- Child protective services.
- The program for abused women.
- The district attorney's office.
- The juvenile court, such as a juvenile probation officer.

- The program for abusive men (if there is one).
- The mental health field, such as a child therapist.
- Concerned clergy.

When individuals wearing this range of hats sit down to discuss problems and solutions together, and to share insights and experience, great leaps forward occur. Here are some of the kinds of interdisciplinary innovations I have learned about in my research:

- A town where the police department, the abused women's program, and a mental health clinic have collaborated so that a trained child therapist accompanies police on *every* domestic violence call, to speak with the children in the home, assess how much distress they are experiencing from the incident, and inform the mother about how she can get therapeutic help for her children and herself.
- A small city where the school system has formed a working relationship with local therapists and advocates so that counseling groups for children of abused women are available right in the school building, an approach that solves the problems of transportation and scheduling that make it difficult for mothers to get their children to services.
- A town where a communication system has been established between the police department and the schools so that police promptly inform school administrators when domestic violence incidents have occurred with children in the home. This knowledge helps teachers be understanding and supportive when children appear withdrawn, distracted, defiant, or aggressive in school over the days following the assault.

These kinds of interdisciplinary cooperation and information-sharing can mean the difference between a child who, for example, gets labeled as a "bad apple" by the school and the local police and ends up eventually in a juvenile detention center, and a child who is correctly assessed as both traumatized and influenced by an abusive father and is offered counseling, education about abuse, and assistance to repair his or her relationship with the mother.

Some individuals have helped to spawn a task force in their town or city by first holding a conference or forum on children and domestic abuse. You might choose, for example, to work in collaboration with a program for abused women and your nearest hospital or mental health clinic to offer a half-day or full-day training program, bringing in knowledgeable speakers and proposing community collaborations like the ones described above. Such a workshop can be a great kickoff for sustained local efforts to reach out to mothers and children.

Challenge Myths That Leave Children Vulnerable

Part of why children are trapped in unhealthy circumstances is that societal misconceptions abound that contribute to keeping their mothers isolated and unable to get assistance. Make your voice heard to correct the following notions when you hear them arise:

"It's her fault for not leaving him." A woman faces tremendous obstacles, and sometimes danger, when she attempts to leave an abusive man. As we saw above, there is also no guarantee that her children will be better off if she does leave. A good response to this myth is to say, "The great majority of abused women want to take steps to make the abuse stop, and are prepared to leave the relationship eventually if those steps don't work. We need to look at what we can do as a community to make it possible for a woman to end her relationship safely, and what kinds of assistance we can offer abused mothers to make it possible for them to protect their children."

"We don't live in the kind of community where there's much do-mestic violence." Domestic violence is widespread across social classes, levels of education, and racial groups. Some of the high-est rates have been found in the wealthiest families. The published research makes it clear that no community or neighborhood is ex-empt from abuse, and that children need us to pay attention to the many distress signals they put out, even if they don't appear to come from "that kind of a family."

"Being raised by single mothers is bad for children—they need to have a father." Children are far better off—as a number of stud-ies demonstrate—living in peace with their mother than being ex-posed to a man who abuses her. In fact, the studies indicate that children are better off living with a single parent than being around parents who fight frequently even *without* abuse.

The research that purports to show how damaging single moth-ering is to children has failed to control for income and for prior exposure to abuse, so that the difficulties observed are actually the effects of *poverty* and of the fact that many children witnessed abuse while their parents were together—and that is why the mother is now single. The solution is to increase the financial and childcare assistance available to single parents, not to pressure women to stay with abusive partners.

It is worth noting that we never seem to hear reports claiming that children are damaged when they are raised by single *fathers.* The reality is that single parenting is difficult, exhausting, some-times isolating work, but both women and men can do it well, and the world is full of well-adjusted, successful people who grew up with one primary parent, male or female. What matters above all is to live in a home where there is safety, love, and kindness—and adequate economic resources.

"People on welfare are a burden to society." More than half of welfare recipients, according to research, are abused women. Part of what keeps children trapped in homes with abusive men is that

their mothers have no way to survive if they leave except by going on public assistance, but they don't want the stigma that comes with welfare. If we want mothers to be able to get their children safe from exposure to domestic abuse, we have to raise welfare benefits to a livable level, ease time limits, treat recipients with respect, and stop speaking negatively about people who receive public assistance. We also have to continue to improve child support enforcement—abusive men are chronically irresponsible about their support payments, but rarely seem to face any consequences.

"Boys will be boys." Glaring signals that a boy is modeling himself after his abusive father are sometimes dismissed with a quick wave of the hand and the comment, "That's just the way boys are." Taking this view not only amounts to abandoning the boy himself, who desperately needs us to notice the distress he is acting out, but also condemns future girls and women in his life to be targets of his aggression and contempt. We should pay careful heed to the bumper sticker that restates the old saying in much more accurate—and ominous—terms: "Boys Will Be Men." By showing boys a greater degree of caring and sensitivity than they currently receive from many adults, while also holding the line in a no-nonsense fashion against the sexist, violent behaviors and attitudes that they begin to manifest, we can give them the opportunity to grow into good men.

"Teen boys need to break away from their mother's influence in order to enter manhood." The longevity and popularity of this myth is matched only by the thoroughness of its inaccuracy. As Dr. William Pollack explains in his book *Real Boys,* the *closer* boys remain to their mothers during their adolescence, the happier and higher-functioning they are as adults. When we see a boy becoming severely rejecting toward his mother, we sometimes are witnessing the influence of an abusive father. Both boys and girls need to develop identities separate from those of their parents

during their teen years, but that doesn't mean they need to break their bonds of affection; in fact, they fare better if they don't.

Challenging these myths calls upon us to replace them with a positive alternative. That vision is one of equality and respect between parents, recognition that children have rights, too, and remembering that children hate to see other people suffer. The concepts of justice, peace, and democracy need to be brought inside our homes, not left on the doorstep as if they applied to the rest of the world but not to family life. In fact, family life is perhaps where those noble values matter most.

Make a Difference to Children You Know

I have often trained daycare providers on how to assist children who live with domestic abuse. The people in these audiences tend to be exceptionally sensitive and concerned, perhaps because they make their living by caring. The providers sometimes have tears streaming down their faces as they tell me of children they've looked after who have been torn apart by cruelty at home. Over and over again I hear these hardworking caregivers say, "I don't feel like I have anything to offer the children except my love."

QUESTION #20:
How can I help children I know who are suffering from exposure to abuse?

My first response is, "You are already helping more than you could ever know. Loving them is no small thing. In fact, it's the greatest gift they can receive." Love is a powerful healing force, though it can take years to see fully the impact that it has.

I wish to send the same call out to anyone who comes in contact with the children of an abused woman: Love them. If you have only ten minutes to spend with them in their whole lives, as might be true of a police officer or a crisis worker, make sure you spend at least five of those just showing them that you notice them and that you care. If children feel seen and understood they can hold onto hope, and if they can hope they can heal.

From a foundation of love and concern, go on to do the following:

Ask children how they are feeling. "Are you okay? What happened? Do you feel like you can tell me about it? I would really like to know how you are, and it's okay to talk about anything."

Name possible feelings for them if they can't tell you. "That seems like it must have been frightening for you. Were you scared? I think I would have been scared if I'd been there. Are you feeling sad today? Children who hear their parents fighting can get pretty sad sometimes. Is there anything you're mad about? It's okay to feel angry when things happen in your home that you don't like."

Reinforce children for anything they disclose about the abuse. "I know it's really hard to talk about these kinds of things, but I'm proud of you for telling me. It's much better to tell an adult you can trust instead of holding everything inside." Children usually feel, at least in part, that they have done a *bad* thing by revealing the abuse at home; they worry that they have burdened you, that they have proven themselves to be disloyal children, or that they have simply been naughty by telling a secret that they were supposed to keep.

Ask children about their concerns regarding retaliation. "Has anyone in your family ever told you not to talk about what happened? Will anyone at home be mad that you told me? I'm glad you didn't keep this secret, because this isn't a good kind of secret to keep, but I also don't want to see you get in trouble for having told me. Is that something I need to worry about?"

Tell children that the abuse is not their fault, nor is it their mother's fault. "You didn't make these things happen, and it isn't up to you to make them stop. Grown-ups have to solve grown-up problems." Children almost always carry some degree of guilt about the abuse they have seen, either believing that their naughty behavior caused their father's explosion, or feeling that they should have found some way to protect their mother. They also struggle with the question of whether their mother somehow caused or deserved the abuse, often fed directly by statements they hear Dad say during or after an incident. Children need us to relieve both their self-blame and their blaming of the victim.

Tell children that they are safe while they are with you. You can't promise to stop the verbal or physical abuse in the child's home, much as you may long to do so. If you make assurances to a child that you can't keep, you run the risk of becoming another adult whom the child sees as unworthy of trust. But you *can* give him or her a sense of security during the time you are together, and even a brief taste helps to keep a child's spirit alive.

Tell children that you want to speak with their mother about your concerns. While an abused mother may not be able to protect her children this instant, she can do so over time if she gets proper emotional support, financial assistance, and legal protection. One of the best ways to make a difference in the lives of children is to build a relationship with their mother. Most children are relieved to hear that you will talk with Mom about the upsetting events at home; they want someone to help her figure out what to do. However, there are a small but important number of domestic abuse cases in which children are afraid of their mothers as well, not just of the abuser; their mother may hit them sometimes, or may have threatened to harm them if they disclose the man's violence to outsiders (perhaps out of fear of what he will do if they tell). If a child says to you, "Please don't tell my mother that I talked about this, she'll be furious," or "She'll kill me," then you will have to seek ways to help that don't involve letting the mother know that her son or daughter has broken the secrecy. Let the child know that the door is open to discuss the situation further in the future if he or she wants to, and ask the child who else he or she might go to for support.

Build ongoing relationships with children if you can. If you are a relative or family friend, make time to be more involved in the children's lives, bringing them over to your home, taking them on outings, and seeking opportunities to spend special time with them. Along with the healing value to children of becoming close to you, your time with them gives them respite from the tension or fear at home, and allows you to get more opportunities for a close look at what's really going on. Your openings to speak to their mother and help her will also increase. If you are a man, your relationships with children have the additional benefit of teaching them—without ever saying it directly—that their father is not the only model of masculinity, and that there are kind, non-abusive ways to be a man. Girls can learn from your example that they can, and should, expect kindness and respect from men.

Make sure to get support and advice for yourself if situations arise that you aren't sure how to handle. If, for example, children disclose to you that they are being abused by their father or their mother, or that they are planning to assault their father, you should contact a program for abused women about how best to respond.

Should I Confront the Abuser?

Empathy for a child's pain can easily shift into outrage at the abusive man who is the cause. But don't give in to the temptation to confront him about his behavior. *You don't have the power to make him stop*—at least not in the short term—whereas he does have the power to make his child pay for revealing the abuse to you. Well-meaning friends or relatives sometimes think they can intimidate the abuser or shame him into change, but the actual product of their intervention may be beatings, severe verbal lashings, or homicide. I have been involved in cases in which children who disclose abuse experience severe verbal retaliation by their father, so they then begin to recant their story, saying that they made it up or that their mother made them tell lies. So be cautious never to let an abuser know that his children or his partner are telling you the truth.

Confrontations of abusers by several relatives or influential community members at once is a different issue. These interventions reportedly can be effective in some cases, especially if the individuals involved have a way to closely monitor the man's behavior subsequently, so that he knows his community will hold him accountable. Some tribal groups, for example, are striving to address domestic violence with this approach. It is still better, however, not to refer to children's disclosures as you confront the abuser, and to only confront him with the mother's permission.

Should I Make a Child Abuse Report?

Unless you fear that a child is at risk of being killed or severely traumatized, and you have no way to build a positive relationship with the mother to help her, it is generally best not to involve child protective services in domestic abuse cases. Social workers are often not adequately sensitive to the parenting challenges that an abused woman faces, so there is a good chance that she will be blamed for her children's problems, the result being that neither she nor her children will receive effective assistance getting safe or recovering from the abuse. There are some regions where collaboration has developed between child protective workers and abused women's programs, which increases the chances of a well-informed, helpful response; such systems are still more the exception than the rule, however.

If you are concerned about the safety of children in a home where the mother is abused, begin by calling a hotline for abused women. Describe the child's circumstances without providing any names, and ask the advocate whether she is of the opinion that involving child protective services would be a positive step. Ask the advocate how well social workers in your area respond to abused mothers, and seek advice on alternative approaches you could take to help her and the children.

If you do decide that making a child abuse report is the best course of action, please follow these guidelines to proceed as safely as possible:

- Inform the mother ahead of time that you are going to make a report, unless she herself is a serious danger to the child. This will allow her to prepare for the abuser's reaction, which may be a scary one, when he learns that child protective services are about to enter his domain.
- When you make the report, include as much positive information about the mother's parenting as possible, to help steer the social workers away from victim blaming. Emphasize that the case involves domestic violence, and that you are concerned for the well-being of the mother, not just of the children.
- Share as much information as you have. While it is often best not to report at all, when you do make a report it is best to give the most extensive detail possible to help foster a constructive and safe response by the social workers.
- Let your local program for abused women know that you are making the report, and ask if they can advocate for the mother in any way. Ask also if they have connections within the child protective service who should be informed about the case and who might be sympathetic to the mother's position.

- Follow up a few days later with the child protective workers to find out what kind of action is being taken. If the case has been assigned to an investigator, ask to speak to that person.
- Express to the mother your hope that your decision to file will not end communication between you and her, and offer to assist her in any way you can in the weeks ahead.

Support Your Local Program for Abused Women

Over the years, abused women's programs have greatly expanded their efforts to offer children's services. These services can include childcare for women who are attending support groups; therapeutic play groups for children; specialized daycare and school classes within the program's building; advocacy for children's educational and medical needs; and mothers' and children's "psychoeducational" groups that run parallel, so that moms meet in one room while the children meet in another, with both groups receiving education about abuse and opportunities to share and process feelings.

You can help your local program's children's services in any of the following ways:

- Contribute financially, which can help maintain or expand children's programming.
- Volunteer your time to work with children of women in the program.
- Offer pro bono services if you are a therapist, attorney, or pediatric medical or dental provider.

You can also ask the program what kinds of materials, toys, or other donations they may be seeking for their children's activities.

Put Pressure on Media Outlets

Children in our times are bombarded with video, magazine, and Internet images that make violence appear exciting, and that portray guns and fists as effective tools in righting wrongs. Cross-cultural studies have shown that the higher a country's level of approval of violence in general, the higher its level of violence against women specifically. Children are exposed also to a steady stream of messages that support abusive behavior by men and submission by women. They see the Jim Carrey movie in which he pushes aside a nursing baby to put his mouth on the breast of a woman he doesn't know, which is portrayed as funny. They hear interviews with O.J. Simpson in which he blames Nicole for his years of battering her. They hear Britney Spears sing "I Was Born to Make You Happy," or if they are part of the sixties nostalgia trend, they can listen to "He Hit Me (and It Felt Like a Kiss)," by Gerry Goffin and Carole King.

Take a closer look at media images and observe how frequently women are portrayed as sex objects; aggression in relationships is treated as proof of how passionate the person is; men are shown as needing to be in charge in order for crises to be handled well, and females are cast as weak, helpless, or stupid. Make your objections to these images heard through letters and phone calls to advertisers, television stations, newspapers, and magazines. Advertisers are particularly sensitive to criticism, whether about the ad itself or about the broadcast or publication in which the ad appeared, because they do not like to alienate anyone. CBS was flooded with advance protests regarding its broadcast of the Grammy Awards the year that white rapper Eminem won an award for his CD featuring the song "Kim," in which he acts out in gruesome detail murdering his wife. One outcome of the public pressure was that CBS agreed to run a public service announcement about domestic violence during the Grammys. Public pressure made an impact, and will continue to do so. You can also work to bring "media literacy" training into your local school system, so that children are educated to think critically about the messages they are absorbing. (See Resources, page 354.)

Publicly challenging the unhealthy cultural values communicated to children by their society is one of the most important steps you can take to overcome the plague of domestic violence, and to send a message to the children of abused women that their community does not condone the mistreatment they are witnessing.

Support Family Court Reform

If women are to be able to successfully protect their children from exposure to abuse, they have to be backed up by the legal system after they leave the abuser. Unfortunately, family courts often do not treat domestic violence cases with adequate care and seriousness, with the result that children can be sent into unsupervised visitation with the abusive man, or even placed in his custody. Family courts generally do not have to follow the kinds of strict rules of procedure that criminal cases do, with the result that they sometimes become kangaroo courts in practice.

Abused mothers tend to receive a mixed message from our society about protecting their children. While still living with an abusive man, a mother can be harshly criticized for exposing her children to him, and given such labels as "failing to protect," even if she is actually making various efforts to keep her children safe. However, once she leaves the man—which is what the society appears to be asking her to do—she is then at risk of being harshly criticized by family court judges and evaluators *for her reluctance to expose her children to the same man,* and may be labeled vindictive or told that *she* is the one who is failing to focus well on the needs of her children.

The sexual abuse scandal in the Catholic Church contains some instructive lessons. In some ways it is not the actions of the priests that was the most shocking, but of the bishops, cardinals, and mental health professionals who enabled the abuse by reassigning known perpetrators or declaring them to be cured when they were not. Family court judges are playing an analogous role in some cases, requiring children to have unsupervised contact with men who have beaten or threatened their mothers, including in some cases where there is ample evidence that their fathers have also been beating or sexually abusing the children directly. Communities that want to rescue children from the wounds of witnessing abuse have to put a high priority on exposing the actions of family law judges and calling for wide-ranging reform to legal procedure in custody and visitation cases.

The good news is that a broad-based movement advocating for such reform is taking shape, demanding that bias and arbitrariness be stopped, that expensive evaluations be prohibited (since there is no evidence that they lead to better outcomes for families), and that allegations of abuse receive thorough, sophisticated, and evenhanded assessment. Several organizations you can become involved with are listed in the Resources section of this book, under "Child Custody, Divorce, and Child Support," starting on page 345. You can contribute to putting justice back into the "family justice system," and ensuring that courts stop forbidding abused women to protect their children.

The Role of Professionals

Are you a child or family therapist? Schoolteacher? Child protective worker? Advocate for abused women? Counselor for abusive men? Court official? Parent educator? Professionals in a wide range of fields are in a position to reach out to children and their mothers, or to bring about effective service improvements. Here are just a few examples of the kinds of action you can take to make a difference:

- Therapists can develop a specialty in working with children who have been exposed to an abuser's behavior, by receiving training in domestic violence, reading some of the key books recommended here, and developing a cooperative relationship with a program for abused women. Then make your availability known to schools, courts (especially juvenile probation officers), child protective services, and domestic violence programs, which have tremendous need for skilled therapists to whom they can refer children and their mothers.

- Police departments can develop protocols for follow-up calls and visits to homes where police have gone on domestic violence calls, offering the woman information about services for herself and her children that are available in her area.

- Schoolteachers can press the school system to offer in-service training on children's exposure to domestic abuse, and administrators can approve protocols for effective intervention and assistance.

- Abuser programs can make sure to contact not only each client's most recent victim, but also *all women with whom the man has children,* to see if he is causing ongoing psychological harm or is harassing the woman through custody and visitation litigation, and to help her find supportive services. (In this way the man's ex-partners can also be informed that he has been arrested for violence toward a new woman, which is important information for her to have in assessing whether her children can safely go on visits with their father.) Abuser programs can also educate their clients about the effects on children of exposure to violence or verbal degradation toward their mothers, and press their clients to stop undermining mothers' authority.

• Abused women's programs can offer specialized support groups for women who are facing custody and visitation litigation with the abuser, or who have been mistreated by family court judges or custody evaluators. They can also expand activities and support groups that are for mothers and children together, working on rebuilding damaged relationships.

• Child protective workers can develop close communication and collaboration with their nearest abused women's program, offering each other cross-training and seeking ways to protect mothers and children simultaneously.

• All professionals can remember to look carefully for children's courage, strength, resilience, and solidarity with their mothers and siblings, not just their emotional injuries.

• Similarly, professionals can learn about and admire the countless efforts that abused women make to protect their children from exposure to abuse (see chapter 10), rather than assuming that mothers don't care or aren't trying, which is rarely the case.

Look for ways in which you can be involved. Professionals who educate themselves about domestic violence and take leadership in reaching out to children can initiate far-reaching changes, as is currently beginning to happen in cities and towns across the continent. Many additional suggestions are available in the final chapter of my book for professionals, *The Batterer as Parent.*

Create an Abuse-Free World

There is no need for children to continue being exposed to men who verbally or physically abuse their mothers, who drive wedges into mother-child relationships and tear siblings apart, or who hit the children directly and violate their boundaries. Even though individual women do not always have the power to stop domestic abuse, communities and governments do. We have available ample information, including research knowledge, that tells us how abusive men are produced, why they become so attached to coercing women, how they manage to slip through the cracks to avoid accountability, and what kinds of legal and counseling interventions are necessary to make them change. Judges can stop taking domestic violence cases lightly, and instead impose strong, meaningful consequences on abusers. Probation officers can break the habit of buddying up to men who abuse women, and make sure to strictly monitor their compliance with the terms of probation. All community members can step out of victim blaming, no longer making comments such as "I would never take that from a man," or "It's her own fault for putting up with it." Non-abusive men can raise their voices loudly in their communities in protest of the abuse of women. Politicians can refuse to cut funding for services for abused women and their children, pointing out that we always seem to have adequate funds for highways, high-tech weapons, and tax cuts, so the money must be there somewhere.

And there are people taking all of the actions above. Their numbers just need to grow. The voices of women and men who oppose domestic abuse are growing louder and louder. The dawning understanding that children are being wounded by the abuse they witness is further strengthening the movement, already powerful, against the abuse of women. This movement has brought about tremendous social changes in the past thirty years, and is now poised to move on to the next level, where domestic violence is truly eradicated. Then we can arrive at the gateway of a society where every human being has value, male or female, adult or child, where each voice has the right to be heard and understood, where dignity and safety reign. Please join us in making that day come soon.

Key Points to Remember

- If we want to make a difference to children who witness verbal or physical abuse, we have to reach out to their mothers and be there for them. Abused mothers are their children's lifeline, and the rest of us are the mothers' lifeline.
- Children need us to work on changing the social environment *outside* their home as well as inside.
- Women can't protect their children if the courts won't permit them to, so large-scale reform of family law proceedings has to be a top priority.
- Everyone has a role to play in bringing safety, security, and healing to children who have been wounded by the actions of an abusive man.
- If you are an abused mother, seek out people in your community who understand your predicament and want to offer assistance. They are out there.
- Peace truly does begin at home.

Resources

The extensive collection of books, videos, websites, and organizations listed here address a range of issues relevant to women who have been abused. Some are specifically directed at the needs of mothers and children, while others are more general. Although some of the listings make specific reference to violence, they provide information and support that is valuable to women who have faced any type of abuse, coercion, or intimidation in a relationship, including subtler forms of mistreatment such as being constantly made to feel worthless.

If you find Internet resources listed here that interest you, but you do not have a computer, see if you can get on the Web at your public library. Internet information can be especially important for women who are involved in legal battles with abusive men over custody, visitation, or finances.

General Resources for Abused Women

National Domestic Violence Hotline for the United States
and Canada
(800) 799-SAFE
Call this number to receive a referral to the closest hotline for abused women in your area. The use of this number is not restricted

to women who have experienced physical violence. Women and teens are welcome to call with any issue regarding verbal abuse or control in a relationship, or just because something is happening in their relationship that is making them uncomfortable.

Rape, Abuse, and Incest National Network Hotline (RAIN)
(800) 656-4673
Call this number if you have been sexually assaulted or sexually abused by your partner or ex-partner (or by anyone else), and you will be connected immediately to the sexual assault hotline closest to you.

When Love Goes Wrong: What to Do When You Can't Do Anything Right
by Ann Jones and Susan Schechter (HarperPerennial)
This is the essential book for women who are seeking guidance on how to cope with a controlling partner and how to move toward freedom and recovery. It is practical, down-to-earth, and accurate, and covers in detail a wide range of issues that women face.

Why Does He Do That?: Inside the Minds of Angry and Controlling Men
by Lundy Bancroft (Putnam)
Many questions that are important to abused women, and to mothers in particular, are answered here, including how to assess how likely a verbally abusive man is to escalate to violence, how to assess how severely dangerous an abuser is, warning signs to watch for early in a relationship in order to avoid abuse, and how to make a plan to leave a relationship safely if necessary.

*It's My Life Now: Starting Over After an Abusive Relationship
or Domestic Violence*
by Meg Kennedy Dugan and Roger Hook (Routledge)
Despite the title, this book is equally valuable for women who are still involved with an angry or controlling partner. This is a wonderful, warm, compassionate book by authors who deeply understand both emotional and physical abuse.

The Verbally Abusive Relationship: How to Recognize It and How to Respond
by Patricia Evans (Bob Adams)
Evans's book takes the reader through the details of verbally abusive tactics in relationships, and how to understand their effects on you. She offers terrific insight and practical advice.

Into the Light: A Guide for Battered Women
by Leslie Cantrelli (Franklin Press)
This booklet is short and simple, with accurate information and good advice. This is a great resource for women who do not have the time or energy for the longer books listed above, or who want to have quick inspiration handy.

Not to People Like Us: Hidden Abuse in Upscale Marriages
by Susan Weitzman (Basic Books)
A valuable exposé of abuse among the wealthy, with important guidance for abused women.

For Teenagers and Their Parents

What Parents Need to Know About Dating Violence
by Barrie Levy and Patricia Occhiuzzo Giggam (Seal Press)
The essential book for parents who are concerned that their daughters or sons may be involved in abusive dating relationships. Compassionate, insightful, and highly practical, written by people who grasp the wide range of anxieties and challenges that parents face.

In Love and Danger—A Teen's Guide to Breaking Free of Abusive Relationships
by Barrie Levy (Seal Press)
A guide for the teenager herself in responding to an abusive or controlling partner, written in just the right tone and language to reach adolescents—an excellent book. It's out of print, so look for it used or at the library, or try to find it online.

For Women of Color

Chain Chain Change: For Black Women in Abusive Relationships
by Evelyn C. White (Seal Press)
This excellent book remains the key reading resource for any African-American woman involved with a controlling or abusive partner. It provides general information combined with guidance that is specific to the black woman's experience, and includes a section speaking to abused black lesbians.

Mejor Sola Que Mal Acompañada: For the Latina in an Abusive Relationship
by Myrna Zambrano (Seal Press)
Zambrano's book for Latina women in abusive relationships is available in a bilingual edition, making it readable for women whose primary language is Spanish or English. This excellent resource speaks to the cultural context in which Latinas live, and offers specific validation and recommendations.

Black Eyes All of the Time: Intimate Violence, Aboriginal Women,
and the Justice System
by Anne McGillivray and Brenda Comaskey (University of Toronto Press)
The experience of abused indigenous (tribal) women is told largely in their own voices in this wonderful and groundbreaking volume. Although there are a few sections in which the writers use some difficult academic language, the great majority of the book is highly accessible and moving.

Mending the Sacred Hoop
202 E. Superior St.
Duluth, MN 55802
(218) 722-2781
www.duluth-model.org, then select "Mending the Sacred Hoop"
This project of Minnesota Program Development focuses on addressing the abuse of women in tribal cultures.

Institute on Domestic Violence in the African-American
Community

University of Minnesota School of Social Work
290 Peters Hall
1404 Gortner Ave.
St. Paul, MN 55108-6142
(877) 643-8222
www.dvinstitute.org
This organization's website includes resources for abused women themselves, while also reaching out to policy makers, researchers, and other concerned community members.

National Latino Alliance for the Elimination of Domestic Violence
P.O. Box 22086
Ft. Washington Station
New York, NY 10032
(646) 672-1404
www.dvalianza.org
Mostly oriented toward research and policy. Extensive listings.

Asian and Pacific Islander Institute on Domestic Violence
942 Market St., Suite 200
San Francisco, CA 94102
(415) 954-9964
www.apiahf.org, then select "Programs," then select the Institute

For Lesbians

Naming the Violence: Speaking Out About Lesbian Battering
edited by Kerry Lobel (Seal Press)
While this 1986 book is regrettably out of print, you can find it through a library, a used-book store, or online. The personal stories of many abused lesbians are shared here, to help you identify the problem and know that you are not alone.

Woman to Woman Sexual Violence: Does She Call It Rape?
by Lori Girshick (Northeastern University Press)
With the stories of survivors of sexual assaults by same-sex part-

ners woven throughout, this book reports on an important survey and helps bring to light a seldom-examined aspect of intimate partner abuse.

Lesbians Talk: Violent Relationships
by Joelle Taylor and Tracy Chandler (Scarlet Press)
This is a short book that draws from the voices of women themselves to describe the problem of abuse in lesbian relationships and to offer solutions.

Same-Sex Domestic Violence: Strategies for Change
by Beth Leventhal and Sandra Lundy (Sage Publications)
This well-written and insightful book offers guidance to community members who want to address the needs of abused lesbians and gay men, explaining how best to structure services and overcome institutional barriers.

(On the Web, try going to "Gayscape" and doing a search for "Domestic Violence"—many listings are available for organizations, publications, and websites.)

For Immigrant and Refugee Women

Family Violence Prevention Fund
383 Rhode Island St., Suite 304
San Francisco, CA 94103-5133
(415) 252-8900
www.endabuse.org, then select "Immigrant Women," then select "Help is Available"
FVPF helps abused immigrant women get information about their rights and options and find referrals to programs in their area.

NOW Legal Defense and Education Fund
Immigrant Women's Project
1522 K St., NW, Suite 550
Washington, DC 20005
(202) 326-0040

www.nowldef.org, then select "Issues," then select "Immigrant Women"

National Lawyers Guild
National Immigration Project
14 Beacon St., Suite 602
Boston, MA 02108
(617) 227-9727
www.nlg.org, then select "National Immigration Project," then select "Domestic Violence"

Children's Healing

Childhood Experiences of Domestic Violence
by Caroline McGee (Jessica Kingsley)
Although this is a professional book, it is very readable and compassionate. McGee understands the challenges an abused mother faces. Told largely in the words of mothers and children themselves, this is the single best introduction I have found to the experiences of children exposed to an abusive man, with extensive guidance for how to effectively assist them to safety and recovery.

The Batterer as Parent: Addressing the Impact of Domestic Violence on Family Dynamics
by Lundy Bancroft and Jay Silverman (Sage Publications)
This professional book explains many of the core concepts contained in *When Dad Hurts Mom,* with a great deal of additional information specifically related to custody and visitation litigation. It is a good resource to give to attorneys, therapists for women or for children, and other professionals involved with your case.

Children and Trauma: A Parent's Guide to Helping Children Heal
by Cynthia Monahon (Lexington Books)
A compassionate and highly informative guide for parents about how to help children recover from abuse and other traumatic experiences, and how to work cooperatively with professional help when it

is available. The ideal book to put on your shelf next to *When Dad Hurts Mom.*

Children Who See Too Much: Lessons from the Child Witness to Violence Project
by Betsy McAlister Groves (Beacon Press)
This book is for parents or professionals who are assisting children who have been exposed to any type of serious physical violence, including domestic violence, to help them understand children's emotional reactions and their recovery needs. It is brief but very clear and helpful.

Books to Read with Children

A Place for Starr: A Story of Hope for Children Experiencing Family Violence
by Howard Schor (Kidsrights)

A Safe Place to Live: A Story for Children Who Have Experienced Domestic Violence
by Michelle Harrison (Kidsrights)

The above two books tell the stories of families living with violent fathers and then fleeing, and contain excellent messages for children. Both are aimed at children between the ages of two and seven, but can be tried with older children. They are not appropriate for children who have not witnessed physical violence or frightening threats, who would be unnecessarily disturbed by these books.

A Bargain for Frances
by Russel Hoban (HarperCollins)
A perfect book to help children recognize and understand manipulation. Use it as a jumping-off point for discussions. Aimed roughly at ages three to seven, but could be stretched in either direction.

Divorce and Separation Issues

I Don't Want to Talk About It
by Jeanie Franz Ransom, illustrated by Kathryn Kunz Feeney (Magination)
(For reading with children.)

Mama and Daddy Bear's Divorce
by Cornelia Maude Spelman, illustrated by Kathy Parkinson (Albert Whitman & Co.)
(For reading with children.)

Helping Your Kids Cope With Divorce the Sandcastles Way
by Gary Neuman (Times Books)

The first two books listed above are for reading and processing with children, and the third is a widely respected guide for parents. As I mentioned in chapter 12, however, bear in mind that some advice or perspectives in these books might not fit when you are divorcing an abuser. Read all materials carefully yourself before reading them aloud with children, to make sure they are appropriate to your specific circumstances.

Child Custody, Divorce, and Child Support

Resource Center on Domestic Violence: Child Protection and Custody
operated by the National Council of Juvenile and Family Court Judges, (800) 527-3223.

The Resource Center offers a free packet of information for abused women in custody and visitation litigation. It does not become involved in specific cases or provide legal advice. The center offers a book called *Managing Your Divorce: A Guide for Battered Women* that helps women prepare for the process of resolving child custody, visitation, and child support.

Women and Children Last: Custody Disputes and the Family "Justice" System
by Georgina Taylor, Jan Barnsley, and Penny Goldsmith of the Vancouver (B.C.) Custody and Access Support and Advocacy Association

This excellent book prepares abused mothers for the difficult emotional and legal challenges of family court litigation, to help increase their ability to keep their children safe and maintain custody. Advocates and concerned community members can also benefit from the explanations offered here of how the family court system works and why abused women can find the environment so hostile. (For ordering information call Vancouver Status of Women, at [604] 255-6554.)

"Battered Mothers Speak Out: A Human Rights Report on Child Custody and Domestic Violence"
This activist project interviewed forty abused women about their experiences of being revictimized by family courts through the abuser's use of custody and visitation litigation, and also interviewed numerous judges, custody evaluators, and advocates. The project report, which exposes these systemic abuses as violations of women's internationally recognized human rights, is available from: Publication Office, Wellesley Centers for Women, Wellesley College, (781) 283-2510, or at www.wcwonline.org.

"Small Justice: Little Justice in America's Family Courts," a video by Garland Waller, Boston University
This one-hour video documents three cases in which abused women have faced systematic mistreatment by family courts as they attempt to protect their children from domestic violence and sexual abuse. This well-made and carefully researched film is an important resource for community members working for court reforms. (Available from Intermedia, [800] 553-8336.)

Divorced from Justice: The Abuse of Women and Children by
Divorce Lawyers and Judges
by Karen Winner (Regan Books)
This is another out-of-print book, but you can find it at libraries, used-book stores, or online. The stories are painful and make for heavy reading, but Winner offers crucial advice to women and to anyone trying to help them, in addition to giving important suggestions to people interested in working for court reform.

National Child Support Enforcement Association
444 North Capitol St., Suite 414
Washington, DC 20001-1512
(202) 624-8180
www.ncsea.org
NCSEA provides information on child support collection, with links to specific child support resources in your area.

Various Internet resources:
www.canow.org
California Now provides information on battered women in custody litigation.
www.protectiveparents.com
The website of the California Protective Parents Association.
www.nationalcoalition.net
The National Coalition for Family Justice.
There are many other websites for abused women who are in custody and visitation litigation.

Child Sexual Abuse

A Mother's Nightmare—Incest: A Practical Legal Guide for Parents and Professionals
by John E. B. Myers (Sage Publications)
Written by a smart and compassionate attorney, this is a critical book for any woman who has reason to suspect that her child has been sexually abused by the child's father or stepfather, whether or not the child has made any explicit disclosures.

Spiders and Flies: Help for Parents and Teachers of Sexually Abused Children
by Donald Hillman and Janice Solek-Tefft (Rowman & Littlefield)
A sensitive and informative guide.

See also *Children and Trauma* above, under "Children's Healing," page 343.

Parenting Issues

The books listed in this section are general parenting guides, full of tremendous practical help and insight. I have found all of these titles to be terrific. However, two words of caution: (1) these books tend not to address the impact on children of exposure to a man who abuses their mother, including the role that abuse plays in as much as half of divorces, and (2) with the exception of *Real Boys,* these books do not offer detailed guidance to parents who have a gay or lesbian teen (though *Reviving Ophelia* touches on the issue briefly).

You can also find additional parenting resources in your phone book, such as parental stress hotline numbers, Parents Anonymous, and various kinds of parent education classes; or do an Internet search for "Parent Education."

How to Talk So Kids Will Listen and Listen So Kids Will Talk
by Adele Faber and Elaine Mazlish (Avon)
This excellent book receives my highest recommendation.

No More Misbehavior
by Michele Borba (Jossey-Bass)
This book is very practical and down-to-earth for a huge range of behavior problems. An excellent choice for mothers who have been abused and are struggling with the ways in which their children are acting out.

Siblings Without Rivalry
by Adele Faber and Elaine Mazlish (Avon)

The Courage to Raise Good Men
by Olga Silverstein and Beth Rashbaum (Penguin)
Consider this book a *must read* for any parent of a son, especially one who has been exposed to a man who mistreats his mother.

Reviving Ophelia: Saving the Selves of Adolescent Girls
by Mary Pipher (Grosset/Putnam)

Abusive Men

To get a referral to a counseling program for abusive men, call the national Domestic Violence Hotline at (800) 799-SAFE. The organizations listed here offer literature, videos, and training for people interested in starting or improving counseling programs for men who abuse women.

Emerge: Counseling and Education to End Domestic Violence
2380 Massachusetts Ave., Suite 101
Cambridge, MA 02140
(617) 547-9879
www.emergedv.com

Domestic Abuse Intervention Project
206 W. Fourth St.
Duluth, MN 55806
(218) 722-2781
www.duluth-model.org

For Those Assisting Abused Women

To Be an Anchor in the Storm: A Guide for Families and Friends of Abused Women
by Susan Brewster (Ballantine Books)
An outstandingly caring, practical, and wise book for the loved ones of an abused woman. If you are trying to assist a woman who is in a bad relationship, *read this book.* It will help you to feel better and make you a much more effective helper. (However, one word of caution: A section at the end of the book on reporting child abuse contains information that I find ill advised. Before you involve child protective services with a mother you care about, call a program for abused women in your area and seek advice about whether and how to make a child abuse report.)

Safety Planning with Battered Women
by Jill Davies, Eleanor Lyon, and Diane Monti-Catania (Sage Publications)
This is a professional book, but is very readable and helpful for anyone who wants to understand what is really involved when a woman is considering leaving an abusive partner, and provides guidance for how to help her be safer *even if she can't leave or doesn't want to.* The authors talk about much more than just safety planning—they address the full range of practical realities that abused women face in a way that I have found in no other book.

Trauma and Recovery
by Judith Herman (Basic Books)
Dr. Herman's book is the bible of trauma, especially for those kinds of traumatic experiences for which society tends to blame the victim or deny the reality of her/his experience. An outstandingly brilliant work.

About Overcoming Partner Abuse in Communities

National Coalition Against Domestic Violence
1532 16th St., NW
Washington, DC 20036
(202) 745-1211
www.ncadv.org
Join this organization to support policy and service development to benefit abused women and their children. NCADV also has various resources that you can order (at a discount if you are a member), and listings of other sources of information.

Next Time She'll Be Dead: Battering and How to Stop It
by Ann Jones (Beacon Press)
This terrific work elucidates the cultural influences and institutional actions that support abuse, and gives to-the-point suggestions for concerned community members on how to end the abuse of women.

Rural Woman Battering and the Justice System: An Ethnography
by Neil Websdale (Sage Publications)

This excellent book describes the special challenges faced by abused women who live far from large population centers, who may be very isolated and may face local communities that are not supportive of escaping abuse. Groundbreaking and insightful, with concrete strategies for how agencies and institutions can better serve abused women in rural areas.

Coordinating Community Responses to Domestic Violence: Lessons from the Duluth Model
edited by Melanie Shepard and Ellen Pence (Sage Publications)

Detailed guidance on how to draw from the United States's premier model of collaborative work in communities to assist abused women, hold abusers accountable, and change community values about partner abuse.

Pornography: The Production and Consumption of Inequality
by Gail Dines, Robert Jensen, and Ann Russo (Routledge)

This highly readable book provides the most reasonable and persuasive explanations that I have encountered of how pornography can shape men's ways of perceiving and interacting with women, and of the various excuses that groups and individuals use to avoid looking at the damage that pornography can do.

Transforming Communities
734 A St.
San Rafael, CA 94901-3923
(415) 457-2464
www.transformcommunities.org

Transforming Communities has a tremendous collection of resources and ideas for how to combat the abuse of women and children.

Educational Advocacy

Begin by calling your local program for abused women to ask about local resources to help you advocate for your child's educational needs. Next, visit the website of your state's Department of Education (or whatever it may be called) and search for information about parents' rights to request special evaluations, specialized educational plans, services to meet special needs, and similar issues. Try also calling mental health or social service agencies in your area to ask if they know of any local groups or individuals who help parents with educational advocacy.

Media Literacy

All the videos listed under this heading are available from Media Education Foundation, 26 Center St., Northampton, MA 01060, (800) 897-0089, www.mediaed.org. They may also be available through your public library. All three are appropriate for watching with teenage children; before viewing with younger children, watch the video yourself and select an appropriate portion to watch that does not contain disturbing or confusing violent or sexual images.

"Dream Worlds II"
This powerful and disturbing video reveals the attitudes toward women that are taught by today's music videos. It equips the audience with a vocabulary and analytical tools to discuss the messages being sent.

"Tough Guise"
This widely acclaimed video shows how popular portrayals of masculinity force boys and men into unhealthy roles, and teach males to be abusive toward females.

"Wrestling with Manhood"
Professional wrestling is an important influence on the attitudes of male youth. This video examines the messages being communicated,

and opens a critical debate about the need to examine what cultural values are being taught to the next generation.

The Other Parent
by James Steyer (Atria Books)
This book helps parents understand that media influences are "the other parent" forming your children's beliefs, values, and perceptions, and offers strategies for countering the unhealthy messages that they are absorbing. This book is excellent; I consider it a must-read for all parents.

Mentors and Male Allies

Family Violence Prevention Fund
www.endabuse.org
Information is available on the FVPF website about its program "Coaching Boys into Men," with a brochure that you can download; a new initiative for reaching out to boys, called "Teach Early," has recently been launched.

Men Overcoming Violence
1385 Mission St., Suite 300
San Francisco, CA 94103
(415) 626-MOVE
www.menovercomingviolence.org
Public speakers, counseling groups, and opportunities for activism.

Men Can Stop Rape
P.O. Box 57144
Washington, DC 20037
(202) 265-6530
www.mencanstoprape.org
MCSR describes its mission as being "to promote gender equity and build men's capacity to be strong without being violent." Many programs, including outreach to youth and education on teen dating violence.

Men's Initiative for Jane Doe
14 Beacon St., Suite 507
Boston, MA 02108
(617) 248-0922
www.menscampaign.org
A new project that offers various ideas for how men can get involved as allies to abused women.

You can also visit the Campus Outreach Services website at www.
campusoutreachservices.com, go to "Resources," and then select "Men
Against Violence Against Women Organizations" and you will be provided with descriptions and links for *twenty* different men's groups
around the country who are focused on stopping the abuse of women.

Hearing the
Personal Accounts of
Abused Mothers

The world needs to hear the parenting stories of mothers who have been abused, told in their own words. If you are an abused mother, do you have a story you would like to share about your frustrations and successes as a parent? Could you share your wisdom about what works and what doesn't in helping your children heal from witnessing abuse? Can you help the society around you understand what kinds of institutional responses—such as from family courts or child protective services—are helpful to you and your children and what kinds just make things worse?

If you are interested in contributing your story to a future book that highlights the voices of abused mothers, I would love to hear from you. I request that you keep your account to between two and twenty double-spaced pages, and that you include your name, address, and phone number, all of which will be kept confidential. You will be contacted and asked to sign a permission if your story is chosen for inclusion in the book. Please write to me in care of G. P. Putnam's Sons, 375 Hudson St., New York, NY 10014.

Index